Joseph Butler

BRITISH MORAL PHILOSOPHERS

Joseph Butler

Fifteen Sermons Preached at the Rolls Chapel and other writings on ethics

EDITED BY
David McNaughton

OXFORD
UNIVERSITY PRESS

OXFORD
UNIVERSITY PRESS

Great Clarendon Street, Oxford, OX2 6DP,
United Kingdom

Oxford University Press is a department of the University of Oxford.
It furthers the University's objective of excellence in research, scholarship,
and education by publishing worldwide. Oxford is a registered trade mark of
Oxford University Press in the UK and in certain other countries

Published in the United States of America by Oxford University Press
198 Madison Avenue, New York, NY 10016, United States of America

British Library Cataloguing in Publication Data
Data available

Library of Congress Control Number: 2016946924

ISBN 978-0-19-965756-8

SACRED
TO THE MEMORY OF
JOSEPH BUTLER
BISHOP OF DURHAM
BORN A.D. 1692
DIED A.D. 1752
SURPASSED BY NONE
WHETHER ON THE LONG LINE OF BISHOPS OF THE SEE
OR AMONG THE
CHRISTIAN PHILOSOPHERS OF ENGLAND
ADAPTING THE TONE OF HIS LANGUAGE
TO THE EXIGENCIES OF HIS HOLY CAUSE
HE COULD USE A SEVERE SELF-RESTRAINT
BUT COULD ALSO RISE
TO THE HEIGHTS OF A FERVID DEVOTION
HIS CHARACTERISTIC STRENGTH LAY
IN A HABIT PROFOUNDLY MEDITATIVE
IN THE PROPORTION AND MEASURE OF HIS THOUGHT
IN SEARCHING MENTAL VISION
IN THE CONSECRATION OF A LIFE
AND IN HUMBLE UNSWERVING LOYALTY TO TRUTH
THUS HIS WORKS BECAME
A FOUNTAIN OF PERPETUAL INSTRUCTION
ON THE HIGHEST DUTIES AND INTERESTS OF MAN

*Inscription from the memorial tablet to Butler in the Choir of Durham
Cathedral.*

Contents

Contents

Preface

I was extremely fortunate in my undergraduate Philosophy Department in a variety of ways. One was that the curriculum at Newcastle-upon-Tyne was fairly traditional. Butler's moral philosophy was part of the main ethics course, along with Aristotle, Hume, Kant, and Mill. This led to a life-long interest in Butler, whose insights strike me as more profound each time I read him. While there is a steady trickle of papers about Butler's moral philosophy, the works themselves seem to have more or less dropped out of the mainstream curriculum. And when they are included, it is only the famous five of his fifteen sermons that are taught. It is, indeed, a sad reflection on the comparative neglect of his work that there are no fully annotated and referenced editions of his *Fifteen Sermons*, nor indeed of his *Analogy of Religion*, currently in print.[1] I am therefore especially pleased to have been given the opportunity to remedy this defect. (An edition of the *Analogy* is in preparation as a companion volume to this one.)

This is a *reader's* edition of the final version of Butler's *Fifteen Sermons* with relevant related ethical writings. The *Sermons* were first published in 1726. Three years later Butler revised them and added a lengthy preface. It is the text of that second edition that is given here. As this is a reader's edition, I have avoided an apparatus of textual variants that tends to distract the reader. Changes between the first and second edition that struck me as especially important are given in the Editor's Notes. I have added to the *Sermons* three pieces that throw light on Butler's ethical views. The first is the *Dissertation of the Nature of Virtue*, which forms Appendix II of the *Analogy*, and which has been standardly reprinted in all complete editions of the *Sermons*. The others are less well known. The first is one of the *Six Sermons Preached on Public Occasions*, which were included in the fourth edition of the *Sermons*, published in 1749. This sermon, preached before the House of Lords on the anniversary of the execution of Charles I, greatly enlarges what Butler has to say about the relation between self-deception and hypocrisy. The second is that part of the correspondence between Butler and Samuel Clarke (written when Butler was fairly young) that deals with ethical issues. The matter they discuss is freedom and accountability for our actions, and the questions and objections that Butler poses to Clarke are ones to which he returns in the *Sermons*.

I have included an Editor's Introduction, in which I give an outline of Butler's chief views, and discuss his treatment of various issues raised in the less well known of the sermons. The Editor's Notes are designed to (1) aid comprehension, (2) draw attention to corresponding passages in other parts of his work where Butler discusses related themes, (3) direct the reader to the work of earlier philosophers whom Butler is discussing, or who may have influenced his thinking. After those Notes there are brief outlines of the thought of a number of philosophers and schools that had an influence on Butler's thought.

I want to acknowledge the assistance of a large number of people. On textual and related matters I have benefited greatly from the help of David White, who maintains a comprehensive website on Butler, a most valuable resource, at <http://bishopbutler. deviousfish.com>. He kindly supplied me with a copy of Bernard's edition when I had all but despaired of finding one, and also with pdf copies of the various editions of the *Sermons* and the *Analogy* published in Butler's lifetime. I also had similar help and advice from the late Robert Tennant. One of my undergraduate students, Nathan Duddles, received an award from FSU to help me with the initial editing. I thoroughly enjoyed our eight months of working together. With his help we established a modern text, using Bernard's edition as our standard. Nathan also found sources for nearly all the classical allusions, both in Butler's text and in Bernard's notes. In addition, I received invaluable help with finding modern translations of Greek and Latin texts from my colleagues, Russ Dancy, Nat Stein, and David Levenson.

On comparing Bernard's text with the editions published during Butler's lifetime it became clear that Bernard had made considerable changes to Butler's admittedly somewhat erratic punctuation. Since changes in punctuation can affect meaning, I thought it best to restore the original. In this I was helped by a large number of students, both undergraduate and graduate: Jeannine Bailey, C'zar Bernstein, Nathan Helms, Tim Hsiao, Darrell Jordan, Dan Miller, and Samantha Wakil. Jeannine Bailey kindly drafted the bibliography.

Various people have kindly read parts of the Introduction, the Editor's Notes, and the brief intellectual biographies. I am especially indebted to Eve Garrard and Aaron Garrett, each of whom has speedily answered my requests for feedback with any number of helpful suggestions. I am grateful to John Roberts and Michael Robinson for helpful discussion of some of Butler's arguments. My friend, collaborator, colleague, and Chair, Piers Rawling, has helped me get much clearer about the issues surrounding divine utilitarianism. I also owe a considerable debt of gratitude to Peter Momtchiloff. I am sure that the many authors who have been through his capable hands can attest to his unfailing support and encouragement.

Finally, I want to thank my wife for her unfailing love and support throughout. I have also enjoyed the companionship of our various dogs, Sugar, Chance, Molly, and Bella, who made sure I got plenty of invigorating exercise and relaxation.

Note

1. David White's complete edition of Butler's works has, for reasons of space, only very limited notes and introduction.

Introduction

Life

The main public events in Butler's fairly uneventful life can be delineated reasonably quickly.[1] Of his private life or opinions we know little, since he ordered all his papers to be burned on his death.[2] Born on 18 May 1692 into a Presbyterian family dwelling in Wantage, Berkshire, he was educated first at the local grammar school and later at the Dissenting Academy in Gloucester, probably with the intention of entering the Presbyterian ministry. The curriculum included Greek and Latin, logic, mathematics, geography, and biblical studies. It was here that Butler met Thomas Secker, later to become Archbishop of Canterbury, and began his correspondence with Samuel Clarke. The earlier part of their correspondence covers such topics as divine omnipresence and necessity; the later correspondence (reprinted in this volume) concerns ethical questions.

By 1714, however, Butler had decided to conform to the Established Church of England and was thus eligible to enter the ancient universities, which were then closed to non-conformists. He entered Oriel College, Oxford in 1715 where, as was not uncommon in the eighteenth century, he found the education he received deficient. He wrote that he had to 'mis-spend so much time here in attending frivolous lectures and unintelligible disputations'.[3] Butler took his B.A. in October 1718, and was ordained to the priesthood in December of that year.

The following year he was appointed preacher at the Rolls Chapel by Sir Joseph Jekyll, Master of the Rolls. The chapel, located in Chancery Lane, London, served both as a repository for legal records (preserved on rolls of parchment—hence the name) and as a place of worship for the lawyers and clerks who worked in the Court of Chancery which dealt with matters of equity rather than with common law.[4] The *Fifteen Sermons*, first published in 1726, were originally preached to this especially well-educated audience. A second edition followed in 1729; it contained a long Preface intended to summarize, elucidate, and amplify Butler's argument.

In 1721 Butler obtained his Bachelor of Common Law degree from Oxford and in the following year was presented with the living of Haughton-le-Skerne, near Darlington, which he combined with his duties at the Rolls Chapel. This was shortly exchanged for the benefice of Stanhope in County Durham, one of the richest in the country.[5] His income now allowed him to resign the Rolls preachership and he resided entirely at Stanhope until 1733, working on the *Analogy of Religion*.

Secker, fearing that Butler was becoming too isolated in Stanhope,[6] recommended him to Queen Caroline.[7] She expressed some surprise, having supposed him dead. The Archbishop of York is reputed to have quipped: 'No, Madam; but he is buried.' In November 1733 Charles Talbot became Lord Chancellor and, at Secker's suggestion, made Butler his chaplain, the arrangement being that he should continue to spend half the year at Stanhope.[8] In the following month Butler proceeded to the degree of Doctor of Common Law at Oxford. In 1736 *The Analogy* was published and the Queen appointed Butler as her clerk of the closet. His duties included attendance on the Queen for two hours each evening for theological discussion, which necessitated his renting lodgings near the court.

Queen Caroline died in November 1737, commending Butler on her deathbed to the Archbishop of Canterbury. Butler was duly elevated to the see of Bristol in the following year. Butler was appointed to the bench of bishops in the Lords, and so had to maintain a household in London when Parliament was in session. In addition, a bishop was expected to provide hospitality to his clergy and to leading citizens. As Bristol was the poorest see in the country, and consequently had an income insufficient for Butler's needs, he felt some dissatisfaction with his preferment, which he expressed in a letter to Robert Walpole:

Indeed, the bishoprick of Bristol is not very suitable either to the condition of my fortune, or the circumstances of my preferment; nor, as I should have thought, answerable to the recommendation with which I was honoured. (Bartlett 1839: 73–4.)

In 1740 he was appointed to the deanery of St. Paul's Cathedral in London, which finally provided him with an adequate income, enabling him to resign from his other posts.

Butler was well known for his charitable giving: it is reported that he found it difficult to resist giving alms to anyone who begged. He spent the majority of his income on refurbishing ecclesiastical buildings, buying land for a church for the working poor, and aiding the development of Bristol Infirmary.

In 1746 Butler was appointed Clerk of the Closet to the King,[9] a position that promised further promotion, which duly came when he was elevated to the see of Durham in 1750. It is characteristic of Butler's scrupulous nature that he resisted the suggestion that a friend be given a prebendal stall at Durham on his appointment, lest it should smack of cronyism. He wrote to a friend:

It would be a melancholy thing in the close of life, to have no reflections to entertain oneself with, but that one had spent the revenues of the bishoprick of Durham, in a sumptuous course of living, and enriched one's friends with the promotions of it, instead of having really set one's self to do good, and promote worthy men. (Bartlett 1839: 116.)

The see of Durham faced many problems, including significant population changes, and what Butler himself described as the 'general decay of religion' (*Works*, vol. I (ed. Bernard): 271). In his 1751 *Charge to the Clergy of the Diocese of Durham* Butler addresses some of these problems; the *Charge* casts further light on Butler's views on the best way to communicate and instil Christianity.[10] As at Bristol, he was instrumental in the founding of an Infirmary, this time at Newcastle-upon-Tyne, and was the most generous of all the subscribers. After infrequently attending the Lords in the session of 1751–2, Butler was taken ill in the spring of 1752. A visit to Bath to take the waters proved unavailing, and he died on 16 June.

His intellectual legacy was considerable. During the eighteenth century, the *Analogy* went through a total of fifteen editions, and the *Sermons* through five. He influenced, among others, Hutcheson, Kames, Hume, Reid, and Richard Price. In the following century the *Analogy* became the standard theological text at Oxford and Cambridge, and he was admired by Hazlitt and Coleridge. Cardinal Newman described him as 'the greatest name in the Anglican Church' (*Apologia*, 1959: 103), and W. E. Gladstone, who was Prime Minister of Britain on four separate occasions, devoted a considerable part of his formidable energies to editing and writing about Butler. Henry Sidgwick, author of the monumental *Methods of Ethics*, attributed his views about the nature of practical reason to Butler. His influence as a theologian and philosopher of religion declined in the twentieth century, at least in part because his apologetics address only those who already accept some sort of Deity or Intelligent Creator. His moral philosophy remained on many undergraduate curricula until the mid-century, and is still a topic of debate in academic circles, but his stature has diminished and few would now endorse C. D. Broad's verdict: '[T]hough his system is incomplete, it does seem to contain the prolegomena to any system of ethics that can claim to do justice to the facts of moral experience' (Broad 1930: 83).[11]

Moral Psychology

In my view, this comparative neglect of Butler, both as theologian and as philosopher, is an unfortunate error, since we have much to learn from him. Perhaps his most important contribution to ethics, as the quotation from Broad suggests, is to what used to be called moral psychology. Somewhat confusingly, this term is now often used to refer to the empirical study of moral thought and behaviour, within the discipline of psychology, utilizing such instruments as questionnaires, experiments, and MRI scans. One striking result from these behavioural studies is that people seem to be influenced, both in their judgement and behaviour, by comparatively trivial and irrelevant external factors, of which they may be largely unconscious, such as whether they are holding a hot or a cold drink, or the degree of tidiness of their surroundings. MRI scans are used to track which parts of the brain are most active when people make moral judgements. The results have been thought to suggest that there is a division of labour between the cognitive, or calculative, parts of the brain and the regions that are connected to emotion and affect. Interesting though these studies are, they need very careful interpretation. For a start, they can only tell us how many people do in fact act and think; they are necessarily silent on how we *ought* to think. More importantly, perhaps, the empirical data need to be carefully assessed if they are to be properly understood. Several prominent figures, in the fields of philosophy as well as of psychology, have leaped to some dramatic and premature conclusions on their basis. For example, it has been claimed that the data about the factors that influence behaviour undermine the viability of the sort of virtue theory advocated by the followers of Aristotle. It has also been maintained that these studies demonstrate the unreliability of our moral intuitions, or suggest that certain of our moral judgements are occasioned by emotional triggers rather than being based on reason.

These conclusions rest on shaky foundations because their proponents either have an inadequate conception of the nature of moral experience, or have failed to draw subtle distinctions between different mental states or, more commonly, both. Proper interpretation of these and other findings must rest on an adequate philosophical understanding of our moral psychology and it is in this area, especially, that Butler's strengths lie.

Moreover, psychological studies can only look at ethical thought from the outside, but moral psychology, as traditionally understood, approaches the moral life from the inside, by reflection on our lived ethical experience, and on what it is like to be a responsible and responsive moral agent. In the hands of Butler and others, this entails paying close attention to the moral phenomenology—to the precise nature of, for example, what it is to recognize a moral obligation, or to experience moral emotions, such as pity, indignation, guilt, or compunction. Moral psychology also engages in the traditional philosophical task of drawing distinctions between phenomena that might at first glance seem somewhat similar: between, say, resentment and indignation, or envy and jealousy. In such areas Butler is, among modern philosophers, preeminent. His shrewd, wise, and insightful analyses are only surpassed, if at all, by Aristotle's *Nicomachean Ethics*.

Whereas contemporary psychology is, or ought to be, an empirical discipline, moral psychology, traditionally conceived, has a normative as well as a descriptive aspect. It seeks, by reflection on our nature and on our moral experience, to discover how we ought to think, feel, act, and be. Butler's approach to ethics falls squarely in that tradition. It informs not only such well-known sermons as the three on human nature but also less familiar ones on such topics as forgiveness and resentment, self-deception, and compassion.

One source of Butler's strength in moral psychology is his lack of *theoretical* presuppositions. Too many philosophers who venture into ethics have already decided, on other grounds, what shape morality must take, and distort the phenomenology accordingly. It must be acknowledged, of course, that while Butler is not in the grip of a philosophical theory, he is deeply committed to a *theological* position. If there is distortion in his theory, it largely comes from his religious convictions.

Butler's Theistic Background

On Butler's view, we live in a universe created and kept in being by a good and benevolent God. Since God has our temporal and eternal welfare at heart, each aspect of our nature must have been given us for good purposes. No emotion, desire, or instinct can be without a proper purpose, though each may be misused or perverted.

To think productively about such topics as resentment, forgiveness, pity, or love, we need to determine when and how such emotions or feelings are appropriate and thereby determine the abuses of them that we must avoid. Given that we are God's creatures, not only must each part of our nature have a purpose but also the whole must be capable of functioning as a harmonious system. If one part of our nature is at war with another, this is a sign that we are not yet living exactly as we ought (S 3.2n).

One question that much exercises contemporary commentators is whether Butler's claims about how we should live can be detached from their theistic setting. In particular, can Butler's central claim, that conscience has authority to determine how we should act, be defended on a secular metaphysic? In my opinion, the grounds for that claim are weakened, but not fatally undermined, if God is excised from the picture.[12] It can be argued that Butler identifies conscience with reflection or reason. We reflect, among other things, on our reasons: what we have reason to believe or to do. We weigh those reasons with a view to finding out what we have *most* reason to believe or to do. If that is right, then conscience is not some strange additional faculty, a sort of moral sense, but simply one important aspect of reason in its practical mode. On this view, the deliverances of conscience are our considered verdicts, in cases where moral issues are to the fore, about what we have most reason to do. Understood as a request for justification, the question: 'Why ought I to do what I believe I have most reason to do?' is not a sensible one. Similarly, on this view of conscience, the question: 'Why ought I to do what I believe would be morally right?' requires no answer and can receive none. At best, it can invite one to further reflection on one's reasons, but what emerges from that further reflection will still be a judgement about what I take myself, faced with some particular moral question, to have most reason to do.[13]

Most discussions of Butler focus on two important topics that occupy just five of the fifteen sermons: either his account of human nature in general, and of conscience and self-love in particular, or his celebrated attack on psychological egoism, especially in its most common, hedonistic, form. Because these issues have been well covered, I shall only briefly delineate his views, and mention some of the main questions that they raise, before spending more time on the remaining sermons, which repay careful study.

Conscience and Self-Love

The central question that Butler addresses in the first three sermons is:[14] What 'obligations [do we have] to the practice of virtue'? (P 12), i.e. what reasons do we have to live virtuously? His answer is that this is what our nature requires of us. He argues (following ancient moralists, such as the Stoics) that 'virtue consists in following [nature] and vice in deviating from it' (P 13).

His account begins, in Sermon 1, by distinguishing between different components of our practical psychology. The most prominent are conscience, self-love, benevolence, and the particular appetites, passions, and affections.[15] The particular passions are many and various; what they have in common is that they seek to attain some particular object. Hunger seeks food; compassion, the relief of someone's suffering, and so on. The gratification of any affection gives us pleasure, but gratification of one often impedes the gratification of others. Our overall long-term happiness consists in harmonizing their gratification, so that each affection attains its object within 'its due stint and bound' (S 11.9). This harmonizing is the task of self-love. Finally, conscience, or reflection, alerts us to the moral status of our acts and prompts us to do what is right. As we all know, our various affections and passions can conflict not only with each other but also with self-interest, or with morality.

Merely to enumerate the components of our psychology omits, in Butler's view, its most important feature, namely that the internal principles of rational, reflective creatures, such as humans, are ordered hierarchically. They do not have equal claims, for some are superior to others. To say that a principle is superior is to make a *normative* claim: that it has authority; it has a right to govern. A subordinate principle may be motivationally strong enough to overcome a superior one, but then the agent will not be acting as he ought, and is open to criticism and censure. If no principle were superior (as is, Butler supposes, the case in animals) whatever we did would be natural, because we would always be acting in accordance with *some* principle in our nature. On that account, someone who knowingly embraced his certain ruin to satisfy a whim would not have failed to act as he ought, and would not be open to criticism. Butler thinks that we only have to spell out such a claim to see its absurdity. Similarly, to defy one's conscience is to violate one's nature.

So much is clear. But beyond that there is much disagreement among commentators as to how to understand Butler. Apparent conflicts between different passages have led to complaints that Butler is careless or inconsistent. I think this charge is mistaken. Butler is among the most careful of writers, but his work has to be read with sympathetic care lest one miss the qualifications and caveats. Sometimes these supposed inconsistencies are put down to the fact that these are sermons, and not philosophical treatises, composed on different occasions for different purposes. So they are, but to suppose him to be careless about consistency on that account is to ignore the meticulous revisions he made to the wording of the *Sermons* in the second edition, and the fact that he added a long Preface precisely in order to obviate misunderstandings.

If we bear three things in mind many of the alleged inconsistencies disappear. First, Butler is often concessive to views in opposition to his own, a point that is sometimes missed by readers. His argumentative strategy frequently takes the form of claiming that his main point still stands even were he to grant some claim that he in fact disputes.

Second, he relies on the reader's good sense, rather than spelling out every possible nuance in the mind-numbing detail beloved of contemporary analytic philosophers. Butler does not qualify each and every statement since he relies both on context and the reader's memory of his earlier assertions to guide understanding.

The final interpretative error that commentators often make is to ignore the main body of the *Analogy* altogether, while lumping the *Sermons* and the *Dissertation of Virtue* together as if they were part of a seamless treatise. But the *Dissertation* was part of the *Analogy* and so published ten years after the first edition of the *Sermons*. It is reasonable to assume that Butler's views may have developed over that decade, and some differences between the two works are to be expected. In fact, I would argue, while there were one or two important changes in Butler's thinking about ethical matters, the viewpoint of the *Analogy* is largely consistent with that of the *Sermons*. Moreover, the *Dissertation* is by no means the only part of the *Analogy* that deals with ethical issues. Passages relevant to ethics in the main body of the later work amount to over 12,000 words.[16] The assumptions on which I proceed are these. Where commentators disagree about the claims that Butler makes in the *Sermons*, and some passage(s) in the *Analogy* are clear and decisive on the matter under dispute, I regard the *Analogy* as not only representing Butler's considered view of the matter but as important evidence as to what he probably meant in the *Sermons*. Where there seems to be a clear shift between the viewpoint of the earlier and the later work, I take Butler to have changed his mind, and then an important interpretative question will be: Why did he change it?

We can now apply the first two of these interpretative principles to a question that has probably divided Butler scholars more than any other: are self-love and conscience equally authoritative, or is one supreme?[17] Butler's official answer is uncompromising:

[C]onscience or reflection, compared with the rest as they all stand together in the nature of man, plainly bears upon it the marks of authority over all the rest, and claims the absolute direction of them all. (P 24.)[18]

Nevertheless, there are passages where Butler seems to get close to regarding them as on a par. This led no less a philosopher than Sidgwick to credit Butler with anticipating Sidgwick's own view. Butler, he claimed, treats self-love and conscience as 'independent principles, and so far co-ordinate in authority that it is not "according to nature" that either should be overruled' (Sidgwick, 1967a: 196). I think Sidgwick misunderstood Butler on this point. In the light of the first two of our interpretive principles, all of these passages can plausibly be read as consistent with his official position. Here I have room to discuss just one such passage:[19]

Reasonable self-love and conscience are the chief or superior principles in the nature of man: because an action may be suitable to this nature, though all other principles be violated; but becomes unsuitable, if either of these are. (S 3.9.)

Sidgwick and others read this passage as implicitly denying the supremacy of conscience since Butler here treats both principles alike. A strict reading of 'either' might imply that an action would be unsuitable to our nature not only if it accorded with self-love but conflicted with conscience but also if it accorded with conscience but conflicted with self-love. But to assert the latter would be to deny the supremacy of conscience.

Read in context, this interpretation is hard to maintain. First, Butler has repeatedly stressed, just prior to this passage, that conscience is the supreme principle. Second, he is in the middle of stressing that, *in fact*, self-interest and morality scarcely ever conflict (never, indeed, if we take into account a future life). Third, the sort of case he is here discussing is one in which an agent acts out of an inclination, contrary to the dictates of either conscience, or self-love, or both. He should most plausibly be read as claiming that it is equally a violation of our nature for an agent to follow an *inclination*, in defiance of either superior principle. He is not, in the context, making any claim about the comparative ranking of conscience and self-love.[20]

Benevolence and Egoism

Butler was keen to combat popular errors that might offer people an excuse to avoid the effort to be virtuous. His especial target was a worldly cynicism that denied the reality or even the possibility of disinterested benevolence, of acting from a genuine concern for the welfare of others. If that were true, then the preaching of virtue would itself be merely self-interested cant, and no-one need feel guilty for acting selfishly.

How are we to understand the claim that there are no acts of disinterested benevolence? There are two possible interpretations, not always carefully distinguished. Such claims might be either empirical or conceptual. Understood empirically, they express a very jaundiced view of human nature. On this view, altruistic acts are conceivable, but rare, or even non-existent. If we look carefully at what appear to be disinterested acts of kindness or justice we shall find the agent had some hidden agenda. Thus understood, such claims apparently run counter to observable facts. We can find many cases of heroism or self-sacrifice in which the agent had nothing to gain and a lot to lose.

A more philosophically interesting version of psychological egoism holds that altruism is impossible. It usually takes the specific form of psychological hedonism: the claim that the agent must be motivated by the prospect of pleasure in order to do any act; otherwise why would she do it? Altruistic action is simply inexplicable, and so impossible.

Butler's main arguments against the conceptual version draw on his earlier account of the particular affections and of self-love, and of the distinction between them. The affections are directed towards particular objects or states of affairs; self-love is directed at our happiness, which consists in our affections enjoying their objects. Self-love is thus a second-order affection whose goal is that our first-order affections be satisfied. Psychological egoists hold that, though we may disguise it from ourselves, all human action is self-interested, motivated by a desire for our own good or happiness. Translated into Butler's terminology, this amounts to the claim that we are motivated solely by self-love. But this is incoherent. Self-love achieves its object only if our particular affections achieve their objects: 'take away these affections and you leave self-love absolutely nothing at all to employ itself about' (P 37).

This ingenious argument may seem too quick. The egoist need not deny that we desire particular things and that our happiness consists in achieving them. What he claims is that it is only in virtue of the fact that they give us pleasure that we desire these things. When we desire anything our ultimate goal, and what motivates us to act, is our own pleasure or enjoyment. Thus, our ultimate object in helping others is not their welfare, but our pleasure. So what explains benevolent actions is our desire for the pleasure we expect to receive from our altruism.

Butler's response to this argument is to claim, in effect, that the hedonist reverses the correct direction of explanation:

That all particular appetites and passions are towards *external things themselves*, distinct from the *pleasure arising from them*, is manifested from hence, that there could not be this pleasure, were it not for that prior suitableness between the object and the passion: There could be no enjoyment or delight for one thing more than another, from eating food more than from swallowing a stone, if there were not an affection or appetite to one thing more than another. (S 11.6.)

Only if I desire things other than pleasure for their own sake, and not simply as a means will I get pleasure when my desire is gratified.[21] If I did not care about the welfare of others for their own sakes, I would get no pleasure from helping them.

This is a famous rebuttal but not, perhaps, as decisive a one as Butler believes.[22] As has often been pointed out, there are obvious exceptions to Butler's claim that we cannot find pleasure in an activity unless we already have a desire to engage in it. Some experiences or activities are intrinsically pleasant, and could be enjoyed in the absence of any prior desire: think of suddenly smelling a delightful scent.

However, Butler's claim that there are *some* pleasures whose existence depends on the gratification of a prior desire for something other than pleasure seems plausible.[23] As well as taking pleasure *in* an experience, such as having a warm bath or smelling a rose, we can be pleased *that* our desires are gratified. In the latter case, our pleasure depends on our desire being gratified. Call these desire-dependent pleasures. The benevolent person is pleased that distress is relieved, while a callous person is not. What explains their different reactions? The former desires the relief of distress, whereas the latter is indifferent to it. Thus, in the case of desire-dependent pleasures, Butler's argument seems to go through. One whose goal is to help the needy will indeed feel pleased that he has been able to help, but only because helping, and not being pleased, is his ultimate goal. We are pleased because we want to help, rather than helping because we want to be pleased. Thus there can be disinterested benevolence.

Even if psychological hedonism is false, our happiness is of great importance to us, as Butler frequently acknowledges. But isn't benevolence directly opposed to self-love in a way that other particular passions are not? Some of our affections, such as ambition and desire for esteem, have some good of our own as their primary end. Between such affections and self-love there seems to be no essential conflict. Benevolence, however, aims at the good of *others*, and so seems directly opposed to self-interest.

Butler's exposition of the mistake behind this line of thought is impressive. It falsely presupposes that the more I promote your interests, the less I am advancing my own. Butler has already argued that happiness consists in my desires being gratified. That is as true of a desire for the happiness of others as it is of any other desire. Insofar as I want you to be happy then my happiness depends on, and is bound up with, yours. We must not think of happiness by analogy with property, so that to give happiness to others is necessarily to diminish my own. Benevolence, while distinct from self-love, is no more opposed to it than any other particular passion. Whether self-love endorses or opposes the gratification of any passion depends on whether it happens to threaten my interests.

Even if we concede that acting benevolently is not *intrinsically* opposed to our interests might it not in fact conflict *more often* with my interests than actions from some other motives? Butler's response to this worry is to claim that interest and duty (of which benevolence forms a large part) hardly ever conflict, even in this life, and not at all if we take into account the life to come. Important as that claim is to Butler's view, we have not space to examine it here.

Butler also points out that an excessive preoccupation with one's own happiness is self-defeating. This is the famous paradox of hedonism, which Sidgwick and others have generalized to other cases.[24] An over-anxious concern for our own welfare breeds the sort of temperament that tells against happiness.

Benevolence and Virtue

Where does Butler stand in the long-running dispute between utilitarianism and deontology?[25] In a nutshell, utilitarianism holds that the only morally relevant feature is the amount of happiness or welfare that we can bring about. So what makes an act the right one is that it brings about the most happiness for all affected parties, where the interests of each party are to be given equal weight. (Utilitarians would make similar claims about the right policy, or the right law.) Deontologists deny this, maintaining that sometimes we are permitted, or even morally required, not to bring about the most happiness overall. In particular, deontologists counter utilitarianism by making some or all of the following claims.

- Agents are permitted, or even in some cases required, to give more weight to their own welfare, and to the welfare of those to whom they stand in special relationships, than they give to the welfare of strangers.
- Agents should avoid acting in certain kinds of ways, e.g. lying, breaking one's word, or killing the innocent, even as a means to bring about greater happiness (or to prevent suffering).

- As well as the quantity of happiness, we need to consider its distribution. Some skewed allocations of welfare would be unfair, even if they were to maximize happiness overall. Fairness is perhaps most plausibly viewed as the allocation of goods in accordance with desert. Better a world in which the deserving get more, and the undeserving less, rather than one in which the reverse obtains, even if the amount of happiness is the same in each case. Most pointedly, the wicked may deserve to suffer as a matter of retributive justice, even if that punishment has no effect on the general welfare.

On which side of this debate does Butler fall? He identifies the love of our neighbour with benevolence, which is an affection to the good and happiness of our fellow creatures (S 12.2). He then enquires whether benevolence is the whole of virtue.[26] His initial answer appears to be positive. He opens Sermon 12 by stating that he will show how the commandment to love our neighbour 'comprehends in it all others'. However, Butler progressively qualifies this bold assertion: firstly, in the text of the Sermon; secondly, in a lengthy footnote; finally, in the *Dissertation* where he roundly declares that 'benevolence, and the want of it, singly considered, are in no sort the whole of virtue and vice' (D 8). In light of this, should we see Butler as moving away from utilitarianism towards some form of deontological pluralism? Or should we rather see him as recognizing the need for a more sophisticated utilitarianism?

Here are some of Butler's qualifications. Are we to love the whole of humanity? No. The object of our benevolence should be 'those persons who come under our immediate notice, acquaintance, and influence' (S 12.3). Love of neighbour is to bear *some proportion* to the love we bear ourselves, but must that proportion be one of equality? Butler's discussion is complex and subtle, but he takes us to have a distinct obligation to make adequate provision for ourselves 'because we are in peculiar manner... intrusted with ourselves' (S 12.15). In both Sermon 12 and the *Dissertation* he also points out that we are required to 'do good to some, preferably to others', either because they are especially entrusted to our care, or because of friendship, or former commitments and obligations. So it would seem that we have special obligations to ourselves and to our nearest and dearest.

In a footnote to Sermon 12, and in D 8, Butler points out that conscience approves of certain kinds of action such as 'fidelity, honour, strict justice', and disapproves of others, such as treachery, falsehood, violence, and meanness, 'abstracted from the consideration of their tendency to the happiness or misery of the world' (S 12.31n). Finally, in D 3 (and elsewhere) he stresses that ill-doers deserve punishment, and that the notion of desert is quite distinct from the thought that society would benefit by their incarceration or other penalty. So Butler holds both that certain types of action are, by their nature, not to be done, and that justice (and punishment) should be sensitive to desert.[27]

It is understandable, in the light of these caveats, that some have seen Butler as a staunch advocate of deontology, especially when, in D 10, he claims that 'imagining the whole of virtue to consist in singly aiming, according to the best of our judgement, at promoting the happiness of mankind' is a source of grave moral error. But such a claim is not, in fact, incompatible with being a utilitarian. Writers in that tradition, most notably Sidgwick, often distinguish between what contemporary philosophers dub the criterion of rightness and a decision procedure. The right action (or set of actions) is that which will *in fact* produce the most happiness. However, it does not follow that this should be the sole consideration before our minds when making a decision about what to do. Indeed, making decisions solely on that basis might, paradoxically, do more harm than good.[28]

Many of the consequences of our actions are unavoidably unforeseen, especially ones in the far future. It is also hard to know what will make people happy, and the less we know them, the more that is the case. We are bad at making decisions under uncertainty, and inclined to persuade ourselves that what we want to do, or what is for our benefit, is in fact the action that will produce the most benefit overall. We might, in fact, do more good by adopting a few simple principles or strategies that will prevent our being led too far astray. So it may be best to focus our benevolent activity on those who are close to us, whose needs and wishes are well known to us. Maybe the world would be better if on some occasion I lied, cheated, or killed, but it is unlikely that the greater good will be served by any of us being given that discretion. If so, things might go better, from the perspective of utilitarianism, if we did not think like utilitarians. And the best way not to think like a utilitarian might be to reject utilitarianism as a false doctrine. But if we all rejected it, how would we ensure that the rules we did follow were the ones best suited to increasing welfare? Some secular ethicists have suggested that there might be an elite who, while knowing utilitarianism to be the correct moral theory, brought the rest of us up to accept whatever non-utilitarian moral code would, if generally adopted, be most likely to maximize welfare.[29] But who guards the guardians? How can we prevent them being corrupted?

It is a tribute to Butler's acuity that he saw the possibility of this kind of 'indirect' utilitarianism.[30] He considers, and it is no more than that, the possibility that God might be a utilitarian who, for good utilitarian reasons, has given us a non-utilitarian conscience. This suggestion neatly avoids the problem of who guards the guardians, since there is no possibility that God will be corrupted.

And therefore, were the Author of Nature to propose nothing to himself as an end but the production of happiness, were his moral character merely that of benevolence; yet ours is not so. Upon that supposition indeed, the only reason of his giving us the above-mentioned approbation of benevolence to some persons rather than others, and disapprobation of falsehood, unprovoked violence, and injustice, must be, that he foresaw, this constitution of our nature would produce more happiness, than forming us with a temper of mere general benevolence. But still, since this is our constitution; falsehood, violence, injustice, must be vice in us, and benevolence to some preferably to others, virtue; abstracted from all consideration of the overbalance of evil or good, which they may appear likely to produce. (D 8.)

Butler seems content to leave matters there, given his homiletic aims. Whether what we might, following Louden,[31] dub divine utilitarianism, or deontology, is the correct moral theory, it remains the case that we must *act and think* like deontologists. Practically, then, the choice makes little or no difference, but in terms of theory the issues Butler's suggestion raises are intriguing.

Compassion

Butler included two Sermons on the topic of compassion. Reason, according to Butler, tells us that there are many things we should do: we should eat, or we will starve; we should not be impulsive, lest we come to grief; we should endeavour to avoid harming others and to promote their happiness. However, for such creatures as we, reason is not always a sufficient motive. If we were not hungry, we might forget to eat. So God has implanted in us particular passions, affections, and appetites in order to aid us in obeying reason. Compassion is one such. To 'rejoice in the good of others, is only a consequence of the general affection of love and good-will to them' (S 5.2). The fortunate do not need us, so there is no need of a particular affection to aid us in rejoicing. But the unfortunate do need our aid, and mere awareness of the badness of their plight is likely to be insufficient to motivate us to relieve their suffering—hence the need for an emotion that will *move* us to help.

In the course of his discussion, Butler makes four points that are characteristic of his position. First, he rejects the Stoic idea that we should seek to extirpate the passions and emotions. Emotions need to be controlled by reason, but the claim that we would be better off without some part of our nature is virtually blasphemous. Second, though many are deficient in compassion, there is the possibility of excess—of allowing pity to sway us when it should not. Here, as elsewhere, Butler tends to follow Aristotle: emotions need to be trained to be fitting responses to their objects, and both excess and deficiency are to be avoided. In one notable passage, he offers a clear summary of his view of human nature:

Reason alone, whatever anyone may wish, is not in reality a sufficient motive of virtue in such a creature as man; but this reason joined with those affections which God has impressed upon his heart: and when these are allowed scope to exercise themselves, but under strict government and direction of reason; then it is we act suitably to our nature, and to the circumstances God has placed us in. (S 5.3.)

Third, pain and suffering can last much longer than great pleasure, still less ecstasy. What we should learn from this, and from the role of compassion in our psychology, is that the relief of the suffering of others, and the avoidance of it for ourselves, are of much greater importance than the promotion of happiness, whether in ourselves or others:

> To make pleasure and mirth and jollity our business, and be constantly hurrying about after some gay amusement, some new gratification of sense or appetite, to those who will consider the nature of man and our condition in this world, will appear the most romantic scheme of life that ever entered into thought. (S 6.10.)

This striking passage reflects Butler's sombre, and even gloomy, state of mind. For him, the world is more a vale of tears and a testing ground, rather than a place where we can find joy or even contentment.

Finally, Butler argues that compassion, despite its inconveniences, does more good than harm. That it is useful to the world at large is, indeed, plausible. Whether some individuals might be better off without it is more debatable, and Butler makes a number of points, of varying cogency, to defend the claim that a lack of that emotion is to our individual, as well as to our collective, detriment.

Butler on Self-Deception

'In all common ordinary cases we see intuitively at first view what is our duty, what is the honest part' (S 7.14). Such claims raise an obvious problem for Butler's account of wrongdoing. If conscience judges so reliably it would seem that, in the normal run of things, no-one can do the wrong thing while believing themselves to be doing what is right. Yet some of the greatest crimes in history have been perpetrated by people who believed that what they were doing was morally permissible, and even obligatory.[32]

Butler allows two exceptions to the claim that conscience unhesitatingly comes up with the correct verdict. First, Butler does not suppose that all moral problems are simple ones. Thought is often required and there can be tricky cases in which there is genuine uncertainty about what is right.[33] Second, and somewhat hesitantly, Butler does allow that what he calls 'superstition' may cause conscience to deliver the wrong verdict, even in comparatively clear cases. Exactly what he means by 'superstition' is not entirely clear, especially as, in eighteenth-century parlance, the term is often simply code for the Roman Catholic Church. Read less restrictively, Butler may be claiming that false religious beliefs can lead people's consciences astray. The implication of allowing this as a genuine exception seems to be that, if these religious views are sincerely held, and those who hold them know no better, then such believers would be blameless for the resulting erroneous moral beliefs.

We might wonder whether these two exceptions are adequate to explain all the instances in which people's consciences have led them astray. A definitive answer will depend on what is covered by the term 'superstition', and how complex a case needs to be before it ceases to be a 'common ordinary' one. However, Butler has a third and very interesting suggestion. Conscience will not mislead us in straightforward cases, if we attend to it carefully, and if we are honest with ourselves. But all too often we manage to deceive ourselves into believing that we have not done anything wrong when it is manifest that we have. In such a case, conscience is either corrupted or, at least, stifled or silenced.[34] Such self-deception is itself wrong and blameable:

It is unfairness; it is dishonesty; it is falseness of heart: and is therefore so far from extenuating guilt, that it is itself the greatest of all guilt in proportion to the degree it prevails; for it is a corruption of the whole moral character in its principle. (S 10.11.)

That Butler devotes two of the *Fifteen Sermons* (7 and 10) as well as a considerable portion of the most important public sermon he gave (here reprinted as *A Sermon Preached Before the House of Lords*) to the topic of self-deception shows the import- ance he attached to it. It is what, in Butler's view, most often leads predominantly good people astray. It is a vice, and one for which we can be blamed. So what is it, how does it work, and why is it blameable?

It has often been pointed out that, if we think of self-deception on the model of deceiving others, we seem to run into paradox. In the most typical case where I deceive another person, I intentionally set out to induce a false belief in that other, by misleading implication, planting false evidence, or downright lying. Here the deceiver and the deceived are distinct; the deceiver knows what is going on but, if the deception is successful, she who is deceived does not. But where only one party is involved—where there is supposedly deception *of* the self *by* the self—how can deception occur? Successful deception requires ignorance on the part of the deceived. But how, in this case, can the deceived not know what the deceiver is up to? A familiar array of solutions is to hand. One is to deny that there can be such a thing as full-blooded self-deception. Another is to reject the model. Self-deception requires only that the self be deceived, but not that the self also be the deceiver.[35] On this view, no *agent* deceives; rather, there is some psychic mechanism that does the deceiving. The self-deceived fail to take proper account of the evidence, perhaps through wishful thinking, or some other form of motivated irrationality. Such an account seems too broad, however: not all cases of forming false beliefs through ignorance, inattention, or stupidity count as *self*-deception. One proposed restriction would require that the self-deceived lack self-knowledge; the self-deceived are thus deceived *about* the self.

The problem with such solutions from Butler's perspective is that, because they deny that the self is also the deceiver, they are compatible with the deception being involuntary and unwitting. But if unwitting, how can self-deception be culpable? Some have claimed that, even where the agent is unaware of what she is doing, and so can exercise no control over her thoughts and actions, she may be at fault in some manner.[36] Whether one's character, and the actions that flow therefrom, is good or bad does not depend on whether one was, or even could have been, aware of what one was up to. Discovery of the fault will rightly lead to shame, or even mortification, and an acceptance of responsibility for amending one's character. But if involuntary self-deception is a fault, is that not sufficient to explain why it is to be condemned?

It is clear, however, that this reply would not satisfy Butler. For him blame requires not just that the agent is at fault, and that she can set about changing once she realizes this, but that, *at the time she acted*, the agent did, or could have known better, and so could *then* have exercised control. Butler's strategy is to bite the bullet: self-deception in moral matters is deception of the self, by the self, and about the self. His task, then, is to explain how this is possible. Butler himself is fully aware of the difficulties. He discusses the case of Balaam, who was asked by Balak, the king of a neighbouring tribe, to curse Israel. Balaam is clearly told by God that he cannot curse the chosen people, but instead of rejecting the request outright, he temporizes and prevaricates, in hopes that he can somehow satisfy Balak without disobeying God's injunction. As Butler points out, here is a man who sought to 'die the death of the righteous', yet did all in his power to avoid having to obey God's command and thus forego his reward. Butler writes:

Good God, what inconsistency, what perplexity is here! With what different views of things, with what contradictory principles of action, must such a mind be torn and distracted! ... (S 7.9.)[37]

Such inconsistency, he concedes, appears unaccountable. Self-deception cannot be successful if the agent is fully aware of what is going on, but it cannot be blameable if the agent is precluded from being aware in any way of what he is up to. His solution lies in reminding us of less flagrant cases of self-deception with which we are familiar in our own lives. What characterizes such cases, and makes them explicable, is the recognition that whether we are aware of, believe, or recognize something is not an all-or-nothing matter. In so doing, he rejects what has been termed a 'toggle-switch' conception of such states. On that view we either believe or we do not, we are fully aware or are in blissful ignorance. Butler rightly and subtly highlights the ambiguities and complexities of our self-knowledge. He reminds us that people put

half-deceits upon themselves ... either by avoiding reflection, or (if they do reflect) by religious equivocation, subterfuges, and palliating matters to themselves: by these means conscience may be laid asleep, and they may go on in a course of wickedness with less disturbance. All the various turns, doubles, and intricacies in a dishonest heart, cannot be laid open; but that there is somewhat of that kind is manifest, be it to be called self-deceit, or by any other name. (S 7.10.)

Balaam's case concerns his relation to God as well as to his own conscience. It is a *religious* injunction that he seeks to disobey by repeatedly making sacrifices, hoping to persuade God to let him find a way of satisfying Balak. The religious, Butler reminds us can thus seek to make 'a composition with the Almighty. These of his commands they will obey: but as to others—why they will make all the atonements in their power' (S 7.13). Butler's diagnosis is not, however, restricted to religious observance. We neglect our duty, but make composition with our consciences by 'half-resolves that [we] will, one time or other, make a change' (S 7.13).

Butler explores more strategies of this kind in Sermon 10, where his example is David and Bathsheba. David lusts after Bathsheba, the wife of Uriah the Hittite. In order to marry her, he arranges for Uriah to be in the front line of battle, and for the other soldiers to draw back, leaving him to be killed. David seems quite unaware of the wrongness of his actions until the prophet Nathan opens his eyes by a parable that gets him to see how his actions look from the outside. On Butler's view, we all suffer from partiality to ourselves which leads us, as it did David, to judge ourselves quite differently from others. It can lead to people being 'perfect strangers to their own characters' (S 10.2). Clearly such people are deceived, but are they *self*-deceived? They are, in Butler's view, if they avoid attending to evidence about their own character that might disconcert them. If they do reflect about a course of action, it 'is not to see whether it be right, but to find out reasons to justify or palliate it, not to others, but to themselves' (S 10.4). Butler rightly remarks that such self-deception is easier in cases where 'the vice and wickedness cannot be exactly defined' (S 10.9).

A great part, perhaps the greatest part, of the intercourse amongst mankind, cannot be reduced to fixed determinate rules. Yet in these cases there is a right and a wrong, a merciful, a liberal, a kind and compassionate behaviour, which surely is our duty; and an unmerciful contracted spirit, an hard and oppressive course of behaviour, which is most certainly immoral and vicious. But who can define precisely, wherein that contracted spirit and hard usage consist?...In these cases, there is great latitude left, for everyone to determine for, and consequently to deceive himself. (S 10.10.)

People thus condemn the very vices from which they suffer, failing to recognize that their character falls under the same censure. But that failure often remains culpable because 'there *frequently appears* a suspicion, that all is not right, or as it should be, and perhaps there *is always* at bottom somewhat of the sort' (S 10.11).[38]

Butler is, no doubt, over-sanguine about the extent to which conscience delivers the correct verdict in a wide range of cases. And he may underestimate the number of cases in which our ignorance of our own vice and folly is incorrigible. But that does not impugn the value of his analysis. All of us recognize, if we are honest, that we often deceive ourselves in this way, and that this is a form of dishonesty for which we are to blame.

Self-Deception and 'Internal' Hypocrisy

That Butler accepts the 'traditional' picture of self-deception in which it is modelled on other-deception becomes especially clear when we turn to his notion of 'internal' hypocrisy. The term occurs only once in the *Sermons* (at S 10.11) but is in the foreground in *A Sermon Preached Before the House of Lords*.

In common language...hypocrisy signifies little more than their pretending what they really do not mean, in order to delude one another. But in Scripture, which treats chiefly of our behaviour towards God and our own consciences, it signifies, not only the endeavour to delude our fellow-creatures, but likewise insincerity towards him, and towards ourselves. (SPO 3.2.)

In Butler's view, it is the sin of internal hypocrisy of which Jesus accuses the Pharisees. They were not, in the ordinary sense, hypocrites who were putting on a show of piety to deceive the world; on the contrary, they were zealous in their religious observation. But their religion was, Butler claims, hypocritical in its very nature:

for it was the form, not the reality; it allowed them in immoral practices...as they indulged their pride and uncharitableness under the notion of zeal for it.... [W]hen any one is thus deluded through his own fault...he deludes himself. And this is as properly hypocrisy towards himself, as deluding the world is hypocrisy towards the world. (SPO 3.2n.)

On Butler's account of self-deception, there is indeed great similarity between the internal and the external hypocrite. Both seek to deceive; both wear a mask, and put on a show of piety or virtue to impress. In one case he does so to make others think well of him; in the other, to make him think well of himself. Linguistically, including the latter may seem a stretch—or it would be if there were ever a case of pure internal hypocrisy, with no attempt to put on a show for others: an internal hypocrite who hid his light under a bushel, so to speak.[39] But that seems unlikely, and was certainly not the case with the Pharisees, who are criticized for making a public display of their zeal for the letter of the law, while ignoring its spirit. That we do think of this as hypocrisy, even when the hypocrite is self-deceived, can be seen by comparing two famous exemplars of the vice in the novels of Dickens. Both Uriah Heep and Mr. Pecksniff are hypocrites. Uriah knows full well his own nature, and seeks only to deceive others for his own advancement. Once exposed, he reveals his true character. Pecksniff is a more interesting case; a fine example of what Butler calls an internal hypocrite. Even when exposed, Pecksniff keeps up his pose: his conception of himself as a good man is central to his self-image. His hypocrisy, we might say, comes from the heart, and is thus more likely to deceive others, as being heart-felt: a sincere form of insincerity.

Resentment and Forgiveness

Christians are especially commanded to forgive, that they may be forgiven, and to love their enemies. Yet we find it natural to resent and to hate those who wrong us and ours. Indeed, many find the injunction to forgive either noble but impractical, or else downright objectionable. Butler has two main purposes in Sermons 8 and 9. First, to explain why a benevolent God has given us such a negative and even hostile emotion as resentment, given that it *appears* 'the direct contrary to benevolence' (S 8.1). Second, he wishes to show that the injunction to forgive is neither impossible nor extravagant, but the merest good sense.

In answering the first question, Butler follows his usual line of enquiry. '[S]ince no passion God hath endued us with can be in itself evil' (S 8.3), we must seek to find out what good purpose it serves. Butler begins by distinguishing two kinds of resentment. Sudden resentment or anger is the immediate response to being hurt, or impeded, and need imply no judgement as to whether one was wronged or treated unjustly. This response is something we share with small children and animals, and its purpose, Butler proposes, is to prevent or defeat any sudden violence, irrespective of fault. Sudden anger may prevent or rectify injustice, but its primary purpose is self-defence. Deliberate anger or resentment, by contrast, is directed not at natural but at moral evil, 'it is not suffering, but injury, which raises that anger or resentment' (S 8.7). Its purpose, then, is to prevent or remedy injury and injustice.

Having uncovered their proper purpose, Butler asks what abuses these passions are liable to. Sudden anger can degenerate into a tendency to 'fly off the handle', or into peevishness. Deliberate resentment is inappropriate when the injury is merely imaginary, or much less than we suppose, or the resentment is disproportionately great given the offence, or finally, 'when pain or harm is inflicted merely in consequence of, and to gratify, that resentment, though naturally raised' (S 8.11).

Why are we supplied with such passions? Why cannot 'reason and cool reflection' serve to move us to prevent or remedy injustice? Passions are, by their nature, highly motivating; just as we need compassion to move us to help the afflicted, so we need resentment or indignation to prompt us to take all the steps that may be necessary to secure justice.

So what is forgiveness, and when is it required? Butler has often been credited as one of the originators of the view that forgiveness requires the *overcoming* of resentment, but it is now generally accepted that this is a misreading. The injunction to forgive 'must be understood to forbid only the *excess and abuse* of this natural feeling, in cases of personal and private injury' (S 9.2, my emphasis). Matters are, however, more complicated than most commentators have realized.

The first complexity is one of nomenclature. Butler takes himself to be picking out *one* negative emotional response to injury and injustice, though there are several different terms for it. 'Let this be called anger, indignation, resentment, or by whatever name anyone shall choose' (S 9.2). But this is surely an over-simplification—an ironic one, in virtue of Butler's famous dictum that 'Every thing is what it is, and not another thing' (P 39). He talks of 'sudden anger *or resentment*', but resentment cannot be sudden. Sudden anger, as Butler says, is an instinctive and largely unthinking response, but resentment can only be settled or deliberate, since it necessarily involves some judgement as to the nature and quality of the act resented.

Nor, I suggest, is there just one form of deliberate anger, for resentment differs from indignation. First, resentment is first-personal in a way that indignation is not. I can only resent wrongs done to me, or to those with whom I am in some way identified, but I can be indignant about any wrong done to anyone (including, of course, myself). Second, resentment, at least normally, seems to involve ill-will towards the offender, while indignation need not. When we are indignant about some injustice, we typically feel that the injustice should be rectified, which in many cases may require that the wrongdoer be punished. Putting things right may be costly for the offender, and so damage his interests, but we need harbour no grudge against him. But the resentful typically do hold grudges; they feel vengeful, or vindictive. To have such attitudes is to want the other person to suffer for its own sake, irrespective of whether it would secure any further good—such as the restoration of justice.[40]

More generally, we can distinguish negative attitudes—such as indignation or outrage—from hostile attitudes, such as hatred, bitterness, resentment, thirst for revenge. If this is right, then Butler should have distinguished resentment from indignation. Since the former, but not the latter, involves ill-will, it may turn out (rather ironically) that the best interpretation of Butler's view is the traditional one. Once we have made this distinction, we could see Butler as claiming that forgiveness *does* require the injured party to *overcome resentment*; it is only *indignation* that is acceptable, provided it is kept within due bounds. In the light of this distinction, let's proceed to look at some of Butler's claims.

1 Hatred, malice, and revenge are abuses of resentment (S 8.3).

2 'indignation raised by cruelty and injustice, and the desire of having it punished, which persons unconcerned would feel, is by no means malice' (S 8.7). Proportionate indignation against wrongdoing is natural and proper (S 9.2).

3 Vice deserves punishment (S 8.16).

4 The injunction to forgive applies only to resentment raised by private or personal injury (S 9.2).

5 It is natural and proper to feel more indignation when the injured party is oneself than one feels when others suffer injury (S 9.2).

6 So the commandment to forgive must 'forbid only the excess and abuse of this natural feeling, in cases of personal and private injury' (S 9.2).

7 Private retaliation, rendering evil for evil, where each person is judge and jury in his own case, will lead to a downward spiral of ever more bitter revenge-taking (S 9.5).

8 When society exacts punishment on the offender, it causes pain. So resentment 'ought never to be made use of, but only in order to produce some greater good' (S 9.6). It must 'never be indulged or gratified for itself' (S 9.8).

9 'Malice and revenge meditates evil itself...: this is what it *directly* tends towards, as its proper design' (S 9.10).

10 The 'general obligation to benevolence or good-will towards mankind' requires us to forgive injuries (S 9.12).

11 'Resentment is not inconsistent with good-will.... We may love our enemy, and yet have resentment against him for his injurious behaviour towards us (S 9.13; see also S 9.19).

Butler supposes that, though there are several terms for a negative attitude to wrongdoing, there is only one emotional response in play. He is thus committed to the view that the only possible difference in response must be one of *degree*. The only difference between the natural response to a wrong done to others, and one done to you or yours, is that you will normally have a stronger response to the latter than to the former. And, by parity of reasoning, the only difference between the appropriate response, and one that involves an abuse of the feeling, is that one's negative reaction is excessive. But as I suggested above, it is more plausible to suppose that the difference between resentment and indignation is one of *kind*, rather than merely of degree. First, only a wrong done to oneself can *wound*; it seems plausible, therefore, that the specifically first-personal response of resentment is different from the third-personal one of indignation. Second, the difference between indignation at the wrong, which is compatible with goodwill, and an abuse of that passion, such as malice or revenge, which is not, is surely a difference in kind. It cannot possibly lie, as Butler's analysis seems to require, merely in the *degree* of negative reaction to the wrong; great indignation, even excessive indignation, is quite compatible with the preservation of goodwill towards the offender, in that it need involve no personal animus, or desire that the offender be harmed for its own sake. And the degree of resentment towards some minor offence may be quite low, but is still inappropriate if it involves ill-will.

Once we distinguish resentment and indignation in the way I have suggested, then Butler's view becomes both consistent and plausible. Resentment, hatred, and malice are inappropriate responses to wrongdoing because they involve ill-will; indignation, the desire for just punishment is, however, appropriate, because consistent with the preservation of goodwill, but it should also be properly proportioned to the degree of offence.

The Love of God

The last three sermons concern issues that are as much to do with philosophy of religion as with moral philosophy, and so I will be brief. In Sermons 13 and 14, Butler turns to the topic of the love of God; his love for us and ours for him. In particular, Butler argues that though, perhaps, in this earthly life it is easier to love the creature than the creator, God is in fact 'the natural object' of our affections. Some, but by no means all, of these affections are such that, when we reflect on them, we love or approve of them, and of anyone who has them. These affections include goodness, righteousness, and zeal for justice. We also wish for the esteem and approval of those who have such qualities to a higher degree than we do. Since God is perfect, we will not only love and admire him more than his creation but we will also be submissive to his will, for we desire his esteem. Though God is constantly present to us, we are too much taken up with the objects of the senses always to recognize that presence. Once we have lost our bodily senses after death, however, we shall retain our intellectual and moral faculties and will, no doubt, have some new means of perception.[41] Once seen face to face, God will be a source of complete satisfaction to us; we will want for nothing.

All this is fairly orthodox theology, but raises a number of deep philosophical issues. What kind of faculty of awareness can we have in some post-mortem bodily existence? In what sense could the pre- and post-mortem persons be said to be the same person? In what manner can we 'see' God? These are questions that take us beyond moral philosophy into the most abstruse questions of metaphysics and epistemology. The last Sermon, 'Upon the Ignorance of Man', continues this trend and serves as a foretaste of the later *Analogy*, rather than as a summation of the *Sermons*.

The Butler–Clarke Correspondence

The portion of the correspondence that concerns ethics begins with an issue about whether we have any control over whether we act virtuously. Butler grants that we have, in many cases, the direct power to act or to refrain from acting, and so the power to do what is right rather than what is wrong. We are thus morally responsible for that choice. However, virtuous action requires that we act from certain motives, rather than others, and with certain goals in view, and not others. But our feelings and goals are not immediately subject to the will. 'How then can we be accountable for neglecting the practice of any virtue, when at what time soever we did neglect it we wanted that which was ... absolutely necessary to the performance of it, viz. a disposition to be influenced by the proper motive?' (Letter of 30 Sept. 1717, para. 3).[42]

Clarke's reply does not seem to me very satisfactory, as he appears to miss Butler's point. First, he holds that rationality includes a disposition to do what we ought, including obeying the will of God; but Butler is not denying that we have the power to, say, relieve the poor. His concern is whether we can do this from the correct motives so that we will not only have done what is right but acted virtuously. Clarke further maintains that, when we do God's will from any motive *other than a vicious one* we are acting virtuously. To relieve distress from immediate and natural compassion would thus count as an instance of virtuous behaviour. It seems that the interlocutors are to some extent talking past each other. Clarke has a conception of virtuous action in which I am virtuous provided I do the act, and did not do it from a bad motive. Butler appears to have a more fully Aristotelian conception in which the agent's emotions are in line with his reason. He has moulded his character so that he does what is right willingly, for the right reasons, and from a stable disposition. (Natural compassion is too fluctuating a motive to count as virtuous on Aristotle's view.)

In Butler's next letter, he concedes that we may all have a natural disposition to virtue, but reformulates his question in the light of that concession. Might we not, at least on some occasions, have a stronger disposition to vice? He concedes that it may be the case that, on some occasion, the strength of my vicious disposition is a result of earlier free decisions of my own that have led me into such a deplorable condition. But surely there must have been a first action of mine, where my motive to do the wrong act was the stronger and, *ex hypothesi*, I could not in such a case be responsible for getting into that state by way of earlier acts of mine. In that case, try as I might, I cannot act from the weaker virtuous motive, and so I cannot act virtuously.

Clarke replies that humans have no disposition to be influenced by wrong motives as such. We have strong inclinations to attain various objects. Those inclinations are not in themselves vicious. What is vicious is not the inclinations, but continuing to act from them, when conscience has declared that such an action ought not to be performed. Though Butler's response in the Correspondence is somewhat cautious it is clear that, in the Sermons, he accepts Clarke's claim that no inclination is, in itself, wrong. It is not clear, however, that this solves the problem that Butler raises. Suppose that, though I care about the deprived, my main reason for engaging in charitable endeavours is to receive the praise and admiration of others. To wish to be admired and praised for doing well is not intrinsically vicious, but my charitable deeds cannot be said to be *virtuous* if that was my predominant motive.

One possible answer to Butler's puzzle is not far to seek. I have only indirect control over my character; I can work to change my feelings and emotions, but I cannot change them at will. If I do what is right from inappropriate motives, where my motivation is not a result of earlier actions of mine, then I have done all that can be demanded of me. My act, though right, was not virtuous; I am accountable for doing the right thing, but not for failing to do it in a virtuous manner. All things equal, however, the older I am, and the more opportunities to improve my character I have had, the less can my failure to act from suitable motives be excused.[43]

Notes

1. I have used a common system of abbreviations for referring to different parts of Butler's writings. For a complete explanation of this system see the material at the beginning of the Editor's Notes.
2. For the fullest modern account of his life, see Cunliffe 2008 to which I am much indebted in what follows.
3. (Letter to Clarke, 30 Sept. 1717, *Works*, ed. Bernard, I. 332.)
4. For more details, and the significance of this fact for an appreciation of the content of Butler's Sermons, see Aaron Garrett (2012, and unpublished).
5. The magnificent rectory still stands, though the building has been divided and the interior has been altered.

6. There is some reason to believe that Butler may have been liable to depression, which was relieved by congenial company.

7. Wife of George II, she had been a pupil of Leibniz, and was well versed in both philosophy and theology, summoning—among others—Berkeley, Clarke, and Benjamin Hoadly to discuss theology with her.

8. This seems to have led to some cooling of the friendship between Secker and Butler, the former thinking the latter not grateful for the efforts made on his behalf. Secker also criticized Butler for hypocrisy in attacking the government and its ministers in private, yet usually supporting them in the division lobbies.

9. The Clerk of the Closet is responsible for advising the Sovereign's Private Secretary on the names of candidates to fill vacancies in the Roll of Chaplains to the Sovereign. He presents Bishops for homage to the Sovereign; examines any theological books to be presented to the Sovereign; and preaches annually in the Chapel Royal, St. James's Palace.

10. He stresses the value of external forms of religion in generating a settled faith. This, along with his placing of a white cross in the chapel at Bristol, led to charges after his death that he may have died a Roman Catholic—a charge that casts more light on the paranoia of the times than on the religious leanings of Butler.

11. One indication of that diminished stature is that no complete editions of either of Butler's main works have been in print for a considerable time.

12. See Wedgwood 2007 for an interesting attempt to give an account of authority in Butler that does not rely on theistic underpinnings.

13. In this interpretation, the proper response to doubts about the deliverances of conscience is the one given by Prichard 1912.

14. In the following two sections I have drawn on McNaughton 2013.

15. There seems no reason to suppose that Butler is drawing a sharp distinction between three different types of mental state; he is not very consistent in his usage.

16. Relevant paragraphs in the *Analogy* include: Intro. 4, 10; I.2.3; I.3.2–3, 5–6, 9–10, 12–15, 17, 19–20, 25, 27–8; I.4.1, 4, 7; I.5.4, 12–13, 18–21; I.6.11–12, 14; I.7.11; II.1.16–17, 21–7; II.3.1, 13, 15; II.5.3–8, 11; II.6.8–9, 11, 13, 17; II.8.9, 11.

17. A less important question is whether benevolence should be regarded as a superior principle. I have dealt with this issue at length in McNaughton 1992.

18. See also, e.g., S 2.8–9.

19. For further discussion see McNaughton 2013.

20. The evidence of the *Analogy* (the third interpretative guide) requires careful treatment. In that work, Butler talks much more about prudence than about self-love. He takes prudence to be a part of morality, and prudent and imprudent actions to be judged by the *same* approving and disapproving faculty as moral and immoral actions. To what extent this represents a shift from his position in the *Sermons* rather than mere clarification is a difficult question, but one rarely addressed by commentators on Butler.

21. As I am using the terms, a desire is *satisfied* if the desired state of affairs comes about. But *gratification* requires that the desirer be aware that her desire has been satisfied.

   That Butler has the contrast between desiring for its own sake and merely as a means in mind is brought out when he writes that 'The principle we call self-love never seeks anything external for the sake of the thing, but only as a means of happiness or good: particular affections rest in the external things themselves' (S 11.5).

22. Butler's attack on psychological hedonism was often regarded as decisive (e.g. Broad 1930: 54–5) but of late there have been a number of sceptical voices: Sober 1992; Stewart 1992; Phillips 2000. For a partial defence of Butler against Sober see Zellner 1999.

23. For a good discussion of this point see Irwin 2008: 499f. See also Sidgwick's partial endorsement of Butler's argument (1967b: 44–56).

24. Sidgwick 1967b: 48–51. The same point is often extended to consequentialism: she whose sole aim is to maximize the good directly may produce less good than someone who has other motivations (see, e.g., Railton 1984).

25. Utilitarianism is a species of consequentialism, and a full discussion would look at other consequentialist theories, many of which can accommodate some or all of these three objections to utilitarianism. Butler, however, considers only a version of utilitarianism. I am also ignoring, for the sake of simplicity, satisficing versions of these theories.

26. In these discussions, Butler probably has Hutcheson's early version of utilitarianism in mind (see esp. Hutcheson, *An Inquiry into the Original of our Ideas of Beauty and Virtue*, Treatise II, Section 3: 116–35). The famous phrase 'greatest happiness for the greatest numbers' is at p. 125. Note that Butler does not try to offer a complete moral theory, but merely to suggest the constraints that the successful theory must meet.

27. A full discussion would require distinguishing what justifies human systems of punishment from what justifies divine punishment.

28. Much as the single-minded pursuit of happiness may make us less happy.

29. Bernard Williams aptly dubbed this view 'Government House utilitarianism' (1985: 108–10).

30. No doubt this was another instance where Sidgwick owed a great deal to Butler.

31. Louden, 1995.

32. Anscombe raises this objection: 'Butler exalts conscience, but appears ignorant that a man's conscience may tell him to do the vilest things' (1958: 2).

33. In a letter to a lady asking him about 'a case of conscience' concerning property formerly owned by the Church, Butler notes that

> The corruption and disorder of human affairs is such as has perplexed the rule of right, and made it hard in some cases to say how one ought to act. (Bartlett 1839: 99.)

In other cases, however, perplexity is self-induced and, to that degree, blameable.

> And persons, by their own negligence and folly in their temporal affairs, no less than by a course of vice, bring themselves into new difficulties … and one irregularity after another, embarrasses things to such a degree, that they know not whereabout they are; and often make the path of conduct so intricate and perplexed, that it is difficult to trace it out; difficult even to determine what is the prudent or the moral part. (A I.4.7: 72.)

34. Whether conscience can be corrupted, so as to give the wrong verdict, or merely silenced, is unclear. Butler's language usually suggests the latter, but occasionally the former. This question is not relevant, however, to our main purpose for, in either case, the false moral belief will be due to self-deception.

35. See Holton 2001.

36. See, e.g., Adams 1985.

37. Here, and elsewhere, Butler likens such cases to full-blown weakness of will, but there is not space to pursue this suggestion.

38. 'It is as easy to close the eyes of the mind, as those of the body: and the former is more frequently done with wilfulness, and yet not attended to, than the latter' (S 10.11). Such wilful blindness extends beyond moral issues; Butler reminds us how often people fail to look into their financial affairs because they fear that they are bad. On discovering their debt, they plead ignorance. 'And yet no one will take this as an excuse, who is sensible that their ignorance of their particular circumstances was owing to their general knowledge of them; that is, their general knowledge, that matters were not well with them, prevented their looking into particulars' (S 10.11).

39. For Butler, of course, there is always an audience, and thus there cannot truly be pure internal hypocrisy. Whoever is guilty of internal hypocrisy 'acts as if he could deceive and mock God, and therefore is an hypocrite towards him, in as strict and literal a sense as the nature of the subject will admit' (SPO 3.2n).

40. It may be that usage has changed since Butler's day, and that his original hearers would not have thus distinguished indignation and resentment. But Butler's identification of the two is bound to confuse the modern reader.

41. See S 14.10.

42. Ross (1939: 114–22) later wrestled with the same problem, and concluded that, since virtuous action was not in our immediate power, we could have no duty to act from certain motives, and were only accountable for what was in our immediate power, viz. to do the right or wrong act.

43. In the *Analogy* Butler takes a fairly wide view as to what counts as a suitable motive. 'For, veracity, justice, and charity, regard to God's authority, and to our own chief interest, are not only all three coincident; but each of them is, in itself, a just and natural motive or principle of action' (A I.5.19: 95), though he does seem to hold that only a concern for veracity, justice, and charity is strictly speaking a moral motive. The whole of chapter 5 of Part I is worth reading in this context.

Notes on the Text

The Sermons and Other Writings

The *Fifteen Sermons Preached at the Rolls Chapel* were first published in 1726; a second edition followed in 1729, in which Butler made a number of changes, including the addition of a lengthy preface. A third edition followed in 1736 to which Butler made a few further very minor corrections. The text reproduced here is essentially that of the second edition, incorporating the very few alterations made in the third edition. Where there is any doubt about the text, I compared the third edition with both the second and the fourth (1749) editions, these being the only ones published in Butler's lifetime.

Bernard's (1900) two-volume edition of Butler's works has long been the standard text that subsequent editors have followed in style, spelling, and layout. I also largely follow Bernard in these, but depart from it in some ways (explained below), and silently correct such errors as I have found. My main alteration is that I have restored Butler's punctuation, which Bernard silently 'regularized'. Bernard numbers Butler's paragraphs, and I follow him in this, for ease of reference. These numbers occur at the beginning of each paragraph, set out to the edge of the text, without brackets.

As I previously noted, Butler made a number of changes when the second edition was published, some of which were fairly substantial. Bernard, and some subsequent editors, includes all differences between first and second editions in the main text or in footnotes. This can lead to a tangle of square brackets and lengthy footnotes. This is distracting and often not especially helpful. I have sought to make this an uncluttered reader's edition of the revised text as Butler finally wished it to be presented. Where the difference between first and second editions appears philosophically significant, I indicate this in the accompanying Editor's Notes.

In addition to the *Sermons* I have included three other significant writings of Butler's. The first is *A Dissertation of the Nature of Virtue*. This was originally printed as an Appendix to the *Analogy of Religion Natural and Revealed*, first published in 1736; it is now almost uniformly printed in editions of the *Sermons*. The second and third are somewhat less well known. In the fourth edition of the *Sermons* (1749) Butler included *Six Sermons Preached upon Public Occasions*. I have decided to include one of them, namely *A Sermon Preached Before the House of Lords*. While all of Butler's six sermons on public occasions contain some material on moral matters they are largely (though not wholly) exhortatory rather than analytical. But the sermon I have selected discusses issues central to the Fifteen

Sermons—hypocrisy, its relation to self-deceit, obedience to authority, and the need for hierarchy in society.

Finally, I include that part of his early correspondence with Clarke that concerns moral motivation and responsibility. This consists of three letters from Butler and two replies by Clarke. (I have edited out extraneous matter.) The other parts of the correspondence are on proofs of the existence of God and so more relevant to the *Analogy* than to the *Sermons*.

Capitalization, Punctuation, and Spelling

Nouns that essentially serve as names of God have an initial capital, e.g. 'Author of Nature', 'Creator', etc. Pronouns referring to the deity, however, as is becoming standard, have no initial capital. Butler's eighteenth-century use of initial capitals for nouns is also dropped, but his use of capitalization for the next word after *First*, *Secondly*, etc. has been retained. His somewhat eccentric punctuation (which may indicate the way the text would be read aloud) is retained, but spelling is modernized, except for words where an old form is still current, e.g. 'shew'. Standard eighteenth-century abbreviations, such as 'tis instead of 'it is', are avoided as a distraction and such words are spelled out in full.

Italics and Quotations

Butler uses italics for at least six different purposes.

1 emphasis
2 quotation
3 names of biblical characters
4 statement of a thesis
5 to indicate a word is being talked about
6 numbering of points, e.g. *First*

I follow Butler in this, except for 2 and 3. Quotations are within single quotation marks with two exceptions. First, where there is a quotation within a quotation. Second, to indicate the interpolations of an imaginary interlocutor or objector who appears a number of times in the text. In both these cases double quotation marks are used. The names of biblical authors are not italicized.

Endnotes

Butler's own notes were originally printed as footnotes, and are here reproduced as endnotes to each Sermon. These notes are here numbered rather than, as in the original, indicated by the use of asterisks, daggers, etc. Butler's references to authors are, of course, to eighteenth-century editions, or earlier. Those references are retained, but a reference to a modern edition, where available, is given in the Editor's Notes. From time to time Butler quotes or alludes to a biblical passage without referencing it. In all such cases, a note enclosed in square brackets will give the reference. Where it would help the reader to have the original biblical text it will be given in the Editor's Notes. Biblical references are given in the original text by abbreviated book headings in italics, followed by chapter in roman numerals, and verse number in Arabic numerals, e.g. *Eccles.* ii.3. I have retained this style both in the text and in the Editor's Notes.

Butler uses the Authorized Version (AV) of the Christian Bible (usually referred to outside the UK as the King James Version) for all quotations, with the exception of the Psalms, where he normally uses the earlier translation by Coverdale that was retained in the 1662 Book of Common Prayer (BCP). It was retained because of its familiarity, and because any change would disrupt musical settings that had long been in use. (For more detail see Cummings 2011: 783–5.)

Editor's Notes

These notes follow immediately after Butler's texts. They refer back to that text by Sermon number followed by paragraph number. A discreet asterisk in the main text will indicate an editorial note at end of text. Further details about referencing the texts are given at the beginning of the Editor's Notes.

References to works in the bibliography are as follows. References to historical texts are, initially, by longer title, and then by book, section, chapter, paragraph (as appropriate) followed by a colon and the page number in the edition cited in the bibliography. Subsequent references will be by shorter title, with abbreviated references to book, section etc. Here is an example. My initial reference to Locke looks like this:

John Locke, *An Essay Concerning Human Understanding*, Book III, ch. 9, para. 6: vol. II, 78.

Second and subsequent references have this form:

Locke, *Essay*, IV.20.6: vol. II, 300.

References to contemporary works are by the author–date method.

On quite a number of occasions I draw from the notes of earlier editors, especially Bernard. Rather than mention this on each occasion I acknowledge my general indebtedness and only reference the editor who drew attention to this point where it seems appropriate.

Butler's use of Greek and Latin words and quotations is extremely sparing. Translations and explanations are given in the Editor's Notes.

Butler's Predecessors

Rather than clutter up the notes with too many details of the main thinkers with whom Butler engaged, I include brief summaries of the views of these thinkers, insofar as their thought is relevant to Butler. Writers covered are the Stoics, Hobbes, Shaftesbury, Clarke, Wollaston, and Hutcheson.

Bibliography

This is selective rather than comprehensive, but includes significant commentaries and articles, as well as works cited. It is divided into the following headings:

Works by Butler Published during his Lifetime
Modern Editions of Butler's Works
Biographical Works
Works by Butler's Predecessors and Contemporaries
Books about Butler's Moral Philosophy
Articles and Chapters about Butler
Internet Entries about Butler
Other Works Cited

Fifteen Sermons Preached at the Rolls Chapel

TO THE
RIGHT HONOURABLE
SIR JOSEPH JEKYLL
MASTER OF THE ROLLS, ETC.
THE FOLLOWING SERMONS, PREACHED IN HIS CHAPEL
ARE, WITH ALL HUMILITY
DEDICATED BY
HIS MOST DUTIFUL AND MOST OBEDIENT
SERVANT
JOSEPH BUTLER

The Preface*

Though it is scarce possible to avoid judging, in some way or other, of almost every 1
thing which offers itself to one's thoughts; yet it is certain, that many persons, from
different causes, never exercise their judgement, upon what comes before them, in
the way of determining whether it be conclusive, and holds. They are perhaps
entertained with some things, not so with others; they like, and they dislike: but
whether that which is proposed to be made out be really made out or not; whether a
matter be stated according to the real truth of the case, seems to the generality of
people merely a circumstance of no consideration at all. Arguments are often wanted
for some accidental purpose: but proof, as such, is what they never want for
themselves; for their own satisfaction of mind, or conduct in life. Not to mention
the multitudes who read merely for the sake of talking, or to qualify themselves for
the world, or some such kind of reasons; there are, even of the few who read for their
own entertainment, and have a real curiosity to see what is said, several, which is
prodigious, who have no sort of curiosity to see what is true: I say, curiosity; because
it is too obvious to be mentioned, how much that religious and sacred attention,
which is due to truth, and to the important question, What is the rule of life? is lost
out of the world.

For the sake of this whole class of readers, for they are of different capacities, 2
different kinds, and get into this way from different occasions, I have often wished
that it had been the custom to lay before people nothing in matters of argument but
premises, and leave them to draw conclusions themselves; which, though it could not
be done in all cases, might in many.

The great number of books and papers of amusement, which, of one kind or 3
another, daily come in one's way, have in part occasioned, and most perfectly fall in
with and humour, this idle way of reading and considering things. By this means,
time even in solitude is happily got rid of, without the pain of attention: neither is any
part of it more put to the account of idleness, one can scarce forbear saying, is spent
with less thought, than great part of that which is spent in reading.

Thus people habituate themselves to let things pass through their minds, as one 4
may speak, rather than to think of them. Thus by use they become satisfied merely
with seeing what is said, without going any further. Review and attention, and even
forming a judgement, become fatigue; and to lay any thing before them that requires
it, is putting them quite out of their way.

There are also persons, and there are at least more of them than have a right to 5
claim such superiority, who take for granted, that they are acquainted with every
thing; and that no subject, if treated in the manner it should be, can be treated in any
manner but what is familiar and easy to them.

6   It is true indeed, that few persons have a right to demand attention; but it is also true, that nothing can be understood without that degree of it, which the very nature of the thing requires. Now morals, considered as a science, concerning which speculative difficulties are daily raised, and treated with regard to those difficulties, plainly require a very peculiar attention. For here ideas never are in themselves determinate, but become so by the train of reasoning and the place they stand in; since it is impossible that words can always stand for the same ideas, even in the same author, much less in different ones.* Hence an argument may not readily be apprehended, which is different from its being mistaken; and even caution to avoid being mistaken, may, in some cases, render it less readily apprehended. It is very unallowable for a work of imagination or entertainment not to be of easy comprehension, but may be unavoidable in a work of another kind, where a man is not to form or accommodate, but to state things as he finds them.

7   It must be acknowledged, that some of the following discourses are very abstruse and difficult; or, if you please, obscure; but I must take leave to add, that those alone are judges, whether or no and how far this is a fault, who are judges, whether or no and how far it might have been avoided—those only who will be at the trouble to understand what is here said, and to see how far the things here insisted upon, and not other things, might have been put in a plainer manner; which yet I am very far from asserting that they could not.

8   This* much however will be allowed, that general criticisms concerning obscurity considered as a distinct thing from confusion and perplexity of thought, as in some cases there may be ground for them; so in others, they may be nothing more at the bottom than complaints, that every thing is not to be understood with the same ease that some things are. Confusion and perplexity in writing is indeed without excuse, because anyone may, if he pleases, know whether he understands and sees through what he is about: and it is unpardonable for a man to lay his thoughts before others, when he is conscious that he himself does not know whereabouts he is, or how the matter before him stands. It is coming abroad in disorder which he ought to be dissatisfied to find himself in at home.

9   But even obscurities, arising from other causes than the abstruseness of the argument, may not be always inexcusable. Thus a subject may be treated in a manner, which all along supposes the reader acquainted with what has been said upon it, both by ancient and modern writers; and with what is the present state of opinion in the world concerning such subject. This will create a difficulty of a very peculiar kind, and even throw an obscurity over the whole before those who are not thus informed; but those who are, will be disposed to excuse such a manner, and other things of the like kind, as a saving of their patience.

10   However upon the whole, as the title of Sermons gives some right to expect what is plain and of easy comprehension, and as the best auditories* are mixed, I shall not set about to justify the propriety of preaching, or under that title publishing, discourses so abstruse as some of these are. Neither is it worth while to trouble the reader with

the account of my doing either. He must not however impute to me, as a repetition of the impropriety, this second edition, but to the demand for it.

Whether he will think he has any amends made him by the following illustrations   11 of what seemed most to require them, I myself am by no means a proper judge.

There are two ways in which the subject of morals may be treated. One begins   12 from inquiring into the abstract relations of things: the other, from a matter of fact, namely, what the particular nature of man is, its several parts, their economy or constitution; from whence it proceeds to determine what course of life it is, which is correspondent to this whole nature. In the former method the conclusion is expressed thus, that vice is contrary to the nature and reasons of things: in the latter, that it is a violation or breaking in upon our own nature. Thus they both lead us to the same thing, our obligations to the practice of virtue; and thus they exceedingly strengthen and enforce each other. The first seems the most direct formal proof, and in some respects the least liable to cavil and dispute: the latter is in a peculiar manner adapted to satisfy a fair mind: and is more easily applicable to the several particular relations and circumstances in life.*

The following discourses proceed chiefly in this latter method. The three first   13 wholly. They were intended to explain what is meant by the nature of man, when it is said that virtue consists in following, and vice in deviating from it; and by explaining to that the assertion is true. That the ancient moralists had some inward feeling or other, which they chose to express in this manner, that man is born to virtue, that it consists in following nature, and that vice is more contrary to this nature than tortures or death, their works in our hands are instances.* Now a person who found no mystery in this way of speaking of the ancients; who, without being very explicit with himself, kept to his natural feeling, went along with them, and found within himself a full conviction, that what they laid down was just and true; such an one would probably wonder to see a point, in which he never perceived any difficulty, so laboured as this is, in the second and third sermons; insomuch perhaps as to be at a loss for the occasion, scope, and drift of them. But it need not to be thought strange, that this manner of expression, though familiar with them, and, if not usually carried so far, yet not uncommon amongst ourselves, should want explaining; since there are several perceptions daily felt and spoken of, which yet it may not be very easy at first view to explicate, to distinguish from all others, and ascertain exactly what the idea or perception is. The many treatises upon the passions are a proof of this; since so many would never have undertaken to unfold their several complications, and trace and resolve them into their principles, if they had thought what they were endeavouring to shew was obvious to everyone who felt and talked of those passions. Thus, though there seems no ground to doubt, but that the generality of mankind have the inward perception expressed so commonly in that manner by the ancient moralists, more than to doubt whether they have those passions; yet it appeared of use to unfold that inward conviction, and lay it open in a more explicit manner, than I had seen done; especially when there were not wanting persons, who manifestly mistook the whole thing, and so had great reason to express themselves dissatisfied with it. A late author of great and deserved reputation says, that to place virtue in following nature, is, at best, a loose way of talk. And he has reason to say this, if what I think he intends to express, though with great decency, be true, that scarce any other sense can be put upon those words, but acting as any of the several parts, without distinction, of a man's nature happened most to incline him.[1]

14   Whoever thinks it worth while to consider this matter thoroughly, should begin with stating to himself exactly the idea of a system, economy or constitution of any particular nature, or particular any thing: and he will, I suppose, find, that it is an one or a whole, made up of several parts; but yet, that the several parts even considered as a whole, do not complete the idea, unless in the notion of a whole, you include the relations and respects, which those parts have to each other. Every work both of nature and of art is a system: and as every particular thing both natural and artificial is for some use or purpose out of and beyond itself, one may add, to what has been already brought into the idea of a system, its conduciveness to this one or more ends. Let us instance in a watch—suppose the several parts of it taken to pieces, and placed apart from each other: let a man have ever so exact a notion of these several parts, unless he considers the respects and relations which they have to each other, he will not have any thing like the idea of a watch. Suppose these several parts brought together and any how united: neither will he yet, be the union ever so close, have an idea which will bear any resemblance to that of a watch. But let him view those several parts put together, or consider them as to be put together in the manner of a watch; let him form a notion of the relations which those several parts have to each other—all conducive in their respective ways, to this purpose, shewing the hour of the day; and then he has the idea of a watch. Thus it is with regard to the inward frame of man. Appetites, passions, affections, and the principle of reflection, considered merely as the several parts of our inward nature, do not at all give us an idea of the system or constitution of this nature; because the constitution is formed by somewhat not yet taken into consideration, namely by the relations, which these several parts have to each other; the chief of which is the authority of reflection or conscience.* It is from considering the relations which the several appetites and passions in the inward frame have to each other, and above all the supremacy of reflection or conscience, that we get the idea of the system or constitution of human nature. And from the idea itself it will as fully appear, that this our nature, i.e. constitution is adapted to virtue, as from the idea of a watch it appears, that its nature, i.e. constitution or system is adapted to measure time.* What in fact or event commonly happens, is nothing to this question. Every work of art is apt to be out of order: but this is so far from being according to its system, that let the disorder increase, and it will totally destroy it. This is merely by way of explanation what an economy, system or constitution is. And thus far the cases are perfectly parallel. If we go further, there is indeed a difference, nothing to the present purpose, but too important an one ever to be omitted. A machine is inanimate and passive: but we are agents. Our constitution is

put in our own power. We are charged with it: and therefore are accountable for any disorder or violation of it.

Thus nothing can possibly be more contrary to nature than vice; meaning by 15 nature, not only *the several parts* of our internal frame, but also the *constitution* of it. Poverty and disgrace, tortures and death are not so contrary to it. Misery and injustice are indeed equally contrary to some different parts of our nature taken singly: but injustice is moreover contrary to the whole constitution of the nature.

If it be asked whether this constitution be really what those philosophers meant, 16 and whether they would have explained themselves in this manner: the answer is the same, as if it should be asked, whether a person, who had often used the word resentment and felt the thing, would have explained this passion exactly in the same manner, in which it is done in one of these discourses. As I have no doubt, but that this is a true account of that passion, which he referred to and intended to express by the word, resentment; so I have no doubt, but that this is the true account of the ground of that conviction, which they referred to, when they said, vice was contrary to nature. And though it should be thought that they meant no more than that vice was contrary to the higher and better part of our nature; even this implies such a constitution as I have endeavoured to explain. For the very terms, higher and better, imply a relation or respect of parts to each other; and these relative parts, being in one and the same nature, form a constitution and are the very idea of it. They had a perception that injustice was contrary to their nature, and that pain was so also. They observed these two perceptions totally different, not in degree, but in kind: and the reflecting upon each of them as they thus stood in their nature, wrought a full intuitive conviction, that more was due and of right belonged to one of these inward perceptions, than to the other; that it demanded in all cases to govern such a creature as man. So that upon the whole, this is a fair and true account of what was the ground of their conviction; of what they intended to refer to when they said, virtue consisted in following nature: a manner of speaking not loose and undeterminate, but clear and distinct, strictly just and true.

Though I am persuaded the force of this conviction is felt by almost everyone; yet 17 since, considered as an argument and put in words, it appears somewhat abstruse, and since the connection of it is broken in the three first sermons, it may not be amiss to give the reader the whole argument here in one view.

Mankind has various instincts and principles of action,* as brute creatures have; 18 some leading most directly and immediately to the good of the community, and some most directly to private good.

Man has several which brutes have not; particularly reflection or conscience, an 19 approbation of some principles or actions, and disapprobation of others.

Brutes obey their instincts or principles of action, according to certain rules; 20 suppose the constitution of their body, and the objects around them.

The generality of mankind also obey their instincts and principles, all of them; 21 those propensions we call good, as well as the bad, according to the same rules;

namely the constitution of their body, and the external circumstances which they are in. (Therefore it is not a true representation of mankind, to affirm that they are wholly governed by self-love, the love of power and sensual appetites: since, as on the one hand, they are often actuated by these, without any regard to right or wrong; so on the other, it is manifest fact, that the same persons, the generality, are frequently influenced by friendship, compassion, gratitude; and even a general abhorrence of what is base, and liking of what is fair and just, takes its turn amongst the other motives of action. This is the partial inadequate notion of human nature treated of in the first discourse: and it is by this nature, if one may speak so, that the world is in fact influenced, and kept in that tolerable order, in which it is.)

22   Brutes in acting according to the rules before-mentioned, their bodily constitution and circumstances, act suitably to their whole nature. (It is however to be distinctly noted, that the reason why we affirm this, is not merely that brutes in fact act so; for this alone, however universal, does not at all determine, whether such course of action be correspondent to their whole nature: but the reason of the assertion is, that as in acting thus, they plainly act conformably to somewhat in their nature, so from all observations we are able to make upon them, there does not appear the least ground to imagine them to have any thing else in their nature, which requires a different rule or course of action.)

23   Mankind also in acting thus would act suitably to their whole nature, if no more were to be said of man's nature, than what has been now said; if that, as it is a true, were also a complete, adequate account of our nature.

24   But that is not a complete account of man's nature. Somewhat further must be brought in to give us an adequate notion of it; namely, that one of those principles of action, conscience or reflection, compared with the rest as they all stand together in the nature of man, plainly bears upon it marks of authority over all the rest, and claims the absolute direction of them all, to allow or forbid their gratification: a disapprobation of reflection being in itself a principle manifestly superior to a mere propension. And the conclusion is, that to allow no more to this superior principle or part of our nature, than to other parts; to let it govern and guide only occasionally in common with the rest, as its turn happens to come, from the temper and circumstances one happens to be in; this is not to act conformably to the constitution of man: neither can any human creature be said to act conformably to his constitution of nature, unless he allows to that superior principle the absolute authority which is due to it. And this conclusion is abundantly confirmed from hence, that one may determine what course of action the economy of man's nature requires, without so much as knowing in what degrees of *strength* the several principles prevail, or which of them have actually the greatest influence.

25   The practical reason of insisting so much upon this natural authority of the principle of reflection or conscience is, that it seems in great measure overlooked by many, who are by no means the worst sort of men. It is thought sufficient to abstain from gross wickedness, and to be humane and kind to such as happen to come in

their way. Whereas in reality the very constitution of our nature requires, that we bring our whole conduct before this superior faculty; wait its determination; enforce upon ourselves its authority, and make it the business of our lives, as it is absolutely the whole business of a moral agent, to conform ourselves to it. This is the true meaning of that ancient precept, *Reverence thyself.**

The not taking into consideration this authority, which is implied in the idea of reflex approbation or disapprobation, seems a material deficiency or omission in Lord Shaftesbury's *Inquiry concerning Virtue*. He has shewn beyond all contradiction, that virtue is naturally the interest or happiness, and vice the misery of such a creature as man, placed in the circumstances which we are in this world. But suppose there are particular exceptions; a case which this author was unwilling to put, and yet surely it is to be put: or suppose a case which he has put and determined, that of a sceptic not convinced of this happy tendency of virtue, or being of a contrary opinion. His determination is, that it would be 'without remedy'.[2]* One may say more explicitly, that leaving out the authority of reflex approbation or disapprobation, such an one would be under an obligation to act viciously; since interest, one's own happiness, is a manifest obligation, and there is not supposed to be any other obligation in the case. "But does it much mend the matter, to take in that natural authority of reflection? There indeed would be an obligation to virtue; but would not the obligation from supposed interest on the side of vice remain?" If it should, yet to be under two contrary obligations, *i.e.* under none at all, would not be exactly the same as to be under a formal obligation to be vicious, or to be in circumstances in which the constitution of man's nature plainly required, that vice should be preferred. But the obligation on the side of interest really does not remain. For the natural authority of the principle of reflection, is an obligation the most near and intimate, the most certain and known: whereas the contrary obligation can at the utmost appear no more than probable;* since no man can be *certain* in any circumstances, that vice is his interest in the present world, much less can he be certain against another: and thus the certain obligation would entirely supersede and destroy the uncertain one; which yet would have been of real force without the former.

In truth the taking in this consideration, totally changes the whole state of the case; and shews, what this author does not seem to have been aware of, that the greatest degree of scepticism which he thought possible, will still leave men under the strictest moral obligations, whatever their opinion be concerning the happiness of virtue.* For that mankind upon reflection felt an approbation of what was good, and disapprobation of the contrary, he thought a plain matter of fact, as it undoubtedly is, which none could deny, but from mere affectation. Take in then that authority and obligation, which is a constituent part of this reflex approbation, and it will undeniably follow, though a man should doubt of every thing else, yet, that he would still remain under the nearest and most certain obligation to the practice of virtue; an obligation implied in the very idea of virtue, in the very idea of reflex approbation.

28   And how little influence soever this obligation alone, can be expected to have in fact upon mankind, yet one may appeal even to interest and self-love, and ask, since from man's nature, condition and the shortness of life, so little, so very little indeed, can possibly in any case be gained by vice; whether it be so prodigious a thing to sacrifice that little, to the most intimate of all obligations; and which a man cannot transgress without being self-condemned, and, unless he has corrupted his nature, without real self-dislike: this question I say may be asked, even upon supposition that the prospect of a future life were ever so uncertain.

29   The observation that man is thus by his very nature a law to himself, pursued to its just consequences, is of the utmost importance; because from it it will follow, that though men should, through stupidity or speculative scepticism, be ignorant of or disbelieve any authority in the universe to punish the violation of this law; yet, if there should be such authority, they would be as really liable to punishment, as though they had been beforehand convinced, that such punishment would follow. For in whatever sense we understand justice, even supposing, what I think would be very presumptuous to assert, that the end of divine punishment is no other than that of civil punishment, namely, to prevent future mischief; upon this bold supposition, ignorance or disbelief of the sanction would by no means exempt even from this justice; because it is not foreknowledge of the punishment, which renders us obnoxious to it; but merely violating a known obligation.

30   And here it comes in one's way to take notice of a manifest error or mistake, in the author now cited, unless perhaps he has incautiously expressed himself so as to be misunderstood; namely, that 'it is malice only, and not goodness, which can make us afraid'.[3]* Whereas in reality, goodness is the natural and just object of the greatest fear to an ill man. Malice may be appeased or satiated; humour may change: but goodness is a fixed, steady, immovable principle of action. If either of the former holds the sword of justice, there is plainly ground for the greatest of crimes to hope for impunity: but if it be goodness, there can be no possible hope, whilst the reasons of things, or the ends of government, call for punishment. Thus everyone sees, how much greater chance of impunity, an ill man has, in a partial administration, than in a just and upright one. It is said, that *the interest or good of the whole, must be the interest of the Universal Being, and that he can have no other.* Be it so. This author has proved, that vice is naturally the misery of mankind in this world. Consequently it was for the good of the whole that it should be so. What shadow of reason then is there to assert, that this may not be the case hereafter? Danger of future punishment (and if there be danger, there is ground of fear) no more supposes malice, than the present feeling of punishment does.

31   The sermon *Upon the Character of Balaam,* and that *Upon Self-Deceit* both relate to one subject.* I am persuaded, that a very great part of the wickedness of the world, is, one way or other, owing to the self-partiality, self-flattery and self-deceit endeavoured there to be laid open and explained. It is to be observed amongst persons of the lowest rank, in proportion to their compass of thought, as much as amongst men of

education and improvement. It seems, that people are capable of being thus artful with themselves, in proportion as they are capable of being so with others. Those who have taken notice that there is really such a thing, namely, plain falseness and insincerity in men with regard to themselves, will readily see the drift and design of these discourses: and nothing, that I can add, will explain the design of them to him, who has not beforehand remarked, at least, somewhat of the character. And yet, the admonitions they contain, may be as much wanted by such a person, as by others; for it is to be noted, that a man may be entirely possessed by this unfairness of mind, without having the least speculative notion what the thing is.

The account given of *resentment* in the eighth sermon, is introductory to the   32 following one *Upon Forgiveness of Injuries*. It may possibly have appeared to some, at first sight, a strange assertion, that injury is the only natural object of settled resentment, or that men do not in fact resent deliberately any thing but under this appearance of injury. But I must desire the reader not to take any assertion alone by itself, but to consider the whole of what is said upon it: because this is necessary, not only in order to judge of the truth of it, but often, such is the nature of language, to see the very meaning of the assertion. Particularly as to this, injury and injustice is, in the sermon itself, explained to mean, not only the more gross and shocking instances of wickedness, but also contempt, scorn, neglect, any sort of disagreeable behaviour towards a person, which he thinks other than what is due to him. And the general notion of injury or wrong, plainly comprehends this, though the words are mostly confined to the higher degrees of it.

Forgiveness of injuries is one of the very few moral obligations which has been   33 disputed. But the proof that it is really an obligation, what our nature and condition require, seems very obvious, were it only from the consideration that revenge is doing harm merely for harm's sake. And as to the love of our enemies: resentment cannot supersede the obligation to universal benevolence, unless they are in the nature of the thing inconsistent, which they plainly are not.[4]

This divine precept, to forgive injuries and love our enemies, though to be met   34 with in Gentile moralists,* yet is in a peculiar sense a precept of Christianity; as our Saviour has insisted more upon it, than upon any other single virtue. One reason of this doubtless is, that it so peculiarly becomes an imperfect, faulty creature. But it may be observed also, that a virtuous temper of mind, consciousness of innocence and good meaning towards everybody, and a strong feeling of injustice and injury, may itself, such is the imperfection of our virtue, lead a person to violate this obligation, if he be not upon his guard. And it may well be supposed, that this is another reason why it is so much insisted upon by him, who 'knew what was in man'.[5]

The chief design of the eleventh discourse is to state the notion of self-love and   35 disinterestedness, in order to shew that benevolence is not more unfriendly to self-love, than any other particular affection whatever. There is a strange affectation in many people of explaining away all particular affections, and representing the whole of life as nothing but one continued exercise of self-love. Hence arises that surprising confusion and perplexity in the Epicureans[6] of old, Hobbes, the author of *Reflexions Sentences et Maximes Morales,** and this whole set of writers; the confusion of calling actions interested which are done in contradiction to the most manifest known interest, merely for the gratification of a present passion. Now all this confusion might easily be avoided, by stating to ourselves wherein the idea of self-love in general consists, as distinguished from all particular movements towards particular external objects; the appetites of sense, resentment, compassion, curiosity, ambition and the rest.[7] When this is done, if the words 'selfish' and 'interested' cannot be parted with, but must be applied to every thing; yet, to avoid such total confusion of all language, let the distinction be made by epithets: and the first may be called cool or settled selfishness, and the other passionate or sensual selfishness. But the most natural way of speaking plainly is, to call the first only, self-love, and the actions proceeding from it, interested: and to say of the latter, that they are not love to ourselves, but movements towards somewhat external: honour, power, the harm or good of another: and that the pursuit of these external objects, so far as it proceeds from these movements (for it may proceed from self-love)[8] is no otherwise interested, than as every action of every creature must, from the nature of the thing, be; for no one can act but from a desire, or choice, or preference of his own.

36   Self-love and any particular passion may be joined together; and from this complication, it becomes impossible in numberless instances to determine precisely, how far an action, perhaps even of one's own; has for its principle general self-love, or some particular passion. But this need create no confusion in the ideas themselves of self-love and particular passions. We distinctly discern what one is, and what the other are: though we may be uncertain how far one or the other influences us. And though from this uncertainty, it cannot but be, that there will be different opinions concerning mankind, as more or less governed by interest; and some will ascribe actions to self-love, which others will ascribe to particular passions: yet it is absurd to say that mankind are wholly actuated by either; since it is manifest that both have their influence. For as on the one hand, men form a general notion of interest, some placing it in one thing, and some in another, and have a considerable regard to it throughout the course of their life, which is owing to self-love; so on the other hand, they are often set on work by the particular passions themselves, and a considerable part of life is spent in the actual gratification of them, *i.e.* is employed, not by self-love, but by the passions.

37   Besides, the very idea of an interested pursuit, necessarily presupposes particular passions or appetites; since the very idea of interest or happiness consists in this, that an appetite or affection enjoys its object.* It is not because we love ourselves that we find delight in such and such objects, but because we have particular affections towards them. Take away these affections, and you leave self-love absolutely nothing at all to employ itself about;[9] no end or object for it to pursue, excepting only that of

avoiding pain. Indeed the Epicureans, who maintained that absence of pain, was the highest happiness, might, consistently with themselves, deny all affection, and, if they had so pleased, every sensual appetite too: but the very idea of interest or happiness other than absence of pain, implies particular appetites or passions; these being necessary to constitute that interest or happiness.

The observation that benevolence is no more disinterested than any of the common particular passions,[10] seems in itself worth being taken notice of; but is insisted upon to obviate that scorn, which one sees rising upon the faces of people who are said to know the world, when mention is made of a disinterested, generous or public-spirited action. The truth of that observation might be made appear, in a more formal manner of proof: for whoever will consider all the possible respects and relations which any particular affection can have to self-love and private interest, will, I think, see demonstrably, that benevolence is not in any respect more at variance with self-love, than any other particular affection whatever, but that it is in every respect, at least, as friendly to it.

If the observation be true, it follows, that self-love and benevolence, virtue and interest are not to be opposed, but only to be distinguished from each other; in the same way as virtue and any other particular affection, love of arts, suppose, are to be distinguished. Every thing is what it is, and not another thing.* The goodness or badness of actions does not arise from hence, that the epithet, interested or disinterested, may be applied to them, any more than that any other indifferent epithet, suppose inquisitive or jealous may or may not be applied to them; not from their being attended with present or future pleasure or pain; but from their being what they are: namely, what becomes such creatures as we are, what the state of the case requires, or the contrary. Or in other words, we may judge and determine, that an action is morally good or evil, before we so much as consider, whether it be interested or disinterested. This consideration no more comes in to determine, whether an action be virtuous, than to determine whether it be resentful. Self-love in its due degree is as just and morally good, as any affection whatever. Benevolence towards particular persons may be to a degree of weakness, and so be blameable: and disinterestedness is so far from being in itself commendable, that the utmost possible depravity, which we can in imagination conceive, is that of disinterested cruelty.

Neither does there appear any reason to wish self-love were weaker in the generality of the world, than it is. The influence which it has, seems plainly owing to its being constant and habitual, which it cannot but be, and not to the degree or strength of it. Every caprice of the imagination, every curiosity of the understanding, every affection of the heart, is perpetually shewing its weakness by prevailing over it. Men daily, hourly sacrifice the greatest known interest, to fancy, inquisitiveness, love or hatred, any vagrant inclination. The thing to be lamented is, not that men have so great regard to their own good or interest in the present world, for they have not enough;[11] but that they have so little to the good of others.* And this seems plainly owing to their being so much engaged in the gratification of particular passions unfriendly to benevolence, and which happen to be most prevalent in them, much more than to self-love. As a proof of this may be observed, that there is no character more void of friendship, gratitude, natural affection, love to their country, common justice, or more equally and uniformly hard-hearted, than the *abandoned* in, what is called, the way of pleasure—hard-hearted and totally without feeling in behalf of others; except when they cannot escape the sight of distress, and so are interrupted by it in their pleasures. And yet it is ridiculous to call such an abandoned course of pleasure interested, when the person engaged in it knows beforehand, and goes on under the feeling and apprehension, that it will be as ruinous to himself, as to those who depend upon him.

41   Upon the whole, if the generality of mankind were to cultivate within themselves the principle of self-love; if they were to accustom themselves often to set down and consider, what was the greatest happiness they were capable of attaining for themselves in this life, and if self-love were so strong and prevalent, as that they would uniformly pursue this their supposed chief temporal good, without being diverted from it by any particular passion; it would manifestly prevent numberless follies and vices. This was in a great measure the Epicurean system of philosophy. It is indeed by no means the religious, or even moral institution of life.* Yet, with all the mistakes men would fall into about interest, it would be less mischievous, than the extravagancies of mere appetite, will and pleasure: for certainly self-love, though confined to the interest of this life, is, of the two, a much better guide than passion,[12] which has absolutely no bound nor measure, but what is set to it by this self-love, or moral considerations.

42   From the distinction above made between self-love, and the several particular principles or affections in our nature, we may see how good ground there was for that assertion, maintained by the several ancient schools of philosophy, against the Epicureans, namely, that virtue is to be pursued as an end, eligible in and for itself. For, if there be any principles or affections in the mind of man distinct from self-love, that the things those principles tend towards, or that the objects of those affections are, each of them, in themselves eligible, to be pursued upon its own account, and to be rested in as an end, is implied in the very idea of such principle or affection.[13] They indeed asserted much higher things of virtue, and with very good reason; but to say thus much of it, that it is to be pursued for itself, is to say no more of it, than may truly be said of the object of every natural affection whatever.

43   The question, which was a few years ago disputed in France* concerning *the love of God*, which was there called enthusiasm, as it will every where by the generality of the world; this question I say, answers in *religion*, to that old one in *morals* now mentioned. And both of them are, I think, fully determined by the same observation,

namely, that the very nature of affection, the idea itself, necessarily implies resting in its object as an end.

I shall not here add any thing further, to what I have said in the two discourses 44 upon that most important subject, but only this: that if we are constituted such sort of creatures, as from our very nature, to feel certain affections or movements of mind, upon the sight or contemplation of the meanest inanimate part of the creation, for the flowers of the field have their beauty; certainly there must be somewhat due to him himself, who is the Author and Cause of all things; who is more intimately present to us, than any thing else can be, and with whom we have a nearer and more constant intercourse, than we can have with any creature: there must be some movements of mind and heart which correspond to his perfections, or of which those perfections are the natural object. And that when we are commanded to 'love the Lord our God, with all our heart, and with all our mind, and with all our soul';[14] somewhat more must be meant than merely that we live in hope of rewards, or fear of punishments from him; somewhat more than this must be intended: though these regards themselves are most just and reasonable, and absolutely necessary to be often recollected, in such a world as this.

It may be proper just to advertise the reader, that he is not to look for any particular 45 reason for the choice of the greatest part of these discourses; their being taken from amongst many others, preached in the same place, through a course of eight years, being in great measure accidental. Neither is he to expect to find any other connection between them, than that uniformity of thought and design, which will always be found in the writings of the same person, when he writes with simplicity and in earnest.

STANHOPE, *Sept.* 16, 1729.

Notes

1. *Religion of Nature Delineated*. Ed. 1724. Pages 22, 23.*
2. *Characteristics* [ed. 1727], vol. ii. p. 69.*
3. *Characteristics*, vol. i. p. 39.*
4. S 9.13.
5. [*John* ii. 25.]
6. One need only look into Torquatus's account of the Epicurean system, in Cicero's first book *de Finibus*, to see in what a surprising manner this was done by them. Thus the desire of praise, and of being beloved, he explains to no other, than desire of safety: regard to our country, even in the most virtuous character, to be nothing but regard to ourselves.* The author of *Reflexions etc. Morales* says, 'Curiosity proceeds from interest or pride; which pride also would doubtless have been explained to be self-love' (p. 85, ed. 1725). As if there were no such passions in mankind, as desire of esteem, or of being beloved, or of knowledge. Hobbes's account of the affections of good-will and pity, are instances of the same kind.*

7. S 11.5.
8. S 1.6n.
9. S 11.9.
10. S 11.11.
11. S 1.14.
12. S 2.25.
13. S 12.5.
14. [*Matt.* xxii. 37.]

Sermon 1

Upon Human Nature*

For as we have many members in one body, and all members have not the same office: so we being many, are one body in Christ, and every one members one of another.

(*Romans* xii.4, 5)

The Epistles in the New Testament have all of them a particular reference to the condition and usages of the Christian world at the time they were written. Therefore as they cannot be thoroughly understood, unless that condition and those usages are known and attended to: so further, though they be known, yet if they be discontinued or changed; exhortations, precepts, and illustrations of things, which refer to such circumstances now ceased or altered, cannot at this time be urged in that manner, and with that force which they were to the primitive Christians. Thus the text now before us, in its first intent and design, relates to the decent management of those extraordinary gifts which were then in the church,[1] but which are now totally ceased.* And even as to the allusion that 'we are one body in Christ'; though what the apostle here intends is equally true of Christians in all circumstances; and the consideration of it is plainly still an additional motive, over and above moral considerations, to the discharge of the several duties and offices of a Christian: yet it is manifest this allusion must have appeared with much greater force to those, who by the many difficulties they went through for the sake of their religion, were led to keep always in view the relation they stood in to their Saviour, who had undergone the same; to those, who from the idolatries of all around them, and their ill treatment, were taught to consider themselves as not of the world in which they lived, but as a distinct society of themselves; with laws, and ends, and principles of life and action, quite contrary to those which the world professed themselves at that time influenced by. Hence the relation of a Christian was by them considered as nearer than that of affinity and blood; and they almost literally esteemed themselves as members one of another.

1

It cannot indeed possibly be denied, that our being God's creatures, and virtue being the natural law we are born under, and the whole constitution of man being plainly adapted to it, are prior obligations to piety and virtue, than the consideration that God sent his Son into the world to save it, and the motives which arise from the peculiar relations of Christians, as members one of another under Christ our head.

2

However, though all this be allowed, as it expressly is by the inspired writers; yet it is manifest that Christians at the time of the revelation, and immediately after, could not but insist mostly upon considerations of this latter kind.

3   These observations shew the original particular reference of the text; and the peculiar force with which the thing intended by the allusion in it, must have been felt by the primitive Christian world. They likewise afford a reason for treating it at this time in a more general way.

4   The relation, which the several parts or members of the natural body have to each other and to the whole body, is here compared to the relation which each particular person in society has to other particular persons and to the whole society; and the latter is intended to be illustrated by the former.* And if there be a likeness between these two relations, the consequence is obvious: that the latter shews us we were intended to do good to others, as the former shews us that the several members of the natural body were intended to be instruments of good to each other and to the whole body.* But as there is scarce any ground for a comparison between society and the mere material body, this without the mind being a dead unactive thing; much less can the comparison be carried to any length. And since the apostle speaks of the several members as having distinct offices, which implies the mind; it cannot be thought an unallowable liberty; instead of the *body* and *its members*, to substitute the *whole nature of man*, and *all the variety of internal principles which belong to it*. And then the comparison will be between the nature of man as respecting self, and tending to private good, his own preservation and happiness; and the nature of man as having respect to society, and tending to promote public good, the happiness of that society. These ends do indeed perfectly coincide; and to aim at public and private good are so far from being inconsistent, that they mutually promote each other: yet in the following discourse they must be considered as entirely distinct; otherwise the nature of man as tending to one, or as tending to the other, cannot be compared. There can no comparison be made, without considering the things compared as distinct and different.

5   From this review and comparison of the nature of man as respecting self, and as respecting society, it will plainly appear, that *there are as real and the same kind of indications in human nature, that we were made for society and to do good to our fellow-creatures; as that we were intended to take care of our own life and health and private good: and that the same objections lie against one of these assertions, as against the other.* For

6   *First*, There is a natural principle of *benevolence*[2] in man; which is in some degree to *society*, what *self-love* is to the *individual*. And if there be in mankind any disposition to friendship; if there be any such thing as compassion, for compassion is momentary love; if there be any such thing as the paternal or filial affections; if there be any affection in human nature, the object and end of which is the good of another; this is itself benevolence, or the love of another. Be it ever so short, be it in ever so low a degree, or ever so unhappily confined; it proves the assertion, and points out what we were designed for, as really as though it were in a higher degree and

more extensive. I must however remind you, that though benevolence and self-love are different; though the former tends most directly to public good, and the latter to private: yet they are so perfectly coincident, that the greatest satisfactions to ourselves depend upon our having benevolence in a due degree;* and that self-love is one chief security of our right behaviour towards society. It may be added, that their mutual coinciding, so that we can scarce promote one without the other, is equally a proof that we were made for both.

Secondly, This will further appear, from observing that the *several passions* and affections, which are distinct[3] both from benevolence and self-love, do in general contribute and lead us to *public* good as really as to *private*. It might be thought too minute and particular, and would carry us too great a length, to distinguish between and compare together the several passions or appetites distinct from benevolence, whose primary use and intention is the security and good of society; and the passions distinct from self-love, whose primary intention and design is the security and good of the individual.[4] It is enough to the present argument, that desire of esteem from others, contempt and esteem of them, love of society as distinct from affection to the good of it, indignation against successful vice, that these are public affections or passions; have an immediate respect to others, naturally lead us to regulate our behaviour in such a manner as will be of service to our fellow-creatures. If any or all of these may be considered likewise as private affections, as tending to private good; this does not hinder them from being public affections too, or destroy the good influence of them upon society, and their tendency to public good. It may be added, that as persons without any conviction from reason of the desirableness of life, would yet of course preserve it merely from the appetite of hunger; so by acting merely from regard (suppose) to reputation, without any consideration of the good of others, men often contribute to public good. In both these instances they are plainly instruments in the hands of another, in the hands of Providence, to carry on ends, the preservation of the individual and good of society, which they themselves have not in their view or intention. The sum is, men have various appetites, passions, and particular affections, quite distinct both from self-love and from benevolence: all of these have a tendency to promote both public and private good, and may be considered as respecting others and ourselves equally and in common: but some of them seem most immediately to respect others, or tend to public good; others of them most immediately to respect self, or tend to private good: as the former are not benevolence, so the latter are not self-love: neither sort are instances of our love either to ourselves or others; but only instances of our Maker's care and love both of the individual and the species, and proofs that he intended we should be instruments of good to each other, as well as that we should be so to ourselves.

Thirdly, There is a principle of reflection in men, by which they distinguish between, approve and disapprove their own actions.* We are plainly constituted such sort of creatures as to reflect upon our own nature. The mind can take a view of what passes within itself, its propensions, aversions, passions, affections, as respecting such objects, and in such degrees; and of the several actions consequent thereupon. In this survey it approves of one, disapproves of another, and towards a third is affected in neither of these ways, but is quite indifferent. This principle in man, by which he approves or disapproves his heart, temper, and actions, is conscience; for this is the strict sense of the word, though sometimes it is used so as to take in more. And that this faculty tends to restrain men from doing mischief to each other, and leads them to do good, is too manifest to need being insisted upon. Thus a parent has the affection of love to his children: this leads him to take care of, to educate, to make due provision for them; the natural affection leads to this: but the reflection that it is his proper business, what belongs to him, that it is right and commendable so to do; this added to the affection, becomes a much more settled principle, and carries him on through more labour and difficulties for the sake of his children, than he would undergo from that affection alone; if he thought it, and the course of action it led to, either indifferent or criminal. This indeed is impossible, to do that which is good and not to approve of it; for which reason they are frequently not considered as distinct, though they really are: for men often approve of the actions of others, which they will not imitate, and likewise do that which they approve not. It cannot possibly be denied that there is this principle of reflection or conscience in human nature. Suppose a man to relieve an innocent person in great distress; suppose the same man afterwards, in the fury of anger, to do the greatest mischief to a person who had given no just cause of offence; to aggravate the injury, add the circumstances of former friendship, and obligation from the injured person; let the man who is supposed to have done these two different actions, coolly reflect upon them afterwards, without regard to their consequences to himself: to assert that any common man would be affected in the same way towards these different actions, that he would make no distinction between them, but approve or disapprove them equally, is too glaring a falsity to need being confuted. There is therefore this principle of reflection or conscience in mankind. It is needless to compare the respect it has to private good, with the respect it has to public; since it plainly tends as much to the latter as to the former, and is commonly thought to tend chiefly to the latter. This faculty is now mentioned merely as another part in the inward frame of man, pointing out to us in some degree what we are intended for, and as what will naturally and of course have some influence. The particular place assigned to it by nature, what authority it has, and how great influence it ought to have, shall be hereafter considered.

9   From this comparison of benevolence and self-love, of our public and private affections, of the courses of life they lead to, and of the principle of reflection or conscience as respecting each of them, it is as manifest, that *we were made for society, and to promote the happiness of it; as that we were intended to take care of our own life, and health, and private good.*

10   And from this whole review must be given a different draught of human nature from what we are often presented with. Mankind are by nature so closely united,

there is such a correspondence between the inward sensations of one man and those of another, that disgrace is as much avoided as bodily pain, and to be the object of esteem and love as much desired as any external goods: and in many particular cases, persons are carried on to do good to others, as the end their affections tend to and rest in; and manifest that they find real satisfaction and enjoyment in this course of behaviour. There is such a natural principle of attraction in man towards man, that having trod the same tract of land, having breathed in the same climate, barely having been born in the same artificial district or division, becomes the occasion of contracting acquaintances and familiarities many years after: for any thing may serve the purpose. Thus relations merely nominal are sought and invented, not by governors, but by the lowest of the people; which are found sufficient to hold mankind together in little fraternities and copartnerships: weak ties indeed, and what may afford fund enough for ridicule, if they are absurdly considered as the real principles of that union: but they are in truth merely the occasions, as any thing may be of any thing, upon which our nature carries us on according to its own previous bent and bias; which occasions therefore would be nothing at all, were there not this prior disposition and bias of nature. Men are so much one body, that in a peculiar manner they feel for each other, shame, sudden danger, resentment, honour, prosperity, distress; one or another, or all of these, from the social nature in general, from benevolence, upon the occasion of natural relation, acquaintance, protection, dependence; each of these being distinct cements of society. And therefore to have no restraint from, no regard to others in our behaviour, is the speculative absurdity of considering ourselves as single and independent, as having nothing in our nature which has respect to our fellow-creatures, reduced to action and practice. And this is the same absurdity, as to suppose a hand, or any part to have no natural respect to any other, or to the whole body.

But allowing all this, it may be asked, "Has not man dispositions and principles **11** within which lead him to do evil to others, as well as to do good? Whence come the many miseries else, which men are the authors and instruments of to each other?" These questions, so far as they relate to the foregoing discourse, may be answered by asking, Has not man also dispositions and principles within, which lead him to do evil to himself, as well as good? Whence come the many miseries else, sickness, pain and death, which men are the instruments and authors of to themselves?

It may be thought more easy to answer one of these questions than the other, but **12** the answer to both is really the same; that mankind have ungoverned passions which they will gratify at any rate, as well to the injury of others, as in contradiction to known private interest: but that as there is no such thing as self-hatred, so neither is there any such thing as ill-will in one man towards another, emulation and resentment being away;* whereas there is plainly benevolence or good-will: there is no such thing as love of injustice, oppression, treachery, ingratitude; but only eager desires after such and such external goods; which, according to a very ancient observation, the most abandoned would choose to obtain by innocent means,* if they were as easy, and as effectual to their end: that even emulation and resentment, by anyone who will consider what these passions really are in nature,[5] will be found nothing to the purpose of this objection: and that the principles and passions in the mind of man, which are distinct both from self-love and benevolence, primarily and most directly lead to right behaviour with regard to others as well as himself, and only secondarily and accidentally to what is evil. Thus, though men to avoid the shame of one villainy are sometimes guilty of a greater, yet it is easy to see, that the original tendency of shame is to prevent the doing of shameful actions; and its leading men to conceal such actions when done, is only in consequence of their being done; *i.e.* of the passion's not having answered its first end.

13   If it be said, that there are persons in the world, who are, in great measure without the natural affections towards their fellow-creatures: there are likewise instances of persons without the common natural affections to themselves: but the nature of man is not to be judged by either of these, but by what appears in the common world, in the bulk of mankind.

14   I am afraid it would be thought very strange, if to confirm the truth of this account of human nature, and make out the justness of the foregoing comparison, it should be added, that from what appears, men in fact as much and as often contradict that *part* of their nature which respects *self*, and which leads them to their *own private* good and happiness; as they contradict that *part* of it which respects *society*, and tends to *public* good: that there are as few persons, who attain the greatest satisfaction and enjoyment which they might attain in the present world; as who do the greatest good to others which they might do: nay, that there are as few who can be said really and in earnest to aim at one, as at the other. Take a survey of mankind: the world in general, the good and bad, almost without exception, equally are agreed, that were religion out of the case, the happiness of the present life would consist in a manner wholly in riches, honours, sensual gratifications; insomuch that one scarce hears a reflection made upon prudence, life, conduct, but upon this supposition. Yet on the contrary, that persons in the greatest affluence of fortune are no happier than such as have only a competency; that the cares and disappointments of ambition for the most part far exceed the satisfactions of it; as also the miserable intervals of intemperance and excess, and the many untimely deaths occasioned by a dissolute course of life: these things are all seen, acknowledged, by every one acknowledged; but are thought no objections against, though they expressly contradict, this universal principle, that the happiness of the present life consists in one or other of them. Whence is all this absurdity and contradiction? Is not the middle way obvious? Can any thing be more manifest, than that the happiness of life consists in these possessed and enjoyed only to a certain degree; that to pursue them beyond this degree, is always attended with more inconvenience than advantage to a man's self, and often with extreme misery and unhappiness. Whence then, I say, is all this absurdity and contradiction? Is it really the result of consideration in mankind, how they may become most easy to themselves, most free from care, and enjoy the chief happiness attainable in this

world? Or is it not manifestly owing either to this, that they have not cool and reasonable concern enough for themselves, to consider wherein their chief happiness in the present life consists; or else, if they do consider it, that they will not act conformably to what is the result of that consideration: *i.e.* reasonable concern for themselves, or cool self-love is prevailed over by passion and appetite. So that from what appears, there is no ground to assert that those principles in the nature of man, which most directly lead to promote the good of our fellow-creatures, are more generally or in a greater degree violated, than those, which most directly lead us to promote our own private good and happiness.*

The sum of the whole is plainly this. The nature of man considered in his single   15
capacity, and with respect only to the present world, is adapted and leads him to attain the greatest happiness he can for himself in the present world. The nature of man considered in his public or social capacity leads him to a right behaviour in society, to that course of life which we call virtue. Men follow or obey their nature in both these capacities and respects to a certain degree, but not entirely: their actions do not come up to the whole of what their nature leads them to in either of these capacities or respects; and they often violate their nature in both, *i.e.* as they neglect the duties they owe to their fellow-creatures, to which their nature leads them; and are injurious, to which their nature is abhorrent: so there is a manifest negligence in men of their real happiness or interest in the present world, when that interest is inconsistent with a present gratification; for the sake of which they negligently, nay, even knowingly are the authors and instruments of their own misery and ruin. Thus they are as often unjust to themselves as to others, and for the most part are equally so to both by the same actions.

Notes

1. *I Cor.* xii.
2. Suppose a man of learning to be writing a grave book upon *human nature*, and to shew in several parts of it that he had an insight into the subject he was considering: amongst other things, the following one would require to be accounted for; the appearance of benevolence or good-will in men towards each other in the instances of natural relation, and in others (Hobbes, *Of Human Nature*, c. 9. §. 17).* Cautious of being deceived with outward shew, he retires within himself to see exactly, what that is in the mind of man from whence this appearance proceeds; and, upon deep reflection, asserts the principle in the mind to be only the love of power, and delight in the exercise of it. Would not every body think here was a mistake of one word for another? That the philosopher was contemplating and accounting for some other *human actions*, some other behaviour of man to man? And could anyone be thoroughly satisfied, that what is commonly called benevolence or good-will was really the affection meant, but only by being made to understand that this learned person had a general hypothesis, to which the appearance of good-will could no otherwise be reconciled? That what has this appearance is often nothing but ambition; that delight in superiority often (suppose always) mixes itself with benevolence, only makes it more specious to call it

ambition than hunger, of the two: but in reality that passion does no more account for the whole appearances of good-will, than this appetite does. Is there not often the appearance of one man's wishing that good to another, which he knows himself unable to procure him; and rejoicing in it, though bestowed by a third person? And can love of power any way possibly come in to account for this desire or delight? Is there not often the appearance of men's distinguishing between two or more persons, preferring one before another to do good to, in cases where love of power cannot in the least account for the distinction and preference? For this principle can no otherwise distinguish between objects, than as it is a greater instance and exertion of power to do good to one rather than to another. Again, suppose good-will in the mind of man to be nothing but delight in the exercise of power: men might indeed be restrained by distant and accidental considerations; but these restraints being removed, they would have a disposition to, and delight in mischief as an exercise and proof of power: and this disposition and delight would arise from or be the same principle in the mind, as a disposition to and delight in charity. Thus cruelty, as distinct from envy and resentment, would be exactly the same in the mind of man as good-will: that one tends to the happiness, the other to the misery of our fellow-creatures, is it seems merely an accidental circumstance, which the mind has not the least regard to. These are the absurdities which even men of capacity run into, when they have occasion to belie their nature, and will perversely disclaim that image of God which was originally stamped upon it; the traces of which, however faint, are plainly discernible upon the mind of man.

If any person can in earnest doubt, whether there be such a thing as good-will in one man towards another; (for the question is not concerning either the degree or extensiveness of it, but concerning the affection itself;) let it be observed, that *whether man be thus or otherwise constituted, what is the inward frame in this particular,* is a mere question of fact or natural history, not provable immediately by reason. It is therefore to be judged of and determined in the same way other facts or matters of natural history are: by appealing to the external senses, or inward perceptions, respectively, as the matter under consideration is cognizable by one or the other: by arguing from acknowledged facts and actions; for a great number of actions in the same kind, in different circumstances, and respecting different objects, will prove, to a certainty, what principles they do not, and, to the greatest probability, what principles they do proceed from: and lastly, by the testimony of mankind. Now that there is some degree of benevolence amongst men, may be as strongly and plainly proved in all these ways, as it could possibly be proved, supposing there was this affection in our nature. And should any one think fit to assert, that resentment in the mind of man was absolutely nothing but reasonable concern for our own safety; the falsity of this, and what is the real nature of that passion, could be shewn in no other ways than those in which it may be shewn, that there is such a thing in *some degree* as *real* good-will in man towards man. It is sufficient that the seeds of it be implanted in our nature by God. There is, it is owned, much left for us to do upon our own heart and temper; to cultivate, to improve, to call it forth, to exercise it in a steady, uniform manner. This is our work: this is virtue and religion.

3. Every body makes a distinction between self-love, and the several particular passions, appetites, and affections; and yet they are often confounded again. That they are totally different will be seen by anyone who will distinguish between the passions and appetites *themselves*, and *endeavouring* after the means of their gratification. Consider the appetite of hunger, and the desire of esteem; these being the occasion both of pleasure and pain, the

coolest *self-love*, as well as the appetites and passions themselves, may put us upon making use of the *proper methods of obtaining* that pleasure, and avoiding that pain; but the *feelings* themselves, the pain of hunger and shame, and the delight from esteem, are no more self-love than they are any thing in the world. Though a man hated himself, he would as much feel the pain of hunger as he would that of the gout: and it is plainly supposable there may be creatures with self-love in them to the highest degree, who may be quite insensible and indifferent (as men in some cases are) to the contempt and esteem of those, upon whom their happiness does not in some further respects depend. And as self-love and the several particular passions and appetites are in themselves totally different; so, that some actions proceed from one, and some from the other, will be manifest to any who will observe the two following very supposable cases. One man rushes upon certain ruin for the gratification of a present desire: no body will call the principle of this action self-love. Suppose another man to go through some laborious work upon promise of a great reward, without any distinct knowledge what the reward will be: this course of action cannot be ascribed to any particular passion. The former of these actions is plainly to be imputed to some particular passion or affection, the latter as plainly to the general affection or principle of self-love. That there are some particular pursuits or actions concerning which we cannot determine how far they are owing to one, and how far to the other, proceeds from this, that the two principles are frequently mixed together, and run up into each other. This distinction is further explained in the Eleventh Sermon.

4. If any desire to see this distinction and comparison made in a particular instance, the appetite and passion now mentioned may serve for one. Hunger is to be considered as a private appetite; because the end for which it was given us is the preservation of the individual. Desire of esteem is a public passion; because the end for which it was given us is to regulate our behaviour towards society. The respect which this has to private good is as remote as the respect that has to public good: and the appetite is no more self-love, than the passion is benevolence. The object and end of the former is merely food; the object and end of the latter is merely esteem: but the latter can no more be gratified, without contributing to the good of society; than the former can be gratified, without contributing to the preservation of the individual.

5. Emulation is merely the desire and hope of equality with or superiority over others, with whom we compare ourselves. There does not appear to be any *other grief* in the natural passion, but only *that want* which is implied in desire. However this may be so strong as to be the occasion of great *grief*. To desire the attainment of this equality or superiority by the *particular means* of others, being brought down to our own level, or below it, is, I think, the distinct notion of envy. From whence it is easy to see, that the real end, which the natural passion emulation, and which the unlawful one envy aims at, is exactly the same; namely, that equality or superiority: and consequently, that to do mischief is not the end of envy, but merely the means it makes use of to attain its end.* As to resentment, see the Eighth Sermon.

Sermon 2
Upon Human Nature

For when the Gentiles which have not the law, do by nature the things contained
in the law, these having not the law, are a law unto themselves.

(Romans ii.14)

1   As speculative truth admits of different kinds of proof, so likewise moral obligations
may be shewn by different methods. If the real nature of any creature leads him and is
adapted to such and such purposes only, or more than to any other; this is a reason to
believe the Author of that nature intended it for those purposes.* Thus there is no
doubt the eye was intended for us to see with. And the more complex any constitution is, and the greater variety of parts there are which thus tend to some one end, the
stronger is the proof that such end was designed. However, when the inward frame of
man is considered as any guide in morals, the utmost caution must be used that none
make peculiarities in their own temper, or any thing which is the effect of particular
customs, though observable in several, the standard of what is common to the
species; and above all, that the highest principle be not forgot or excluded, that to
which belongs the adjustment and correction of all other inward movements and
affections: which principle will of course have some influence, but which being in
nature supreme, as shall now be shewn, ought to preside over and govern all the rest.
The difficulty of rightly observing the two former cautions; the appearance there is of
some small diversity amongst mankind with respect to this faculty, with respect to
their natural sense of moral good and evil; and the attention necessary to survey with
any exactness what passes within, have occasioned that it is not so much agreed what
is the standard of the internal nature of man, as of his external form. Neither is this
last exactly settled. Yet we understand one another when we speak of the shape of a
human body: so likewise we do when we speak of the heart and inward principles,
how far soever the standard is from being exact or precisely fixed. There is therefore
ground for an attempt of shewing men to themselves, of shewing them what course
of life and behaviour their real nature points out and would lead them to. Now
obligations of virtue shewn, and motives to the practice of it enforced, from a review
of the nature of man, are to be considered as an appeal to each particular person's
heart and natural conscience: as the external senses are appealed to for the proof of
things cognizable by them. Since then our inward feelings, and the perceptions we

receive from our external senses are equally real; to argue from the former to life and conduct, is as little liable to exception, as to argue from the latter to absolute speculative truth. A man can as little doubt whether his eyes were given him to see with, as he can doubt of the truth of the science of *optics*, deduced from ocular experiments. And allowing the inward feeling, shame; a man can as little doubt whether it was given him to prevent his doing shameful actions, as he can doubt whether his eyes were given him to guide his steps. And as to these inward feelings themselves; that they are real, that man has in his nature passions and affections, can no more be questioned, than that he has external senses. Neither can the former be wholly mistaken; though to a certain degree liable to greater mistakes than the latter.

There can be no doubt but that several propensions or instincts, several principles **2** in the heart of man, carry him to society, and to contribute to the happiness of it, in a sense and a manner in which no inward principle leads him to evil.* These principles, propensions or instincts which lead him to do good, are approved of by a certain faculty within, quite distinct from these propensions themselves. All this hath been fully made out in the foregoing discourse.

But it may be said, "What is all this, though true, to the purpose of virtue and **3** religion? These require, not only that we do good to others when we are led this way, by benevolence or reflection, happening to be stronger than other principles, passions, or appetites; but likewise that the *whole* character be formed upon thought and reflection; that *every* action be directed by some determinate rule, some other rule than the strength and prevalency of any principle or passion. What sign is there in our nature (for the inquiry is only about what is to be collected from thence) that this was intended by its Author? Or how does so various and fickle a temper as that of man appear adapted thereto? It may indeed be absurd and unnatural for men to act without any reflection; nay, without regard to that particular kind of reflection which you call conscience; because this does belong to our nature. For as there never was a man but who approved one place, prospect, building, before another: so it does not appear that there ever was a man who would not have approved an action of humanity rather than of cruelty; interest and passion being quite out of the case. But interest and passion do come in, and are often too strong for and prevail over reflection and conscience. Now as brutes have various instincts, by which they are carried on to the end the Author of their nature intended them for: is not man in the same condition; with this difference only, that to his instincts (*i.e.* appetites and passions) is added the principle of reflection or conscience? And as brutes act agreeably to their nature, in following that principle or particular instinct which for the present is strongest in them: does not man likewise act agreeably to his nature, or obey the law of his creation, by following that principle, be it passion or conscience, which for the present happens to be strongest in him? Thus different men are by their particular nature hurried on to pursue honour, or riches, or pleasure: there are also persons whose temper leads them in an uncommon degree to kindness, compassion, doing good to their fellow-creatures: as there are others who are given to suspend their judgement, to weigh and consider things, and to act upon thought and reflection. Let every one then quietly follow his nature; as passion, reflection, appetite, the several parts of it, happen to be strongest: but let not the man of virtue take upon him to blame the ambitious, the covetous, the dissolute; since these equally with him obey and follow their nature. Thus, as in some cases we follow our nature in doing the works 'contained in the law', so in other cases we follow nature in doing contrary."

4   Now all this licentious talk entirely goes upon a supposition, that men follow their nature in the same sense, in violating the known rules of justice and honesty for the sake of a present gratification, as they do in following those rules when they have no temptation to the contrary.* And if this were true, that could not be so which St. Paul asserts, that men are 'by nature a law to themselves'. If by following nature were meant only acting as we please, it would indeed be ridiculous to speak of nature as any guide in morals: nay the very mention of deviating from nature would be absurd; and the mention of following it, when spoken by way of distinction, would absolutely have no meaning. For did ever anyone act otherwise than as he pleased? And yet the ancients speak of deviating from nature as vice; and of following nature so much as a distinction, that according to them the perfection of virtue consists therein. So that language itself should teach people another sense to the words *following nature*, than barely acting as we please. Let it however be observed, that though the words *human nature* are to be explained, yet the real question of this discourse is not concerning the meaning of words, any otherwise than as the explanation of them may be needful to make out and explain the assertion, that *every man is naturally a law to himself*, that *everyone may find within himself the rule of right, and obligations to follow it*. This St. Paul affirms in the words of the text, and this the foregoing objection really denies by seeming to allow it. And the objection will be fully answered, and the text before us explained, by observing that *nature* is considered in different views, and the word used in different senses; and by shewing in what view it is considered, and in what sense the word is used, when intended to express and signify that which is the guide of life, that by which men are a law to themselves. I say, the explanation of the term will be sufficient, because from thence it will appear, that in some senses of the word, *nature* cannot be, but that in another sense it manifestly is, a law to us.

5   I. By *nature* is often meant no more than some principle in man, without regard either to the kind or degree of it. Thus the passion of anger, and the affection of parents to their children, would be called equally *natural*. And as the same person hath often contrary principles, which at the same time draw contrary ways, he may by the same action both follow and contradict his nature in this sense of the word; he may follow one passion and contradict another.

6   II. *Nature* is frequently spoken of as consisting in those passions which are strongest, and most influence the actions; which being vicious ones, mankind is in this sense naturally vicious, or vicious by nature. Thus St. Paul says of the Gentiles, 'who were dead in trespasses and sins, and walked according to the spirit of

disobedience, that they were by nature the children of wrath'.[1] They could be no otherwise 'children of wrath' by nature, than they were vicious by nature.

Here then are two different senses of the word *nature*, in neither of which men can   7 at all be said to be a law to themselves. They are mentioned only to be excluded; to prevent their being confounded, as the latter is in the objection, with another sense of it, which is now to be inquired after, and explained.

III. The apostle asserts, that 'the Gentiles do by *nature* the things contained in the   8 law'. Nature is indeed here put by way of distinction from revelation, but yet it is not a mere negative. He intends to express more than that by which they *did not*, that by which they *did* the works of the law; namely, by *nature*. It is plain the meaning of the word is not the same in this passage as in the former, where it is spoken of as evil; for in this latter it is spoken of as good; as that by which they acted, or might have acted virtuously. What that is in man by which he is 'naturally a law to himself', is explained in the following words: 'which shews the work of the law written in their hearts, their consciences also bearing witness, and their thoughts the meanwhile accusing or else excusing one another'.[2] If there be a distinction to be made between the 'works written in their hearts', and the 'witness of conscience'; by the former must be meant the natural disposition to kindness and compassion, to do what is of good report, to which this apostle often refers: that part of the nature of man, treated of in the foregoing discourse, which with very little reflection and of course leads him to society, and by means of which he naturally acts a just and good part in it, unless other passions or interest lead him astray. Yet since other passions, and regards to private interest, which lead us (though indirectly, yet they lead us) astray, are themselves in a degree equally natural, and often most prevalent; and since we have no method of seeing the particular degrees in which one or the other is placed in us by nature; it is plain the former, considered merely as natural, good and right as they are, can no more be a law to us than the latter. But there is a superior principle of reflection or conscience in every man, which distinguishes between the internal principles of his heart, as well as his external actions: which passes judgement upon himself and them; pronounces determinately some actions to be in themselves just, right, good; others to be in themselves evil, wrong, unjust: which, without being consulted, without being advised with, magisterially exerts itself, and approves or condemns him the doer of them accordingly: and which, if not forcibly stopped, naturally and always of course goes on to anticipate a higher and more effectual sentence, which shall hereafter second and affirm its own.* But this part of the office of conscience is beyond my present design explicitly to consider. It is by this faculty, natural to man, that he is a moral agent, that he is a law to himself: by this faculty, I say, not to be considered merely as a principle in his heart, which is to have some influence as well as others; but considered as a faculty in kind and in nature supreme over all others, and which bears its own authority of being so.

This *prerogative*, this *natural supremacy*, of the faculty which surveys, approves or   9 disapproves the several affections of our mind, and actions of our lives, being that by which men 'are a law to themselves', their conformity or disobedience to which law of our nature renders their actions, in the highest and most proper sense, natural or unnatural; it is fit it be further explained to you: and I hope it will be so, if you will attend to the following reflections.

10   Man may act according to that principle or inclination which for the present happens to be strongest, and yet act in a way disproportionate to, and violate his real proper nature. Suppose a brute creature by any bait to be allured into a snare, by which he is destroyed. He plainly followed the bent of his nature, leading him to gratify his appetite: there is an entire correspondence between his whole nature and such an action: such action therefore is natural. But suppose a man, foreseeing the same danger of certain ruin, should rush into it for the sake of a present gratification. He in this instance would follow his strongest desire, as did the brute creature: but there would be as manifest a disproportion, between the nature of a man and such an action, as between the meanest work of art and the skill of the greatest master in that art: which disproportion arises, not from considering the action singly in *itself*, or in its *consequences*; but from *comparison* of it with the nature of the agent.* And since such an action is utterly disproportionate to the nature of man, it is in the strictest and most proper sense unnatural; this word expressing that disproportion. Therefore, instead of the words *disproportionate to his nature*, the word, *unnatural*, may now be put; this being more familiar to us: but let it be observed, that it stands for the same thing precisely.

11   Now what is it which renders such a rash action unnatural? Is it that he went against the principle of reasonable and cool self-love, considered *merely* as a part of his nature? No: for if he had acted the contrary way, he would equally have gone against a principle or part of his nature, namely, passion or appetite. But to deny a present appetite, from foresight that the gratification of it would end in immediate ruin or extreme misery, is by no means an unnatural action: whereas to contradict or go against cool self-love for the sake of such gratification, is so in the instance before us. Such an action then being unnatural; and its being so not arising from a man's going against a principle or desire barely, nor in going against that principle or desire which happens for the present to be strongest; it necessarily follows, that there must be some other difference or distinction to be made between these two principles, passion and cool self-love, than what I have yet taken notice of. And this difference, not being a difference in strength or degree, I call a difference in *nature* and in *kind*. And since, in the instance still before us, if passion prevails over self-love, the consequent action is unnatural; but if self-love prevails over passion, the action is natural: it is manifest that self-love is in human nature a superior principle to passion. This may be contradicted without violating that nature; but the former cannot. So that, if we will act conformably to the economy of man's nature, reasonable self-love must govern. Thus, without particular consideration of conscience, we may have a clear conception of the *superior nature* of one inward principle to another; and see that there really is this natural superiority, quite distinct from degrees of strength and prevalency.

Let us now take a view of the nature of man, as consisting partly of various   12
appetites, passions, affections, and partly of the principle of reflection or conscience;
leaving quite out all consideration of the different degrees of strength, in which either
of them prevail, and it will further appear that there is this natural superiority of one
inward principle to another, and that it is even part of the idea of reflection or
conscience.*

Passion or appetite implies a direct simple tendency towards such and such   13
objects, without distinction of the means by which they are to be obtained. Consequently, it will often happen there will be a desire of particular objects, in cases where
they cannot be obtained without manifest injury to others. Reflection or conscience
comes in, and disapproves the pursuit of them in these circumstances; but the desire
remains. Which is to be obeyed, appetite or reflection? Cannot this question be
answered from the economy and constitution of human nature merely, without
saying which is strongest? Or need this at all come into consideration? Would not
the question be *intelligibly* and fully answered by saying, that the principle of
reflection or conscience being compared with the various appetites, passions, and
affections in men, the former is manifestly superior and chief, without regard to
strength? And how often soever the latter happens to prevail, it is mere *usurpation*:
the former remains in nature and in kind its superior; and every instance of such
prevalence of the latter is an instance of breaking in upon and violation of the
constitution of man.

All this is no more than the distinction, which every body is acquainted with,   14
between *mere power* and *authority*: only, instead of being intended to express the
difference between what is possible, and what is lawful in civil government; here it
has been shewn applicable to the several principles in the mind of man. Thus that
principle, by which we survey, and either approve or disapprove our own heart,
temper and actions, is not only to be considered as what is in its turn to have some
influence; which may be said of every passion, of the lowest appetites: but likewise as
being superior; as from its very nature manifestly claiming superiority over all others:
insomuch that you cannot form a notion of this faculty, conscience, without taking in
judgement, direction, superintendency. This is a constituent part of the idea, that is,
of the faculty itself: and, to preside and govern, from the very economy and
constitution of man, belongs to it. Had it strength, as it has right; had it power, as
it has manifest authority; it would absolutely govern the world.

This gives us a further view of the nature of man; shews us what course of life we   15
were made for: not only that our real nature leads us to be influenced in some degree
by reflection and conscience; but likewise in what degree we are to be influenced by it,
if we will fall in with, and act agreeably to the constitution of our nature: that this
faculty was placed within to be our proper governor; to direct and regulate all under
principles, passions, and motives of action. This is its right and office: thus sacred is
its authority. And how often soever men violate and rebelliously refuse to submit to
it, for supposed interest which they cannot otherwise obtain, or for the sake of

passion which they cannot otherwise gratify; this makes no alteration as to the *natural right* and *office* of conscience.

16   Let us now turn this whole matter another way, and suppose there was no such thing at all as this natural supremacy of conscience; that there was no distinction to be made between one inward principle and another, but only that of strength; and see what would be the consequence.

17   Consider then what is the latitude and compass of the actions of man with regard to himself, his fellow-creatures, and the Supreme Being? What are their bounds, besides that of our natural power? With respect to the two first, they are plainly no other than these: no man seeks misery as such for himself; and no one unprovoked does mischief to another for its own sake.* For in every degree within these bounds, mankind knowingly from passion or wantonness bring ruin and misery upon themselves and others. And impiety and profaneness, I mean, what every one would call so who believes the being of God, have absolutely no bounds at all. Men blaspheme the Author of Nature, formally and in words renounce their allegiance to their Creator. Put an instance then with respect to any one of these three. Though we should suppose profane swearing, and in general that kind of impiety now mentioned, to mean nothing, yet it implies wanton disregard and irreverence towards an Infinite Being our Creator; and is this as suitable to the nature of man, as reverence and dutiful submission of heart towards that Almighty Being? Or suppose a man guilty of parricide, with all the circumstances of cruelty which such an action can admit of. This action is done in consequence of its principle being for the present strongest: and if there be no difference between inward principles, but only that of strength; the strength being given, you have the whole nature of the man given so far as it relates to this matter. The action plainly corresponds to the principle, the principle being in that degree of strength it was: it therefore corresponds to the whole nature of the man. Upon comparing the action and the whole nature, there arises no disproportion, there appears no unsuitableness between them. Thus the *murder of a father* and the *nature of man* correspond to each other, as the same nature and an act of filial duty. If there be no difference between inward principles, but only that of strength; we can make no distinction between these two actions, considered as the actions of such a creature; but in our coolest hours must approve or disapprove them equally: than which nothing can be reduced to a greater absurdity.*

Notes

1. *Ephes.* ii.3.
2. [*Rom.* ii.15.]

Sermon 3

Upon Human Nature

For when the Gentiles which have not the law, do by nature the things contained in the law, these having not the law, are a law unto themselves.

(*Romans* ii.14)

The natural supremacy of reflection or conscience being thus established; we may 1 from it form a distinct notion of what is meant by *human nature*, when virtue is said to consist in following it, and vice in deviating from it.

As the idea of a civil constitution implies in it united strength, various subordin- 2 ations, under one direction, that of the supreme authority; the different strength of each particular member of the society not coming into the idea; whereas, if you leave out the subordination, the union and the one direction, you destroy and lose it: so reason, several appetites, passions and affections, prevailing in different degrees of strength, is not *that* idea or notion of *human nature*; but *that nature* consists in these several principles considered as having a natural respect to each other, in the several passions being naturally subordinate to the one superior principle of reflection or conscience. Every bias, instinct, propension within, is a real part of our nature, but not the whole: add to these the superior faculty, whose office it is to adjust, manage and preside over them, and take in this its natural superiority, and you complete the idea of human nature. And as in civil government the constitution is broken in upon and violated by power and strength prevailing over authority; so the constitution of man is broken in upon and violated by the lower faculties or principles within prevailing over that which is in its nature supreme over them all. Thus, when it is said by ancient writers,* that tortures and death are not so contrary to human nature as injustice; by this to be sure is not meant, that the aversion to the former in mankind is less strong and prevalent than their aversion to the latter: but that the former is only contrary to our nature considered in a partial view, and which takes in only the lowest part of it, that which we have in common with the brutes; whereas the latter is contrary to our nature, considered in a higher sense, as a system and constitution, contrary to the whole economy of man.[1]

And from all these things put together, nothing can be more evident, than that, 3 exclusive of revelation, man cannot be considered as a creature left by his Maker to act at random, and live at large up to the extent of his natural power, as passion, humour, wilfulness, happen to carry him; which is the condition brute creatures are in: but that *from his make, constitution, or nature, he is in the strictest and most proper sense a law to himself.* He hath the rule of right within: what is wanting is only that he honestly attend to it.

4   The inquiries which have been made by men of leisure after some general rule, the conformity to, or disagreement from which, should denominate our actions good or evil, are in many respects of great service. Yet let any plain honest man, before he engages in any course of action, ask himself, 'Is this I am going about right, or is it wrong? Is it good, or is it evil?' I do not in the least doubt but that this question would be answered agreeably to truth and virtue, by almost any fair man in almost any circumstance.* Neither do there appear any cases which look like exceptions to this; but those of superstition, and of partiality to ourselves. Superstition may perhaps be somewhat of an exception: but partiality to ourselves is not; this being itself dishonesty. For a man to judge that to be the equitable, the moderate, the right part for him to act, which he would see to be hard, unjust, oppressive in another; this is plain vice, and can proceed only from great unfairness of mind.

5   But allowing that mankind hath the rule of right within himself, yet it may be asked, "What obligations are we under to attend to and follow it?" I answer: it has been proved that man by his nature is a law to himself, without the particular distinct consideration of the positive sanctions of that law; the rewards and punishments which we feel, and those which, from the light of reason we have ground to believe, are annexed to it. The question then carries its own answer along with it. Your obligation to obey this law, is its being the law of your nature. That your conscience approves of and attests to such a course of action, is itself alone an obligation. Conscience does not only offer itself to shew us the way we should walk in, but it likewise carries its own authority with it, that it is our natural guide; the guide assigned us by the Author of our nature: it therefore belongs to our condition of being, it is our duty, to walk in that path and follow this guide without looking about to see whether we may not possibly forsake them with impunity.

6   However, let us hear what is to he said against obeying this law of our nature. And the sum is no more than this. "Why should we be concerned about any thing out of and beyond ourselves? If we do find within ourselves regards to others, and restraints of we know not how many different kinds; yet these being embarrassments, and hindering us from going the nearest way to our own good, why should we not endeavour to suppress and get over them?"

7   Thus people go on with words, which, when applied to human nature, and the condition in which it is placed in this world, have really no meaning. For does not all this kind of talk go upon supposition, that our happiness in this world consists in somewhat quite distinct from regards to others; and that it is the privilege of vice to be without restraint or confinement? Whereas on the contrary, the enjoyments, in a

manner all the common enjoyments of life, even the pleasures of vice, depend upon these regards of one kind or another to our fellow-creatures. Throw off all regards to others, and we should be quite indifferent to infamy and to honour; there could be no such thing at all as ambition; and scarce any such thing as covetousness; for we should likewise be equally indifferent to the disgrace of poverty, the several neglects and kinds of contempt which accompany this state; and to the reputation of riches, the regard and respect they usually procure. Neither is restraint by any means peculiar to one course of life: but our very nature, exclusive of conscience, and our condition lays us under an absolute necessity of it. We cannot gain any end whatever without being confined to the proper means, which is often the most painful and uneasy confinement. And in numberless instances a present appetite cannot be gratified without such apparent and immediate ruin and misery, that the most dissolute man in the world chooses to forego the pleasure, rather than endure the pain.

Is the meaning then, to indulge those regards to our fellow-creatures, and submit 8
to those restraints, which upon the whole are attended with more satisfaction than uneasiness, and get over only those which bring more uneasiness and inconvenience than satisfaction? "Doubtless this was our meaning." You have changed sides then. Keep to this; be consistent with yourselves; and you and the men of virtue are *in general* perfectly agreed. But let us take care and avoid mistakes. Let it not be taken for granted that the temper of envy, rage, resentment, yields greater delight than meekness, forgiveness, compassion, and good-will: especially when it is acknowledged that rage, envy, resentment, are in themselves mere misery; and the satisfaction arising from the indulgence of them is little more than relief from that misery; whereas the temper of compassion and benevolence is itself delightful; and the indulgence of it, by doing good, affords new positive delight and enjoyment. Let it not be taken for granted, that the satisfaction arising from the reputation of riches and power however obtained, and from the respect paid to them, is greater than the satisfaction arising from the reputation of justice, honesty, charity, and the esteem which is universally acknowledged to be their due. And if it be doubtful which of these satisfactions is the greatest, as there are persons who think neither of them very considerable, yet there can be no doubt concerning ambition and covetousness, virtue and a good mind, considered in themselves, and as leading to different courses of life; there can, I say, be no doubt, which temper and which course is attended with most peace and tranquil-lity of mind, which with most perplexity, vexation and inconvenience. And both the virtues and vices which have been now mentioned, do in a manner equally imply in them regards of one kind or another to our fellow-creatures. And with respect to restraint and confinement: whoever will consider the restraints from fear and shame, the dissimulation, mean arts of concealment, servile compliances, one or other of which belong to almost every course of vice: will soon be convinced that the man of virtue is by no means upon a disadvantage in this respect. How many instances are there in which men feel and own and cry aloud under the chains of vice with which

they are enthralled, and which yet they will not shake off? How many instances, in which persons manifestly go through more pains and self-denial to gratify a vicious passion, than would have been necessary to the conquest of it? To this is to be added, that when virtue is become habitual, when the temper of it is acquired, what was before confinement ceases to be so, by becoming choice and delight. Whatever restraint and guard upon ourselves may be needful to unlearn any unnatural distortion or odd gesture; yet, in all propriety of speech, natural behaviour must be the most easy and unrestrained. It is manifest that, in the common course of life, there is seldom any inconsistency between our duty and what is *called* interest: it is much seldomer that there is an inconsistency between duty and what is really our present interest; meaning by interest, happiness and satisfaction. Self-love then, though confined to the interest of the present world, does in general perfectly coincide with virtue; and leads us to one and the same course of life. But, whatever exceptions there are to this, which are much fewer than they are commonly thought, all shall be set right at the final distribution of things. It is a manifest absurdity to suppose evil prevailing finally over good, under the conduct and administration of a perfect mind.

9   The whole argument, which I have been now insisting upon, may be thus summed up and given you in one view. The nature of man is adapted to some course of action or other. Upon comparing some actions with this nature, they appear suitable and correspondent to it: from comparison of other actions with the same nature, there arises to our view some unsuitableness or disproportion. The correspondence of actions to the nature of the agent renders them natural: their disproportion to it, unnatural. That an action is correspondent to the nature of the agent, does not arise from its being agreeable to the principle which happens to be the strongest: for it may be so, and yet be quite disproportionate to the nature of the agent. The correspondence therefore, or disproportion, arises from somewhat else. This can be nothing but a difference in nature and kind (altogether distinct from strength) between the inward principles. Some then are in nature and kind superior to others. And the correspondence arises from the action being conformable to the higher principle; and the unsuitableness, from its being contrary to it. Reasonable self-love and conscience are the chief or superior principles in the nature of man: because an action may be suitable to this nature, though all other principles be violated; but becomes unsuitable, if either of those are. Conscience and self-love, if we understand our true happiness, always lead us the same way. Duty and interest are perfectly coincident; for the most part in this world, but entirely and in every instance, if we take in the future, and the whole; this being implied in the notion of a good and perfect administration of things. Thus they who have been so wise in their generation as to regard only their own supposed interest, at the expense and to the injury of others, shall at last find, that he who has given up all the advantages of the present world, rather than violate his conscience and the relations of life, has infinitely better provided for himself, and secured his own interest and happiness.

Note

1. Every man in his physical nature is one individual single agent. He has likewise properties and principles, each of which may be considered separately, and without regard to the respects which they have to each other. Neither of these are the nature we are taking a view of. But it is the inward frame of man considered as a *system* or *constitution*: whose several parts are united, not by a physical principle of individuation, but by the respects they have to each other; the chief of which is the subjection which the appetites, passions, and particular affections have to the one supreme principle of reflection or conscience. The system or constitution is formed by and consists in these respects and this subjection. Thus the body is a *system* or *constitution*: so is a tree: so is every machine. Consider all the several parts of a tree without the natural respects they have to each other, and you have not at all the idea of a tree; but add these respects, and this gives you the idea. The body may be impaired by sickness, a tree may decay, a machine be out of order, and yet the system and constitution of them not totally dissolved. There is plainly somewhat which answers to all this in the moral constitution of man. Whoever will consider his own nature, will see that the several appetites, passions, and particular affections, have different respects amongst themselves. They are restraints upon, and are in a proportion to each other.* This proportion is just and perfect, when all those under principles are perfectly coincident with conscience, so far as their nature permits, and in all cases under its absolute and entire direction. The least excess or defect, the least alteration of the due proportions amongst themselves, or of their coincidence with conscience, though not proceeding into action, is some degree of disorder in the moral constitution. But perfection, though plainly intelligible and supposable, was never attained by any man. If the higher principle of reflection maintains its place, and as much as it can corrects that disorder, and hinders it from breaking out into action, this is all that can be expected in such a creature as man. And though the appetites and passions have not their exact due proportion to each other; though they often strive for mastery with judgement or reflection; yet, since the superiority of this principle to all others is the chief respect which forms the constitution, so far as this superiority is maintained, the character, the man, is good, worthy, virtuous.

Sermon 4
Upon the Government of the Tongue

If any man among you seem to be religious, and bridleth not his tongue, but deceiveth his own heart, this man's religion is vain.

(*James* i.26)

1 The translation of this text would be more determinate by being more literal, thus: 'If any man among you seemeth to be religious, not bridling his tongue, but deceiving his own heart, this man's religion is vain.' This determines that the words, 'but deceiveth his own heart', are not put in opposition to, 'seemeth to be religious', but to, 'bridleth not his tongue'. The certain determinate meaning of the text then being, that he who seemeth to be religious, and bridleth not his tongue, but in that particular deceiveth his own heart, this man's religion is vain; we may observe somewhat very forcible and expressive in these words of St. James. As if the apostle had said, No man surely can make any pretences to religion, who does not at least believe that he bridleth his tongue: if he puts on any appearance or face of religion, and yet does not govern his tongue, he must surely deceive himself in that particular, and think he does: and whoever is so unhappy as to deceive himself in this, to imagine he keeps that unruly faculty in due subjection, when indeed he does not, whatever the other part of his life be, his religion is vain; the government of the tongue being a most material restraint which virtue lays us under: without it no man can be truly religious.

2 In treating upon this subject, I will consider,

First, What is the general vice or fault here referred to: or what disposition in men is supposed in moral reflections and precepts concerning *bridling the tongue*.

Secondly, When it may be said of anyone, that he has a due government over himself in this respect.

3 I. Now the fault referred to, and the disposition supposed, in precepts and reflections concerning the government of the tongue, is not evil-speaking from malice, nor lying or bearing false witness from indirect selfish designs. The disposition to these, and the actual vices themselves, all come under other subjects. The tongue may be employed about and made to serve all the purposes of vice, in tempting and deceiving, in perjury and injustice. But the thing here supposed and

referred to, is talkativeness: a disposition to be talking, abstracted from the consideration of what is to be said; with very little or no regard to, or thought of doing, either good or harm. And let not any imagine this to be a slight matter, and that it deserves not to have so great weight laid upon it; till he has considered, what evil is implied in it, and the bad effects which follow from it. It is perhaps true, that they who are addicted to this folly would choose to confine themselves to trifles and indifferent subjects, and so intend only to be guilty of being impertinent: but as they cannot go on for ever talking of nothing, as common matters will not afford a sufficient fund for perpetual continued discourse: when subjects of this kind are exhausted, they will go on to defamation, scandal, divulging of secrets, their own secrets as well as those of others, any thing rather than be silent. They are plainly hurried on in the heat of their talk to say quite different things from what they first intended, and which they afterwards wish unsaid: or improper things, which they had no other end in saying but only to afford employment to their tongue. And if these people expect to be heard and regarded, for there are some content merely with talking, they will invent to engage your attention: and, when they have heard the least imperfect hint of an affair, they will out of their own head add the circumstances of time and place, and other matters to make out their story, and give the appearance of probability to it: not that they have any concern about being believed, otherwise than as a means of being heard. The thing is, to engage your attention; to take you up wholly for the present time: what reflections will be made afterwards, is in truth the least of their thoughts. And further: when persons, who indulge themselves in these liberties of the tongue, are in any degree offended with another, as little disgusts and misunderstandings will be, they allow themselves to defame and revile such an one without any moderation or bounds; though the offence is so very slight, that they themselves would not do, nor perhaps wish him an injury in any other way. And in this case the scandal and revilings are chiefly owing to talkativeness, and not bridling their tongue; and so come under our present subject. The least occasion in the world will make the humour break out in this particular way, or in another.* It is like a torrent, which must and will flow; but the least thing imaginable will first of all give it either this or another direction, turn it into this or that channel: or like a fire; the nature of which, when in a heap of combustible matter, is to spread and lay waste all around; but any one of a thousand little accidents will occasion it to break out first either in this or another particular part.

The subject then before us, though it does run up into, and can scarce be treated as 4 entirely distinct from all others; yet it needs not be so much mixed or blended with them as it often is. Every faculty and power may be used as the instrument of premeditated vice and wickedness, merely as the most proper and effectual means of executing such designs. But if a man, from deep malice and desire of revenge, should meditate a falsehood with a settled design to ruin his neighbour's reputation, and should with great coolness and deliberation spread it; nobody would choose to say of such an one, that he had no government of his tongue. A man may use the faculty of speech as an instrument of false witness, who yet has so entire a command over that faculty, as never to speak but from forethought and cool design. Here the crime is injustice and perjury: and, strictly speaking, no more belongs to the present subject, than perjury and injustice in any other way. But there is such a thing as a disposition to be talking for its own sake; from which persons often say any thing, good or bad, of others, merely as a subject of discourse, according to the particular temper they themselves happen to be in, and to pass away the present time. There is likewise to be observed in persons such a strong and eager desire of engaging attention to what they say, that they will speak good or evil, truth or otherwise, merely as one or the other seems to be most hearkened to: and this, though it is sometimes joined, is not the same with the desire of being thought important and men of consequence. There is in some such a disposition to be talking, that an offence of the slightest kind, and such as would not raise any other resentment, yet raises, if I may so speak, the resentment of the tongue, puts it into a flame, into the most ungovernable motions. This outrage, when the person it respects is present, we distinguish in the lower rank of people by a peculiar term: and let it be observed, that though the decencies of behaviour are a little kept; the same outrage and virulence, indulged when he is absent, is an offence of the same kind. But not to distinguish any further in this manner: men run into faults and follies, which cannot so properly be referred to any one general head as this, that they have not a due government over their tongue.

5   And this unrestrained volubility and wantonness of speech is the occasion of numberless evils and vexations in life. It begets resentment in him who is the subject of it; sows the seed of strife and dissension amongst others; and inflames little disgusts and offences, which if let alone would wear away of themselves: it is often of as bad effect upon the good name of others, as deep envy or malice; and, to say the least of it in this respect, it destroys and perverts a certain equity of the utmost importance to society to be observed; namely, that praise and dispraise, a good or bad character, should always be bestowed according to desert. The tongue used in such a licentious manner is like a sword in the hand of a madman; it is employed at random, it can scarce possibly do any good, and for the most part does a world of mischief; and implies not only great folly and a trifling spirit, but great viciousness of mind, great indifference to truth and falsity, and to the reputation, welfare, and good of others. So much reason is there for what St. James says of the tongue, 'It is a fire, a world of iniquity, it defileth the whole body, setteth on fire the course of nature, and is itself set on fire of hell.'[1] This is the faculty or disposition which we are required to keep a guard upon: these are the vices and follies it runs into, when not kept under due restraint.

6   II. Wherein the due government of the tongue consists, or when it may be said of anyone in a moral and religious sense that 'he bridleth his tongue', I come now to consider.

7   The due and proper use of any natural faculty or power, is to be judged of by the end and design for which it was given us.* The chief purpose, for which the faculty of

speech was given to man, is plainly that we might communicate our thoughts to each other, in order to carry on the affairs of the world; for business, and for our improvement in knowledge and learning. But the good Author of our nature designed us not only necessaries, but likewise enjoyment and satisfaction, in that being he hath graciously given, and in that condition of life he hath placed us in.* There are secondary uses of our faculties: they administer to delight, as well as to necessity: and as they are equally adapted to both, there is no doubt but he intended them for our gratification, as well as for the support and continuance of our being. The secondary use of speech is to please and be entertaining to each other in conversation. This is in every respect allowable and right: it unites men closer in alliances and friendships; gives us a fellow-feeling of the prosperity and unhappiness of each other; and is in several respects serviceable to virtue, and to promote good behaviour in the world. And provided there be not too much time spent in it, if it were considered only in the way of gratification and delight, men must have strange notions of God and of religion, to think that he can be offended with it, or that it is in any way inconsistent with the strictest virtue. But the truth is, such sort of conversation, though it has no particular good tendency, yet it has a general good one: it is social and friendly; and tends to promote humanity, good-nature and civility.

As the end and use, so likewise the abuse of speech, relates to the one or other of 8 these; either to business, or to conversation. As to the former; deceit in the management of business and affairs does not properly belong to the subject now before us: though one may just mention that multitude, that endless number of words, with which business is perplexed; when a much fewer would, as it should seem, better serve the purpose: but this must be left to those who understand the matter. The government of the tongue, considered as a subject of itself, relates chiefly to conversation; to that kind of discourse which usually fills up the time spent in friendly meetings, and visits of civility. And the danger is, lest persons entertain themselves and others at the expense of their wisdom and their virtue, and to the injury or offence of their neighbour. If they will observe and keep clear of these, they may be as free, and easy, and unreserved, as they can desire.

The cautions to be given for avoiding these dangers, and to render conversation 9 innocent and agreeable, fall under the following particulars: silence; talking of indifferent things; and, which makes up too great a part of conversation, giving of characters, speaking well or evil of others.

The Wise Man observes, that 'there is a time to speak and a time to keep silence'.[2] 10 One meets with people in the world, who seem never to have made the last of these observations. And yet these great talkers do not at all speak from their having any thing to say, as every sentence shews, but only from their inclination to be talking. Their conversation is merely an exercise of the tongue: no other human faculty has any share in it. It is strange these persons can help reflecting, that unless they have in truth a superior capacity, and are in an extraordinary manner furnished for conversation; if they are entertaining, it is at their own expense. Is it possible, that it should never come into people's thoughts to suspect, whether or no it be to their advantage to shew so very much of themselves? 'O that you would altogether hold your peace, and it should be your wisdom.'[3] Remember likewise there are persons who love fewer words, an inoffensive sort of people, and who deserve some regard, though of too still and composed tempers for you. Of this number was the Son of Sirach: for he plainly speaks from experience, when he says, 'As hills of sand are to the steps of the aged, so is one of many words to a quiet man.'[4] But one would think it should be obvious to every one, that when they are in company with their superiors of any kind, in years, knowledge and experience; when proper and useful subjects are discoursed of, which they cannot bear a part in; that these are times for silence: when they should learn to hear, and be attentive; at least in their turn. It is indeed a very unhappy way these people are in: they in a manner cut themselves out from all advantage of conversation, except that of being entertained with their own talk: their business in coming into company not being at all to be informed, to hear, to learn; but to display themselves; or rather to exert their faculty, and talk without any design at all. And if we consider conversation as an entertainment, as somewhat to unbend the mind; as a diversion from the cares, the business, and the sorrows of life; it is of the very nature of it, that the discourse be mutual.* This, I say, is implied in the very notion of what we distinguish by conversation, or being in company. Attention to the continued discourse of one alone grows more painful often, than the cares and business we come to be diverted from. He therefore who imposes this upon us, is guilty of a double offence; arbitrarily enjoining silence upon all the rest, and likewise obliging them to this painful attention.

11   I am sensible these things are apt to be passed over, as too little to come into a serious discourse: but in reality men are obliged, even in point of morality and virtue, to observe all the decencies of behaviour. The greatest evils in life have had their rise from somewhat, which was thought of too little importance to be attended to. And as to the matter we are now upon, it is absolutely necessary to be considered. For if people will not maintain a due government over themselves, in regarding proper times and seasons for silence, but *will* be talking; they certainly, whether they design it or not at first, will go on to scandal and evil-speaking, and divulging secrets.

12   If it were needful to say any thing further, to persuade men to learn this lesson of silence; one might put them in mind, how insignificant they render themselves by this excessive talkativeness: insomuch that, if they do chance to say any thing which deserves to be attended to and regarded, it is lost in the variety and abundance which they utter of another sort.

13   The occasions of silence then are obvious, and one would think should be easily distinguished by every body: namely, when a man has nothing to say; or nothing, but what is better unsaid: better, either in regard to the particular persons he is present with; or from its being an interruption to conversation itself; or to conversation of a more agreeable kind; or better, lastly, with regard to himself. I will end this particular with two reflections of the Wise Man: one of which, in the strongest manner, exposes

the ridiculous part of this licentiousness of the tongue; and the other, the great danger and viciousness of it. 'When he that is a fool walketh by the way side, his wisdom faileth him, and he saith to every one that he is a fool.'[5] The other is, 'In the multitude of words there wanteth not sin.'[6]

As to the government of the tongue in respect to talking upon indifferent subjects: after what has been said concerning the due government of it in respect to the occasions and times for silence, there is little more necessary, than only to caution men to be fully satisfied, that the subjects are indeed of an indifferent nature; and not to spend too much time in conversation of this kind. But persons must be sure to take heed, that the subject of their discourse be at least of an indifferent nature: that it be no way offensive to virtue, religion, or good manners; that it be not of a licentious dissolute sort, this leaving always ill impressions upon the mind; that it be no way injurious or vexatious to others; and that too much time be not spent this way, to the neglect of those duties and offices of life which belong to their station and condition in the world. However, though there is not any necessity, that men should aim at being important and weighty in every sentence they speak: yet since useful subjects, at least of some kinds, are as entertaining as others; a wise man, even when he desires to unbend his mind from business, would choose that the conversation might turn upon somewhat instructive.   **14**

The last thing is, the government of the tongue as relating to discourse of the affairs of others, and giving of characters. These are in a manner the same: and one can scarce call it an indifferent subject, because discourse upon it almost perpetually runs into somewhat criminal.   **15**

And first of all, it were very much to be wished that this did not take up so great a part of conversation; because it is indeed a subject of a dangerous nature. Let anyone consider the various interests, competitions, and little misunderstandings which arise amongst men; and he will soon see, that he is not unprejudiced and impartial, that he is not, as I may speak, neutral enough, to trust himself with talking of the character and concerns of his neighbour, in a free, careless, and unreserved manner. There is perpetually, and often it is not attended to, a rivalship amongst people of one kind or another, in respect to wit, beauty, learning, fortune; and that one thing will insensibly influence them to speak to the disadvantage of others, even where there is no formed malice or design. Since therefore it is so hard to enter into this subject without offending, the first thing to be observed is, that people should learn to decline it; to get over that strong inclination most have to be talking of the concerns and behaviour of their neighbour.   **16**

But since it is impossible that this subject should be wholly excluded conversation; and since it is necessary that the characters of men should be known: the next thing is, that it is a matter of importance what is said; and therefore, that we should be religiously scrupulous and exact to say nothing, either good or bad, but what is true. I put it thus, because it is in reality of as great importance to the good of society, that the characters of bad men should be known, as that the characters of good men   **17** should. People, who are given to scandal and detraction, may indeed make an ill use of this observation: but truths, which are of service towards regulating our conduct, are not to be disowned, or even concealed, because a bad use may be made of them. This however would be effectually prevented, if these two things were attended to. *First*, That, though it is equally of bad consequence to society, that men should have either good or ill characters which they do not deserve; yet, when you say somewhat good of a man which he does not deserve, there is no wrong done him in particular; whereas, when you say evil of a man which he does not deserve, here is a direct formal injury, a real piece of injustice, done him. This therefore makes a wide difference; and gives us, in point of virtue, much greater latitude in speaking well, than ill, of others. *Secondly*, A good man is friendly to his fellow-creatures, and a lover of mankind; and so will, upon every occasion, and often without any, say all the good he can of every body: but, so far as he is a good man, will never be disposed to speak evil of any, unless there be some other reason for it, besides barely that it is true. If he be charged with having given an ill character, he will scarce think it a sufficient justification of himself to say it was a true one; unless he can also give some further account how he came to do so: a just indignation against particular instances of villainy, where they are great and scandalous; or to prevent an innocent man from being deceived and betrayed, when he has great trust and confidence in one who does not deserve it. Justice must be done to every part of a subject, when we are considering it. If there be a man, who bears a fair character in the world, whom yet we know to be without faith or honesty, to be really an ill man; it must be allowed in general, that we shall do a piece of service to society, by letting such an one's true character be known. This is no more, than what we have an instance of in our Saviour himself;[7] though he was mild and gentle beyond example.* However, no words can express too strongly the caution which should be used in such a case as this.

18   Upon the whole matter: if people would observe the obvious occasions of silence; if they would subdue the inclination to tale-bearing; and that eager desire to engage attention, which is an original disease in some minds; they would be in little danger of offending with their tongue; and would, in a moral and religious sense, have due government over it.

19   I will conclude with some precepts and reflections of the Son of Sirach upon this subject. 'Be swift to hear: and, if thou hast understanding, answer thy neighbour; if not, lay thy hand upon thy mouth. Honour and shame is in talk. A man of an ill tongue is dangerous in his city, and he that is rash in his talk shall be hated. A wise man will hold his tongue, till he see opportunity; but a babbler and a fool will regard no time. He that useth many words shall be abhorred; and he that taketh to himself authority therein, shall be hated. A back-biting tongue hath disquieted many; strong cities hath it pulled down, and overthrown the houses of great men. The tongue of a man is his fall; but if thou love to hear, thou shalt receive understanding.'[8]*

Notes

1. *James* iii.6.
2. [*Eccles.* iii.7.]
3. *Job* xiii.5.
4. [*Ecclus.* xxv.20.]
5. *Ecclus.* x.3.
6. *Prov.* x.19.
7. *Mark* xii.38, 40.
8. [*Ecclus.* v.11, 12, 13; ix.18; xx.7, 8; xxviii.14; v.13; vi.33.]

Sermon 5

Upon Compassion

Rejoice with them that do rejoice, and weep with them that weep.

(*Romans* xii.15)

1   Every man is to be considered in two capacities, the private and public; as designed to pursue his own interest, and likewise to contribute to the good of others. Whoever will consider, may see, that in general there is no contrariety between these; but that from the original constitution of man, and the circumstances he is placed in, they perfectly coincide, and mutually carry on each other. But, amongst the great variety of affections or principles of action in our nature, some in their primary intention and design seem to belong to the single or private, others to the public or social capacity. The affections required in the text are of the latter sort. When we rejoice in the prosperity of others, and compassionate their distresses, we, as it were, substitute them for ourselves, their interest for our own; and have the same kind of pleasure in their prosperity and sorrow in their distress, as we have from reflection upon our own. Now there is nothing strange or unaccountable in our being thus carried out, and affected towards the interests of others. For, if there be any appetite, or any inward principle besides self-love; why may there not be an affection to the good of our fellow-creatures, and delight from that affection's being gratified, and uneasiness from things going contrary to it?[1]

2   Of these two, delight in the prosperity of others and compassion for their distresses, the last is felt much more generally than the former. Though men do not universally rejoice with all whom they see rejoice, yet, accidental obstacles removed, they naturally compassionate all in some degree whom they see in distress, so far as they have any real perception or sense of that distress: insomuch that words expressing this latter, pity, compassion, frequently occur; whereas we have scarce any single one, by which the former is distinctly expressed. Congratulation indeed answers condolence: but both these words are intended to signify certain forms of civility, rather than any inward sensation or feeling. This difference or inequality is so remarkable, that we plainly consider compassion as itself an original, distinct, particular affection in human nature; whereas to rejoice in the good of others, is only a consequence of the general affection of love and good-will to them. The reason

and account of which matter is this. When a man has obtained any particular advantage or felicity, his end is gained; and he does not in that particular want the assistance of another: there was therefore no need of a distinct affection towards that felicity of another already obtained; neither would such affection directly carry him on to do good to that person: whereas men in distress want assistance; and compassion leads us directly to assist them. The object of the former is the present felicity of another; the object of the latter is the present misery of another: it is easy to see that the latter wants a particular affection for its relief, and that the former does not want one, because it does not want assistance. And upon supposition of a distinct affection in both cases, the one must rest in the exercise of itself, having nothing further to gain; the other does not rest in itself, but carries us on to assist the distressed.*

But, supposing these affections natural to the mind, particularly the last; "Has not   3 each man troubles enough of his own? must he indulge an affection which appropriates to himself those of others? which leads him to contract the least desirable of all friendships, friendships with the unfortunate? Must we invert the known rule of prudence, and choose to associate ourselves with the distressed? Or allowing that we ought, so far as it is in our power, to relieve them; yet is it not better to do this from reason and duly? Does not passion and affection of every kind perpetually mislead us? Nay, is not passion and affection itself a weakness, and what a perfect being must be entirely free from?" Perhaps so: but it is mankind I am speaking of; imperfect creatures, and who naturally and, from the condition we are placed in, necessarily depend upon each other. With respect to such creatures, it would be found of as bad consequence to eradicate all natural affections, as to be entirely governed by them. This would almost sink us to the condition of brutes; and that would leave us without a sufficient principle of action. Reason alone, whatever anyone may wish, is not in reality a sufficient motive of virtue in such a creature as man; but this reason joined with those affections which God has impressed upon his heart: and when these are allowed scope to exercise themselves, but under strict government and direction of reason; then it is we act suitably to our nature, and to the circumstances God has placed us in. Neither is affection itself at all a weakness; nor does it argue defect, any otherwise than as our senses and appetites do; they belong to our condition of nature, and are what we cannot be without. God Almighty is to be sure unmoved by passion or appetite, unchanged by affection: but then it is to be added, that he neither sees, nor hears, nor perceives things by any senses like ours; but in a manner infinitely more perfect. Now, as it is an absurdity almost too gross to be mentioned, for a man to endeavour to get rid of his senses, because the Supreme Being discerns things more perfectly without them; it is as real, though not so obvious an absurdity, to endeavour to eradicate the passions he has given us, because he is without them. For, since our passions are as really a part of our constitution as our senses; since the former as really belong to our condition of nature as the latter; to get rid of either, is equally a violation of and breaking in upon that nature and constitution he has given us. Both our senses and our passions are a supply to the imperfection of our nature: thus they shew that we are such sort of creatures, as to stand in need of those helps which higher orders of creatures do not. But it is not the supply, but the deficiency; as it is not a remedy, but a disease, which is the imperfection. However, our appetites, passions, senses, no way imply disease: nor indeed do they imply deficiency or imperfection of any sort; but only this, that the constitution of nature according to which God has made us, is such as to require them. And it is so far from being true, that a wise man must entirely suppress compassion, and all fellow-feeling for others, as a weakness; and trust to reason alone, to teach and enforce upon him the practice of the several charities we owe to our kind; that on the contrary, even the bare exercise of such affections would itself be for the good and happiness of the world; and the imperfection of the higher principles of reason and religion in man, the little influence they have upon our practice, and the strength and prevalency of contrary ones, plainly require these affections, to be a restraint upon these latter, and a supply to the deficiencies of the former.*

4   *First,* The very exercise itself of these affections, in a just and reasonable manner and degree, would upon the whole increase the satisfactions, and lessen the miseries of life.

5   It is the tendency and business of virtue and religion to procure, as much as may be, universal good-will, trust and friendship amongst mankind. If this could be brought to obtain; and each man enjoyed the happiness of others, as everyone does that of a friend; and looked upon the success and prosperity of his neighbour, as every one does upon that of his children and family; it is too manifest to be insisted upon, how much the enjoyments of life would be increased. There would be so much happiness introduced into the world, without any deduction or inconvenience from it, in proportion as the precept of 'rejoicing with those who rejoice' was universally obeyed. Our Saviour has owned this good affection as belonging to our nature, in the parable of the Lost Sheep;[2] and does not think it to the disadvantage of a perfect state, to represent its happiness as capable of increase from reflection upon that of others.

6   But since in such a creature as man, compassion or sorrow for the distress of others, seems so far necessarily connected with joy in their prosperity, as that whoever rejoices in one must unavoidably compassionate the other; there cannot be that delight or satisfaction, which appears to be so considerable, without the inconveniences, whatever they are, of compassion.

7   However, without considering this connection, there is no doubt but that more good than evil, more delight than sorrow, arises from compassion itself; there being so many things which balance the sorrow of it. There is first the relief which the distressed feel from this affection in others towards them. There is likewise the additional misery which they would feel from the reflection that no one commiserated their case. It is indeed true, that any disposition, prevailing beyond a certain degree, becomes somewhat wrong; and we have ways of speaking, which, though they do not directly express that excess, yet always lead our thoughts to it, and give us the notion of it. Thus, when mention is made of delight in being pitied, this always

conveys to our mind the notion of somewhat which is really a weakness: the manner of speaking, I say, implies a certain weakness and feebleness of mind, which is and ought to be disapproved. But men of the greatest fortitude would in distress feel uneasiness, from knowing that no person in the world had any sort of compassion or real concern for them; and in some cases, especially when the temper is enfeebled by sickness or any long and great distress, doubtless, would feel a kind of relief even from the helpless good-will and ineffectual assistances of those about them. Over against the sorrow of compassion is likewise to be set a peculiar calm kind of satisfaction, which accompanies it, unless in cases where the distress of another is by some means so brought home to ourselves, as to become in a manner our own; or when from weakness of mind the affection rises too high, which ought to be corrected. This tranquillity or calm satisfaction proceeds, partly from consciousness of a right affection and temper of mind, and partly from a sense of our own freedom from the misery we compassionate. This last may possibly appear to some at first sight faulty; but it really is not so. It is the same with that positive enjoyment, which sudden ease from pain for the present affords, arising from a real sense of misery, joined with a sense of our freedom from it; which in all cases must afford some degree of satisfaction.

To these things must be added the observation, which respects both the affections 8 we are considering; that they who have got over all fellow-feeling for others, have withal contracted a certain callousness of heart, which renders them insensible to most other satisfactions, but those of the grossest kind.

Secondly, Without the exercise of these affections, men would certainly be much 9 more wanting in the offices of charity they owe to each other, and likewise more cruel and injurious, than they are at present.

The private interest of the individual would not be sufficiently provided for by 10 reasonable and cool self-love alone: therefore the appetites and passions are placed within as a guard and further security, without which it would not be taken due care of. It is manifest our life would be neglected, were it not for the calls of hunger, and thirst, and weariness; not withstanding that without them reason would assure us, that the recruits* of food and sleep are the necessary means of our preservation. It is therefore absurd to imagine, that, without affection, the same reason alone would be more effectual to engage us to perform the duties we owe to our fellow-creatures. One of this make would be as defective, as much wanting, considered with respect to society; as one of the former make would be defective, or wanting, considered as an individual, or in his private capacity. Is it possible any can in earnest think, that a public spirit, *i.e.* a settled reasonable principle of benevolence to mankind, is so prevalent and strong in the species, as that we may venture to throw off the under affections, which are its assistants, carry it forward and mark out particular courses for it; family, friends, neighbourhood, the distressed, our country? The common joys and the common sorrows, which belong to these relations and circumstances, are as plainly useful to society; as the pain and pleasure belonging to hunger, thirst, and weariness are of service to the individual. In defect of* that higher principle of reason, compassion is often the only way by which the indigent can have access to us: and therefore to eradicate this, though it is not indeed formally to deny that assistance which is their due; yet it is to cut them off from that which is too frequently their only way of obtaining it. And as for those who have shut up this door against the complaints of the miserable, and conquered this affection in themselves; even these persons will be under great restraints from the same affection in others. Thus a man who has himself no sense of injustice, cruelty, oppression, will be kept from running the utmost lengths of wickedness, by fear of that detestation, and even resentment of inhumanity, in many particular instances of it, which compassion for the object, towards whom such inhumanity is exercised, excites in the bulk of mankind. And this is frequently the chief danger, and the chief restraint, which tyrants and the great oppressors of the world feel.

11   In general, experience will shew, that as want of natural appetite to food supposes and proceeds from some bodily disease; so the apathy the Stoics talk of as much supposes, or is accompanied with somewhat amiss in the moral character, in that which is the health of the mind. Those who formerly aimed at this upon the foot of philosophy, appear to have had better success in eradicating the affections of tenderness and compassion, than they had with the passions of envy, pride, and resentment: these latter, at best, were but concealed, and that imperfectly too. How far this observation may be extended to such as endeavour to suppress the natural impulses of their affections, in order to form themselves for business and the world, I shall not determine. But there does not appear any capacity or relation to be named, in which men ought to be entirely deaf to the calls of affection, unless the judicial one is to be excepted.*

12   And as to those who are commonly called the men of pleasure, it is manifest that the reason they set up for hardness of heart, is to avoid being interrupted in their course, by the ruin and misery they are the authors of: neither are persons of this character always the most free from the impotencies of envy and resentment. What may men at last bring themselves to, by suppressing their passions and affections of one kind, and leaving those of the other in their full strength? But surely it might be expected, that persons who make pleasure their study and their business, if they understood what they profess, would reflect, how many of the entertainments of life, how many of those kind of amusements which seem peculiarly to belong to men of leisure and education, they become insensible to by this acquired hardness of heart.*

13   I shall close these reflections with barely mentioning the behaviour of that Divine Person, who was the example of all perfection in human nature, as represented in the Gospels mourning, and even, in a literal sense, weeping over the distresses of his creatures.*

14   The observation already made, that, of the two affections mentioned in the text, the latter exerts itself much more than the former; that, from the original constitution of human nature we much more generally and sensibly compassionate the distressed,

than rejoice with the prosperous, requires to be particularly considered. This obser-vation therefore, with the reflections which arise out of it, and which it leads our thoughts to, shall be the subject of another discourse.*

For the conclusion of this, let me just take notice of the danger of over-great   15 refinements; of going besides or beyond the plain, obvious, first appearances of things, upon the subject of morals and religion. The least observation will shew, how little the generality of men are capable of speculations. Therefore morality and religion must be somewhat plain and easy to be understood: it must appeal to what we call plain common sense, as distinguished from superior capacity and improve-ment; because it appeals to mankind. Persons of superior capacity and improvement have often fallen into errors, which no one of mere common understanding could.* Is it possible that one of this latter character could ever of himself have thought, that there was absolutely no such thing in mankind as affection to the good of others; suppose of parents to their children; or that what he felt upon seeing a friend in distress, was only fear for himself; or, upon supposition of the affections of kindness and compassion, that it was the business of wisdom and virtue, to set him about extirpating them as fast as he could? And yet each of these manifest contradictions to nature has been laid down by men of speculation, as a discovery in moral philosophy; which they, it seems, have found out through all the specious appearances to the contrary. This reflection may be extended further. The extravagancies of enthusiasm and superstition do not at all lie in the road of common sense; and therefore so far as they are *original mistakes*, must be owing to going beside or beyond it.* Now, since inquiry and examination can relate only to things so obscure and uncertain as to stand in need of it, and to persons who are capable of it; the proper advice to be given to plain honest men, to secure them from the extremes both of superstition and irreligion, is that of the Son of Sirach: 'In every good work trust thy own soul; for this is the keeping of the commandment.'[3]

Notes

1. There being manifestly this appearance of men's substituting others for themselves, and being carried out and affected towards them as towards themselves; some persons, who have a system which excludes every affection of this sort, have taken a pleasant method to solve it; and tell you it is *not another* you are at all concerned about, but your *self only*, when you feel the affection called compassion, *i.e.* here is a plain matter of fact, which men cannot reconcile with the general account they think fit to give of things: they therefore, instead of *that* manifest fact, substitute *another*, which is reconcilable to their own scheme. For does not every body by compassion mean, an affection the object of which is another in distress? Instead of this, but designing to have it mistaken for this, they speak of an affection or passion, the object of which is ourselves, or danger to ourselves. Hobbes defines 'pity, imagination, or fiction of future calamity to ourselves, proceeding from the sense' (he means sight or knowledge) 'of another man's calamity.'* Thus fear and compassion would be the same idea, and a fearful and a compassionate man the same character, which every one

immediately sees are totally different. Further, to those who give any scope to their affections, there is no perception or inward feeling more universal than this: that one who, has been merciful and compassionate throughout the course of his behaviour, should himself be treated with kindness, if he happens to fall into circumstances of distress. Is fear then or cowardice so great a recommendation to the favour of the bulk of mankind? Or is it not plain, that mere fearlessness (and therefore not the contrary) is one of the most popular qualifications? This shews that mankind are not affected towards compassion as fear, but as somewhat totally different.

Nothing would more expose such accounts as these of the affections which are favourable and friendly to our fellow-creatures, than to substitute the definitions which this author, and others who follow his steps, give of such affections, instead of the words by which they are commonly expressed. Hobbes, after having laid down that pity or compassion is only fear for ourselves, goes on to explain the reason why we pity our friends in distress more than others. Now substitute the *definition* instead of the word *pity* in this place, and the inquiry will be, why we fear our friends, etc. which words (since he really does not mean why we are afraid of them) make no question or sentence at all. So that common language, the words *to compassionate, to pity*, cannot be accommodated to his account of compassion. The very joining of the words to *pity our friends*, is a direct contradiction to his definition of pity: because those words so joined, necessarily express that our friends are the objects of the passion; whereas his definition of it asserts, that our selves (or danger to ourselves) are the only objects of it. He might indeed have avoided this absurdity, by plainly saying what he is going to account for; namely, why the sight of the innocent, or of our friends in distress, raises greater fear for ourselves than the sight of other persons in distress. But had he put the thing thus plainly, the fact itself would have been doubted; that *the sight of our friends in distress raises in us greater fear for ourselves, than the sight of others in distress.* And in the next place it would immediately have occurred to every one, that the fact now mentioned, which at least is *doubtful*, whether true or false, was not the same with this fact, which nobody ever doubted, that *the sight of our friends in distress raises in us greater compassion than the sight of others in distress*: every one, I say, would have seen that these are not the *same*, but *two different* inquiries; and consequently, that fear and compassion are not the same. Suppose a person to be in real danger, and by some means or other to have forgot it; any trifling accident, any sound might alarm him, recall the danger to his remembrance, and renew his fear: but it is almost too grossly ridiculous (though it is to show an absurdity) to speak of that sound or accident as an object of compassion; and yet according to Mr. Hobbes, our greatest friend in distress is no more to us, no more the object of compassion or of any affection in our heart: neither the one nor the other raises any emotion in our mind, but only the thoughts of our liableness to calamity, and the fear of it; and both equally do this. It is fit such sort of accounts of human nature should be shown to be what they really are, because there is raised upon them a general scheme which undermines the whole foundation of common justice and honesty. See Hobbes, *Of Human Nature*, c. 9. sec. 10.

There are often three distinct perceptions or inward feelings upon sight of persons in distress: real sorrow and concern for the misery of our fellow-creatures; some degree of satisfaction from a consciousness of our freedom from that misery; and, as the mind passes on from one thing to another, it is not unnatural from such an occasion to reflect upon our own liableness to the same or other calamities. The two last frequently accompany the first, but it is the first *only* which is properly compassion, of which the distressed are the objects, and which directly carries us with calmness and thought to their assistance. Any one of these, from various and complicated reasons, may in particular cases prevail over the other two; and there are, I suppose, instances where the bare *sight* of distress, without our feeling any compassion for it, may be the occasion of either or both of the two latter perceptions. One might add, that if there be really any such thing as the fiction or imagination of danger to ourselves from sight of the miseries of others, which Hobbes speaks of, and which he has absurdly mistaken for the whole of compassion; if there be any thing of this sort common to mankind, distinct from the reflection of reason, it would be a most remarkable instance of what was furthest from his thoughts, namely, of a mutual sympathy between each particular of the species, a fellow-feeling common to mankind. It would not indeed be an example of our substituting others for ourselves, but it would be an example of our substituting ourselves for others. And as it would not be an instance of benevolence, so neither would it be any instance of self-love: for this phantom of danger to ourselves, naturally rising to view upon sight of the distresses of others, would be no more an instance of love to ourselves, than the pain of hunger is.*

2. [*Luke* xv.7.]

3. *Ecclus.* xxxii.23.

Sermon 6

Upon Compassion*
Preached the first Sunday in Lent

Rejoice with them that do rejoice, and weep with them that weep.

(Romans xii.15)

1   There is a much more exact correspondence between the natural and moral world, than we are apt to take notice of. The inward frame of man does in a peculiar manner answer to the external condition and circumstances of life, in which he is placed. This is a particular instance of that general observation of the Son of Sirach: 'All things are double one against another, and God hath made nothing imper-fect.'[1]* The several passions and affections in the heart of man, compared with the circumstances of life in which he is placed, afford, to such as will attend to them, as certain instances of final causes, as any whatever which are more commonly alleged for such: since those affections lead him to a certain determinate course of action suitable to those circumstances; as (for instance) compassion, to relieve the distressed. And as all observations of final causes, drawn from the principles of action in the heart of man, compared with the condition he is placed in, serve all the good uses which instances of final causes in the material world about us do; and both these are equally proofs of wisdom and design in the Author of Nature: so the former serve to further good purposes; they shew us what course of life we are made for, what is our duty, and in a peculiar manner enforce upon us the practice of it.

2   Suppose we are capable of happiness and of misery in degrees equally intense and extreme, yet, we are capable of the latter for a much longer time beyond all comparison. We see men in the tortures of pain for hours, days, and, excepting the short suspensions of sleep, for months together without intermission; to which no enjoyments of life do, in degree and continuance, bear any sort of proportion. And such is our make and that of the world about us, that any thing may become the instrument of pain and sorrow to us. Thus almost any one man is capable of doing mischief to any other, though he may not be capable of doing him good: and if he be capable of doing him some good, he is capable of doing him more evil. And it is, in numberless cases, much more in our power to lessen the miseries of others, than to

promote their positive happiness, any otherwise than as the former often includes the latter; ease from misery occasioning for some time the greatest positive enjoyment. This constitution of nature, namely, that it is so much more in our power to occasion and likewise to lessen misery, than to promote positive happiness, plainly required a particular affection, to hinder us from abusing, and to incline us to make a right use of the former powers, *i.e.* the powers both to occasion and to lessen misery; over and above what was necessary to induce us to make a right use of the latter power, that of promoting positive happiness. The power we have over the misery of our fellow-creatures, to occasion or lessen it, being a more important trust, than the power we have of promoting their positive happiness; the former requires and has a further, an additional security and guard against its being violated, beyond and over and above what the latter has.* The social nature of man, and general good-will to his species, equally prevent him from doing evil, incline him to relieve the distressed, and to promote the positive happiness of his fellow-creatures: but compassion only restrains from the first, and carries him to the second; it hath nothing to do with the third.

The final causes then of compassion are to prevent and to relieve misery.　　3

As to the former: this affection may plainly be a restraint upon resentment, envy,　4 unreasonable self-love; that is, upon all the principles from which men do evil to one another. Let us instance only in resentment. It seldom happens, in regulated societies, that men have an enemy so entirely in their power, as to be able to satiate their resentment with safety. But if we were to put this case, it is plainly supposable, that a person might bring his enemy into such a condition, as from being the object of anger and rage, to become an object of compassion, even to himself, though the most malicious man in the world: and in this case compassion would stop him, if he could stop with safety, from pursuing his revenge any further. But since nature has placed within us more powerful restraints to prevent mischief, and since the final cause of compassion is much more to relieve misery, let us go on to the consideration of it in this view.

As this world was not intended to be a state of any great satisfaction or high　5 enjoyment; so neither was it intended to be a mere scene of unhappiness and sorrow. Mitigations and reliefs are provided by the merciful Author of Nature, for most of the afflictions in human life. There is kind provision made even against our frailties; as we are so constituted that time abundantly abates our sorrows, and begets in us that resignment of temper, which ought to have been produced by a better cause; a due sense of the authority of God, and our state of dependence. This holds in respect to far the greatest part of the evils of life; I suppose, in some degree, as to pain and sickness. Now this part of the constitution or make of man, considered as some relief to misery, and not as provision for positive happiness, is, if I may so speak, an instance of nature's compassion for us; and every natural remedy or relief to misery, may be considered in the same view.

But since in many cases it is very much in our power to alleviate the miseries of　6 each other; and benevolence, though natural in man to man, yet is in a very low degree, kept down by interest and competitions; and men, for the most part, are so engaged in the business and pleasures of the world, as to overlook and turn away from objects of misery; which are plainly considered as interruptions to them in their way, as intruders upon their business, their gaiety and mirth: compassion is an advocate within us in their behalf, to gain the unhappy admittance and access, to make their case attended to. If it sometimes serves a contrary purpose, and makes men industriously turn away from the miserable, these are only instances of abuse and perversion: for the end, for which the affection was given us, most certainly is not to make us avoid, but to make us attend to the objects of it. And if men would only resolve to allow thus much to it; let it bring before their view, the view of their mind, the miseries of their fellow-creatures; let it gain for them that their case be considered; I am persuaded it would not fail of gaining more, and that very few real objects of charity would pass unrelieved. Pain and sorrow and misery have a right to our assistance: compassion puts us in mind of the debt, and that we owe it to ourselves, as well as to the distressed. For, to endeavour to get rid of the sorrow of compassion by turning from the wretched, when yet it is in our power to relieve them, is as unnatural, as to endeavour to get rid of the pain of hunger by keeping from the sight of food. That we can do one with greater success than we can the other, is no proof that one is less a violation of nature than the other. Compassion is a call, a demand of nature, to relieve the unhappy; as hunger is a natural call for food. This affection plainly gives the objects of it an additional claim to relief and mercy, over and above what our fellow-creatures in common have to our good-will. Liberality and bounty are exceedingly commendable; and a particular distinction in such a world as this, where men set themselves to contract their heart, and close it to all interests but their own. It is by no means to be opposed to mercy, but always accompanies it: the distinction between them is only, that the former leads our thoughts to a more promiscuous and undistinguished distribution of favours; to those who are not, as well as those who are necessitous; whereas the object of compassion is misery. But in the comparison, and where there is not a possibility of both, mercy is to have the preference: the affection of compassion manifestly leads us to this preference. Thus, to relieve the indigent and distressed, to single out the unhappy, from whom can be expected no returns either of present entertainment or future service, for the objects of our favours; to esteem a man's being friendless as a recommendation; dejection, and incapacity of struggling through the world, as a motive for assisting him; in a word, to consider these circumstances of disadvantage, which are usually thought a sufficient reason for neglect and overlooking a person, as a motive for helping him forward: this is the course of benevolence which compassion marks out and directs us to: this is that humanity, which is so peculiarly becoming our nature and circumstances in this world.

7   To these considerations, drawn from the nature of man, must be added the reason of the thing itself we are recommending, which accords to and shews the same. For since it is so much more in our power to lessen the misery of our fellow-creatures,

than to promote their positive happiness; in cases where there is an inconsistency, we shall be likely to do much more good by setting ourselves to mitigate the former, than by endeavouring to promote the latter. Let the competition be between the poor and the rich. It is easy, you will say, to see which will have the preference. True: but the question is, which ought to have the preference? What proportion is there between the happiness produced by doing a favour to the indigent, and that produced by doing the same favour to one in easy circumstances? It is manifest, that the addition of a very large estate to one who before had an affluence, will in many instances yield him less new enjoyment or satisfaction, than an ordinary charity would yield to a necessitous person. So that it is not only true, that our nature, *i.e.* the voice of God within us,* carries us to the exercise of charity and benevolence in the way of compassion or mercy, preferably to any other way; but we also manifestly discern much more good done by the former; or, if you will allow me the expressions, more misery annihilated, and happiness created. If charity and benevolence, and endeavouring to do good to our fellow-creatures, be any thing, this observation deserves to be most seriously considered by all who have to bestow. And it holds with great exactness, when applied to the several degrees of greater and less indigency throughout the various ranks in human life: the happiness or good produced not being in proportion to what is bestowed, but in proportion to this joined with the need there was of it.

It may perhaps be expected, that upon this subject, notice should be taken of 8 occasions, circumstances and characters, which seem at once to call forth affections of different sorts. Thus vice may be thought the object both of pity and indignation:* folly, of pity and of laughter. How far this is strictly true, I shall not inquire; but only observe upon the appearance, how much more human it is to yield and give scope to affections, which are more directly in favour of, and friendly towards our fellow-creatures; and that there is plainly much less danger of being led wrong by these, than by the other.

But, notwithstanding all that has been said in recommendation of compassion, 9 that it is most amiable, most becoming human nature, and most useful to the world; yet it must be owned, that every affection, as distinct from a principle of reason,* may rise too high, and be beyond its just proportion. And by means of this one carried too far, a man throughout his life is subject to much more uneasiness than belongs to his share: and in particular instances, it may be in such a degree, as to incapacitate him from assisting the very person who is the object of it. But, as there are some who upon principle set up for suppressing this affection itself as weakness, there is also I know not what of fashion on this side; and, by some means or other, the whole world almost is run into the extremes of insensibility towards the distresses of their fellow-creatures: so that general rules and exhortations must always be on the other side.

And now to go on to the uses we should make of the foregoing reflections, the 10 further ones they lead to, and the general temper they have a tendency to beget in us. There being that distinct affection implanted in the nature of man, tending to lessen the miseries of life, that particular provision made for abating its sorrows, more than for increasing its positive happiness, as before explained; this may suggest to us, what should be our general aim respecting ourselves, in our passage through this world: namely, to endeavour chiefly to escape misery, keep free from uneasiness, pain and sorrow, or to get relief and mitigation of them; to propose to ourselves peace and tranquillity of mind, rather than pursue after high enjoyments. This is what the constitution of nature before explained marks out as the course we should follow, and the end we should aim at. To make pleasure and mirth and jollity our business, and be constantly hurrying about after some gay amusement, some new gratification of sense or appetite, to those who will consider the nature of man and our condition in this world, will appear the most romantic scheme of life that ever entered into thought. And yet how many are there who go on in this course, without learning better from the daily, the hourly disappointments, listlessness, and satiety, which accompany this fashionable method of wasting away their days?*

11   The subject we have been insisting upon would lead us into the same kind of reflections, by a different connection. The miseries of life brought home to ourselves by compassion, viewed through this affection considered as the sense by which they are perceived, would beget in us that moderation, humility, and soberness of mind, which has been now recommended; and which peculiarly belongs to a season of recollection, the only purpose of which is to bring us to a just sense of things, to recover us out of that forgetfulness of ourselves, and our true state, which it is manifest far the greatest part of men pass their whole life in. Upon this account Solomon says, that 'it is better to go to the house of mourning, than to go to the house of feasting'; *i.e.* it is more to a man's advantage to turn his eyes towards objects of distress, to recall sometimes to his remembrance the occasions of sorrow, than to pass all his days in thoughtless mirth and gaiety. And he represents the wise as choosing to frequent the former of these places; to be sure not for its own sake, but because 'by the sadness of the countenance the heart is made better'.[2] Everyone observes, how temperate and reasonable men are when humbled and brought low by afflictions, in comparison of what they are in high prosperity. By this voluntary resort to the house of mourning which is here recommended, we might learn all those useful instructions which calamities teach, without undergoing them ourselves; and grow wiser and better at a more easy rate than men commonly do. The objects themselves, which in that place of sorrow lie before our view, naturally give us a seriousness and attention, check that wantonness which is the growth of prosperity and ease, and lead us to reflect upon the deficiencies of human life itself; that 'every man at his best estate is altogether vanity'.[3] This would correct the florid and gaudy prospects and expectations which we are too apt to indulge, teach us to lower our notions of happiness and enjoyment, bring them down to the reality of things, to what is attainable, to what the frailty of our condition will admit of, which, for any continuance, is only tranquillity, ease, and moderate satisfactions. Thus we might at once become proof against the temptations, with which the whole world almost is

carried away; since it is plain, that not only what is called a life of pleasure, but also vicious pursuits in general, aim at somewhat besides and beyond these moderate satisfactions.

And as to that obstinacy and wilfulness, which renders men so insensible to the   12 motives of religion; this right sense of ourselves and of the world about us would bend the stubborn mind, soften the heart, and make it more apt to receive impression: and this is the proper temper in which to call our ways to remembrance, to review and set home upon ourselves the miscarriages of our past life. In such a compliant state of mind, reason and conscience will have a fair hearing; which is the preparation for, rather the beginning of that repentance, the outward show of which we all put on at this season.*

Lastly, The various miseries of life which lie before us wherever we turn our eyes,   13 the frailty of this mortal state we are passing through, may put us in mind that the present world is not our home; that we are merely strangers and travellers in it, as all our fathers were. It is therefore to be considered as a foreign country; in which our poverty and wants, and the insufficient supplies of them were designed to turn our views to that higher and better state we are heirs to: a state where will be no follies to be overlooked, no miseries to be pitied, no wants to be relieved; where the affection we have been now treating of will happily be lost, as there will be no objects to exercise it upon: for 'God shall wipe away all tears from their eyes, and there shall be no more death, neither sorrow, nor crying, neither shall there be any more pain; for the former things are passed away'.[4]*

Notes

1. *Ecclus.* xlii.24.
2. [*Eccles.* vii.2, 3.]
3. [*Ps.* xxxix.5.*]
4. [*Rev.* xxi.4.]

Sermon 7

Upon the Character of Balaam*
Preached the Second Sunday after Easter

Let me die the death of the righteous, and let my last end be like his.

(*Numbers* xxiii.10)

1   These words, taken alone, and without respect to him who spoke them, lead our thoughts immediately to the different ends of good and bad men. For, though the comparison is not expressed, yet it is manifestly implied; as is also the preference of one of these characters to the other in that last circumstance, death. And, since dying the death of the righteous or of the wicked, necessarily implies men's being righteous or wicked, *i.e.* having lived righteously or wickedly; a comparison of them in their lives also might come into consideration from such a single view of the words themselves. But my present design is, to consider them with a particular reference or respect to him who spoke them; which reference, if you please to attend, you will see. And if what shall be offered to your consideration at this time, be thought a discourse upon the whole history of this man, rather than upon the particular words I have read, this is of no consequence: it is sufficient, if it afford reflections of use and service to ourselves.

2   But, in order to avoid cavils respecting this remarkable relation in Scripture, either that part of it which you have heard in the first lesson for the day,* or any other; let me just observe, that as this is not a place for answering them, so they no way affect the following discourse; since the character there given is plainly a real one in life, and such as there are parallels to.*

3   The occasion of Balaam's coming out of his own country into the land of Moab, where he pronounced this solemn prayer or wish, he himself relates in the first parable or prophetic speech, of which it is the conclusion. In which is a custom referred to, proper to be taken notice of: that of devoting enemies to destruction, before the entrance upon a war with them. This custom appears to have prevailed over a great part of the world, for we find it amongst the most distant nations. The Romans had public officers, to whom it belonged as a stated part of their office. But there was somewhat more particular in the case now before us; Balaam being looked

upon as an extraordinary person, whose blessing or curse was thought to be always effectual.

In order to engage the reader's attention to this passage, the sacred historian has   4 enumerated the preparatory circumstances, which are these. Balaam requires the king of Moab to build him seven altars, and to prepare him the same number of oxen and of rams. The sacrifice being over, he retires alone to a solitude sacred to these occasions, there to await the divine inspiration or answer, for which the foregoing rites were the preparation. 'And God met Balaam, and put a word in his mouth,'[1]* upon receiving which, he returns back to the altars; where was the king, who had all this while attended the sacrifice, as appointed; he and all the princes of Moab standing, big with expectation of the prophet's reply. 'And he took up his parable and said, Balak the King of Moab hath brought me from Aram, out of the mountains of the east; saying, come, curse me Jacob, and come, defy Israel. How shall I curse, whom God hath not cursed? Or how shall I defy, whom the Lord hath not defied? For from the top of the rocks I see him, and from the hills I behold him: lo, the people shall dwell alone, and shall not be reckoned among the nations. Who can count the dust of Jacob, and the number of the fourth part of Israel? Let me die the death of the righteous, and let my last end be like his.'[2]

It is necessary, as you will see in the progress of this discourse, particularly to   5 observe what he understood by *righteous*. And he himself is introduced in the book of Micah[3] explaining it; if by *righteous* is meant *good*, as to be sure it is. 'O my people, remember now what Balak king of Moab consulted, and what Balaam the son of Beor answered him from Shittim unto Gilgal.' From the mention of Shittim it is manifest, that it is this very story which is here referred to, though another part of it, the account of which is not now extant; as there are many quotations in Scripture out of books which are not come down to us. 'Remember what Balaam answered, that ye may know the righteousness of the Lord,' i.e. the righteousness which God will accept. Balak demands, 'Wherewith shall I come before the Lord, and bow myself before the high God? Shall I come before him with burnt-offerings, with calves of a year old? Will the Lord be pleased with thousands of rams, or with ten thousands of rivers of oil? Shall I give my first born for my transgression, the fruit of my body for the sin of my soul?' Balaam answers him, 'He hath shewed thee, O man, what is good: and what doth the Lord require of thee, but to do justly, and to love mercy, and to walk humbly with thy God?'[4] Here is a good man expressly characterized, as distinct from a dishonest, and a superstitious man. No words can more strongly exclude dishonesty and falseness of heart, than 'doing justice' and 'loving mercy': and both these, as well as 'walking humbly with God', are put in opposition to those cere-monial methods of recommendation, which Balak hoped might have served the turn. From hence appears what he meant by the *righteous*, whose *death* he desires to die.

Whether it was his own character shall now be inquired: and in order to determine   6 it, we must take a view of his whole behaviour upon this occasion. When the elders of Moab came to him, though he appears to have been much allured with the rewards offered, yet he had such regard to the authority of God, as to keep the messengers in suspense until he had consulted his will. 'And God said to him, Thou shalt not go with them, thou shalt not curse the people, for they are blessed.'[5] Upon this he dismisses the ambassadors, with an absolute refusal of accompanying them back to their king. Thus far his regard to his duty prevailed, neither does there any thing appear as yet amiss in his conduct. His answer being reported to the king of Moab, a more honourable embassy is immediately dispatched, and greater rewards proposed. Then the iniquity of his heart began to disclose itself. A thorough honest man would without hesitation have repeated his former answer, that he could not be guilty of so infamous a prostitution of the sacred character with which he was invested, as in the name of a prophet to curse those, whom he knew to be blessed. But instead of this, which was the only honest part in these circumstances that lay before him, he desired the princes of Moab to tarry that night with him also; and for the sake of the reward deliberates, whether by some means or other he might not be able to obtain leave to curse Israel; to do that, which had been before revealed to him to be contrary to the will of God, which yet he resolves not to do without that permission. Upon which, as when this nation afterwards rejected God from reigning over them, he gave them a king in his anger; in the same way, as appears from other parts of the narration, he gives Balaam the permission he desired: for this is the most natural sense of the words. Arriving in the territories of Moab, and being received with particular distinction by the king, and he repeating in person the promise of the rewards he had before made to him by his ambassadors: he seeks, the text says, by 'sacrifices' and 'enchantments',* (what these were is not to our purpose) to obtain leave of God to curse the people; keeping still his resolution, not to do it without that permission: which not being able to obtain, he had such regard to the command of God, as to keep this resolution to the last. The supposition of his being under a supernatural restraint is a mere fiction of Philo:* he is plainly represented to be under no other force or restraint, than the fear of God. However, he goes on persevering in that endeavour, after he had declared, that 'God had not beheld iniquity in Jacob, neither had he seen perverseness in Israel';[6] i.e. they were a people of virtue and piety so far as not to have drawn down, by their iniquity, that curse which he was soliciting leave to pronounce upon them. So that the state of Balaam's mind was this: he wanted to do what he knew to be very wicked, and contrary to the express command of God; he had inward checks and restraints, which he could not entirely get over; he therefore casts about for ways to reconcile this wickedness with his duty. How great a paradox soever this may appear, as it is indeed a contradiction in terms, it is the very account which the Scripture gives us of him.

7   But there is a more surprising piece of iniquity yet behind. Not daring in his religious character as a prophet to assist the king of Moab, he considers whether there might not be found some other means of assisting him against that very people, whom he himself by the fear of God was restrained from cursing in words. One would not think it possible, that the weakness, even of religious self-deceit in its

utmost excess, could have so poor a distinction, so fond an evasion, to serve itself of. But so it was: and he could think of no other method, than to betray the children of Israel to provoke his wrath, who was their only strength and defence. The temptation which he pitched upon, was that concerning which Solomon afterwards observed, that it had 'cast down many wounded; yea, many strong men had been slain by it':[7] and of which he himself was a sad example, when 'his wives turned away his heart after other gods'.[8] This succeeded: the people sin against God; and thus the prophet's counsel brought on that destruction, which he could by no means be prevailed upon to assist with the religious ceremony of execration, which the king of Moab thought would itself have effected it. Their crime and punishment are related in Deuteronomy[9] and Numbers.[10] And from the relation repeated in Numbers,[11] it appears, that Balaam was the contriver of the whole matter. It is also ascribed to him in the Revelation,[12] where he is said to have 'taught Balak to cast a stumbling-block before the children of Israel'.*

This was the man, this Balaam, I say, was the man who desired to 'die the death of the righteous', and that his 'last end might be like his': and this was the state of his mind, when he pronounced these words.   8

So that the object we have now before us is the most astonishing in the world: a very wicked man, under a deep sense of God and religion, persisting still in his wickedness, and preferring the wages of unrighteousness, even when he had before him a lively view of death, and that approaching period of his days, which should deprive him of all those advantages for which he was prostituting himself; and likewise a prospect, whether certain or uncertain, of a future state of retribution: all this joined with an explicit ardent wish, that, when he was to leave this world, he might be in the condition of a righteous man. Good God, what inconsistency, what perplexity is here! With what different views of things, with what contradictory principles of action, must such a mind be torn and distracted! It was not unthinking carelessness, by which he run on headlong in vice and folly, without ever making a stand to ask himself what he was doing: No; he acted upon the cool motives of interest and advantage. Neither was he totally hard and callous to impressions of religion, what we call abandoned; for he absolutely denied to curse Israel. When reason assumes her place, when convinced of his duty, when he owns and feels, and is actually under the influence of the divine authority; whilst he is carrying on his views to the grave, the end of all temporal greatness; under this sense of things, with the better character and more desirable state present—full before him—in his thoughts, in his wishes, voluntarily to choose the worse—what fatality is here! Or how otherwise can such a character be explained? And yet, strange as it may appear, it is not altogether an uncommon one: Nay, with some small alterations, and put a little lower, it is applicable to a very considerable part of the world. For, if the reasonable choice be seen and acknowledged, and yet men make the unreasonable one, is not this the same contradiction; that very inconsistency, which appeared so unaccountable?   9

10   To give some little opening to such characters and behaviour, it is to be observed in general, that there is no account to be given in the way of reason, of men's so strong attachments to the present world: our hopes and fears and pursuits are in degrees beyond all proportion to the known value of the things they respect. This may be said without taking into consideration religion and a future state; and when these are considered, the disproportion is infinitely heightened. Now when men go against their reason, and contradict a more important interest at a distance, for one nearer, though of less consideration; if this be the whole of the case, all that can be said is, that strong passions, some kind of brute force within, prevails over the principle of rationality. However, if this be with a clear, full and distinct view of the truth of things, then it is doing the utmost violence to themselves, acting in the most palpable contradiction to their very nature. But if there be any such thing in mankind, as putting half-deceits upon themselves; which there plainly is, either by avoiding reflection, or (if they do reflect) by religious equivocation, subterfuges, and palliating matters to themselves; by these means conscience may be laid asleep, and they may go on in a course of wickedness with less disturbance. All the various turns, doubles and intricacies in a dishonest heart, cannot be unfolded or laid open; but that there is somewhat of that kind is manifest, be it to be called self-deceit, or by any other name. Balaam had before his eyes the authority of God, absolutely forbidding him what he, for the sake of a reward, had the strongest inclination to: he was likewise in a state of mind sober enough to consider death and his last end: by these considerations he was restrained, first from going to the king of Moab; and after he did go, from cursing Israel. But notwithstanding this, there was great wickedness in his heart. He could not forego the rewards of unrighteousness: he therefore first seeks for indulgences; and when these could not be obtained, he sins against the whole meaning, end and design of the prohibition, which no consideration in the world could prevail with him to go against the letter of. And surely that impious counsel he gave to Balak against the children of Israel, was, considered in itself, a greater piece of wickedness, than if he had cursed them in words.

11   If it be inquired what his situation, his hopes and fears were, in respect to this his wish: the answer must be, that consciousness of the wickedness of his heart must necessarily have destroyed all settled hopes of dying the death of the righteous: he could have no calm satisfaction in this view of his last end: yet, on the other hand, it is possible that those partial regards to his duty, now mentioned, might keep him from perfect despair.

12   Upon the whole, it is manifest that Balaam had the most just and true notions of God and religion; as appears, partly from the original story itself, and more plainly from the passage in Micah; where he explains religion to consist in real virtue and real piety, expressly distinguished from superstition, and in terms which most strongly exclude dishonesty and falseness of heart. Yet you see his behaviour: he seeks indulgences for plain wickedness; which not being able to obtain, he glosses over that same wickedness, dresses it up in a new form, in order to make it pass off

more easily with himself. That is, he deliberately contrives to deceive and impose upon himself, in a matter which he knew to be of the utmost importance.

To bring these observations home to ourselves. It is too evident that many persons **13** allow themselves in very unjustifiable courses, who yet make great pretences to religion; not to deceive the world, none can be so weak as to think this will pass in our age; but from principles, hopes, and fears, respecting God and a future state; and go on thus with a sort of tranquillity and quiet of mind. This cannot be upon a thorough consideration, and full resolution, that the pleasures and advantages they propose are to be pursued at all hazards, against reason, against the law of God, and though everlasting destruction is to be the consequence. This would be doing too great violence upon themselves. No, they are for making a composition with the Almighty. These of his commands they will obey: but as to others—why they will make all the atonements in their power; the ambitious, the covetous, the dissolute man, each in a way which shall not contradict his respective pursuit. Indulgences before, which was Balaam's first attempt, though he was not so successful in it as to deceive himself, or atonements afterwards, are all the same. And here perhaps come in faint hopes that they may, and half-resolves that they will, one time or other, make a change.

Besides these, there are also persons, who from a more just way of considering **14** things, see the infinite absurdity of this, of substituting sacrifice instead of obedience; there are persons far enough from superstition, and not without some real sense of God and religion upon their minds; who yet are guilty of most unjustifiable practices, and go on with great coolness and command over themselves. The same dishonesty and unsoundness of heart discovers itself in these another way. In all common ordinary cases we see intuitively at first view what is our duty, what is the honest part.* This is the ground of the observation, that the first thought is often the best. In these cases doubt and deliberation is itself dishonesty; as it was in Balaam upon the second message. That which is called considering what is our duty in a particular case, is very often nothing but endeavouring to explain it away. Thus those courses, which, if men would fairly attend to the dictates of their own consciences, they would see to be corruption, excess, oppression, uncharitableness; these are refined upon— things were so and so circumstantiated—great difficulties are raised about fixing bounds and degrees: and thus every moral obligation whatever may be evaded. Here is scope, I say, for an unfair mind to explain away every moral obligation to itself. Whether men reflect again upon this internal management and artifice, and how explicit they are with themselves, is another question. There are many operations of the mind, many things pass within, which we never reflect upon again; which a by-stander, from having frequent opportunities of observing us and our conduct, may make shrewd guesses at.

That great numbers are in this way of deceiving themselves is certain. There is **15** scarce a man in the world, who has entirely got over all regards, hopes and fears, concerning God and a future state; and these apprehensions in the generality, bad as we are, prevail in considerable degrees: yet men will and can be wicked with calmness and thought; we see they are. There must therefore be some method of making it sit a little easy upon their minds; which, in the superstitious, is those indulgences and atonements before-mentioned,* and this self-deceit of another kind in persons of another character. And both these proceed from a certain unfairness of mind, a peculiar inward dishonesty; the direct contrary to that simplicity which our Saviour recommends, under the notion of 'becoming little children',[13] as a necessary quali-fication for our entering into the kingdom of heaven.*

16   But to conclude: how much soever men differ in the course of life they prefer, and in their ways of palliating and excusing their vices to themselves; yet all agree in the one thing, desiring to 'die the death of the righteous'. This is surely remarkable. The observation may be extended further, and put thus: even without determining what that is which we call guilt or innocence, there is no man but would choose, after having had the pleasure or advantage of a vicious action, to be free of the guilt of it, to be in the state of an innocent man.* This shews at least a disturbance, and implicit dissatisfaction in vice. If we inquire into the grounds of it, we shall find it proceeds partly from an immediate sense of having done evil; and partly from an apprehen-sion, that this inward sense shall one time or other be seconded by an higher judgement, upon which our whole being depends.* Now to suspend and drown this sense, and these apprehensions, be it by the hurry of business or of pleasure, or by superstition, or moral equivocation, this is in a manner one and the same, and makes no alteration at all in the nature of our case. Things and actions are what they are, and the consequences of them will be what they will be: why then should we desire to be deceived? As we are reasonable creatures, and have any regard to ourselves, we ought to lay these things plainly and honestly before our mind, and upon this, act as you please, as you think most fit; make that choice and prefer that course of life, which you can justify to yourselves, and which sits most easy upon your own mind. It will immediately appear, that vice cannot be the happiness, but must upon the whole be the misery, of such a creature as man; a moral, an accountable agent. Superstitious observances, self-deceit though of a more refined sort, will not in reality at all amend matters with us. And the result of the whole can be nothing else, but that with simplicity and fairness we 'keep innocency, and take heed unto the thing that is right; for this alone shall bring a man peace at the last'.[14]*

Notes

1. [*Num.* xxiii] vv.4, 5.
2. [*Num.* xxiii] vv.7–10.
3. *Micah* vi.[5].
4. [*Micah* vi.6–8.]
5. *Num.* xxii.12.
6. [*Num.* xxiii.] 21.

7. [*Proverbs* vii.26.]
8. [*I Kings* xi.4.]
9. *Deut.* iv.[3].
10. *Num.* xxv.
11. *Num.* xxxi.[16].*
12. *Rev.* ii.[14].*
13. [*Matt.* xviii.3.]
14. [*Ps.* xxxvii.37.]*

Sermon 8

Upon Resentment

Ye have heard that it hath been said, Thou shalt love thy neighbour, and hate thine enemy. But I say unto you, Love your enemies, bless them that curse you, do good to them that hate you, and pray for them which despitefully use you, and persecute you.

(Matt. v.43, 44)

1   Since perfect goodness in the Deity is the principle, from whence the universe was brought into being, and by which it is preserved;* and since general benevolence is the great law of the whole moral creation: it is a question which immediately occurs, *Why had man implanted in him a principle, which appears the direct contrary to benevolence?* Now the foot upon which inquiries of this kind should be treated is this: to take human nature as it is, and the circumstances in which it is placed as they are; and then consider the correspondence between that nature and those circumstances, or what course of action and behaviour, respecting those circumstances, any particular affection or passion leads us to.* This I mention to distinguish the matter now before us from disquisitions of quite another kind; namely, *Why we are not made more perfect creatures, or placed in better circumstances?* these being questions which we have not, that I know of, any thing at all to do with.* God Almighty undoubtedly foresaw the disorders, both natural and moral, which would happen in this state of things. If upon this we set ourselves to search and examine, why he did not prevent them; we shall, I am afraid, be in danger of running into somewhat worse than impertinent curiosity.* But upon this to examine, how far the nature which he hath given us hath a respect to those circumstances, such as they are; how far it leads us to act a proper part in them; plainly belongs to us: and such inquiries are in many ways of excellent use. Thus the thing to be considered is, not, *Why we were not made of such a nature, and placed in such circumstances, as to have no need of so harsh and turbulent a passion as resentment*; but, taking our nature and condition as being what they are, *Why or for what end such a passion was given us*: and this chiefly in order to shew, what are the abuses of it.

2   The persons who laid down for a rule, 'Thou shalt love thy neighbour, and hate thine enemy,' made short work with this matter. They did not, it seems, perceive any thing to be disapproved in hatred, more than in good-will: and, according to their

system of morals, our enemy was the proper natural object of one of these passions, as our neighbour was of the other of them.*

This was all they had to say, and all they thought needful to be said, upon the subject. But this cannot be satisfactory; because hatred, malice and revenge, are directly contrary to the religion we profess, and to the nature and reason of the thing itself.* Therefore, since no passion God hath endued us with can be in itself evil; and yet since men frequently indulge a passion in such ways and degrees, that at length it becomes quite another thing from what it was originally in our nature; and those vices of malice and revenge in particular take their occasion from the natural passion of resentment: it will be needful to trace this up to its original, that we may see, *what it is in itself, as placed in our nature by its Author;* from which it will plainly appear, *for what ends it was placed there.* And when we know what the passion is in itself, and the ends of it, we shall easily see, *what are the abuses of it, in which malice and revenge consist;* and which are so strongly forbidden in the text, by the direct contrary being commanded.

Resentment is of two kinds: *hasty and sudden,* or *settled and deliberate.* The former is called anger, and often *passion;* which, though a general word, is frequently appropriated and confined to the particular feeling, sudden anger, as distinct from deliberate resentment, malice and revenge. In all these words is usually implied somewhat vicious; somewhat unreasonable as to the occasion of the passion, or immoderate as to the degree or duration of it. But that the natural passion itself is indifferent, St. Paul has asserted in that precept, 'Be ye angry and sin not':[1] which though it is by no means to be understood as an encouragement to indulge ourselves in anger, the sense being certainly this, 'Though ye be angry, sin not'; yet here is evidently a distinction made between anger and sin; between the natural passion, and sinful anger.*

Sudden anger upon certain occasions is mere instinct: as merely so, as the disposition to close our eyes upon the apprehension of somewhat falling into them; and no more necessarily implies any degree of reason. I say, *necessarily:* for to be sure *hasty,* as well as *deliberate,* anger may be occasioned by injury or contempt; in which cases reason suggests to our thoughts that injury and contempt, which is the occasion of the passion: but I am speaking of the former only so far as it is to be distinguished from the latter. The only way, in which our reason and understanding can raise anger, is by representing to our mind injustice or injury of some kind or other. Now momentary anger is frequently raised, not only without any real, but without any apparent reason; that is, without any appearance of injury, as distinct from hurt or pain. It cannot, I suppose, be thought that this passion, in infants; in the lower species of animals; and, which is often seen, in men towards them; it cannot, I say, be imagined that these instances of this passion are the effect of reason: no, they are occasioned by mere sensation and feeling. It is opposition, sudden hurt, violence, which naturally excites the passion; and the real demerit or fault of him who offers that violence, or is the cause of that opposition or hurt, does not in many cases so much as come into thought.

6   The reason and end, for which man was made thus liable to this passion, is, that he might be better qualified to prevent, and likewise (or perhaps chiefly) to resist and defeat, sudden force, violence and opposition, considered merely as such, and without regard to the fault or demerit of him who is the author of them. Yet, since violence may be considered in this other and further view, as implying fault; and since injury, as distinct from harm, may raise sudden anger; sudden anger may likewise accidentally serve to prevent, or remedy, such fault and injury. But, considered as distinct from settled anger, it stands in our nature for self-defence, and not for the administration of justice. There are plainly cases, and in the uncultivated parts of the world, and, where regular governments are not formed, they frequently happen, in which there is no time for consideration, and yet to be passive is certain destruction; in which, sudden resistance is the only security.

7   But from *this*, *deliberate anger or resentment* is essentially distinguished, as the latter is not naturally excited by, or intended to prevent mere harm without appearance of wrong or injustice. Now, in order to see, as exactly as we can, what is the natural object and occasion of such resentment; let us reflect upon the manner in which we are touched with reading, suppose, a feigned story of baseness and villainy, properly worked up to move our passions. This immediately raises indignation, somewhat of a desire that it should be punished. And though the designed injury be prevented, yet that it was designed is sufficient to raise this inward feeling. Suppose the story true, this inward feeling would be as natural and as just: and one may venture to affirm, that there is scarce a man in the world, but would have it upon some occasions. It seems *in us* plainly connected with a sense of virtue and vice, of moral good and evil. Suppose further, we knew both the persons who did, and who suffered the injury: neither would this make any alteration, only that it would probably affect us more. The indignation raised by cruelty and injustice, and the desire of having it punished, which persons unconcerned would feel, is by no means malice.* No, it is resentment against vice and wickedness: it is one of the common bonds, by which society is held together; a fellow-feeling which each individual has in behalf of the whole species, as well as of himself. And it does not appear that this, generally speaking, is at all too high amongst mankind.* Suppose now the injury I have been speaking of to be done against ourselves; or those whom we consider as ourselves. It is plain, the way, in which we should be affected, would be exactly the same in kind: but it would certainly be in a higher degree, and less transient; because a sense of our own happiness and misery is most intimately and always present to us; and, from the very constitution of our nature, we cannot but have a greater sensibility to, and be more deeply interested in, what concerns ourselves.* And this seems to be the whole of this passion which is, properly speaking, natural to mankind: namely, a resentment against injury and wickedness in general; and in a higher degree when towards ourselves, in proportion to the greater regard which men naturally have for themselves, than for others. From hence it appears, that it is not natural, but moral evil; it is not suffering, but injury, which raises that anger or resentment, which is of

any continuance. The natural object of it is not one, who appears to the suffering person to have been only the innocent occasion of his pain or loss; but one, who has been in a moral sense injurious either to ourselves or others. This is abundantly confirmed by observing, what it is which heightens or lessens resentment; namely, the same which aggravates or lessens the fault: friendship and former obligations, on one hand; or inadvertency, strong temptations and mistake, on the other. All this is so much understood by mankind, how little soever it be reflected upon, that a person would be reckoned quite distracted, who should coolly resent an harm, which had not to himself the appearance of injury or wrong. Men do indeed resent what is occasioned through carelessness: but then they expect observance as their due, and so that carelessness is considered as faulty. It is likewise true, that they resent more strongly an injury done, than one which, though designed, was prevented, in cases where the guilt is perhaps the same: the reason however is, not that bare pain or loss raises resentment, but, that it gives a new, and, as I may speak, additional sense of the injury or injustice. According to the natural course of the passions, the degrees of resentment are in proportion, not only to the degree of design and deliberation in the injurious person; but in proportion to this, joined with the degree of the evil designed or premeditated; since this likewise comes in to make the injustice greater or less. And the evil or harm will appear greater when they feel it, than when they only reflect upon it: so therefore will the injury: and consequently the resentment will be greater.

The natural object, or occasion of, settled resentment then being injury, as distinct   8 from pain or loss; it is easy to see, that to prevent and to remedy such injury, and the miseries arising from it, is the end for which this passion was implanted in man. It is to be considered as a weapon, put into our hands by nature, against injury, injustice and cruelty: how it may be innocently employed and made use of, shall presently be mentioned.

The account, which has been now given of this passion, is in brief, that sudden   9 anger is raised by, and was chiefly intended to prevent or remedy, mere harm distinct from injury: but that it *may* be raised by injury, and *may* serve to prevent or to remedy it; and then the occasions and effects of it are the same, with the occasions and effects of deliberate anger. But they are essentially distinguished in this, that the latter is never occasioned by harm, distinct from injury; and its natural proper end is to remedy or prevent only that harm, which implies, or is supposed to imply, injury or moral wrong. Every one sees that these observations do not relate to those, who have habitually suppressed the course of their passions and affections, out of regard either to interest or virtue; or who, from habits of vice and folly, have changed their nature. But, I suppose, there can be no doubt but this, now described, is the general course of resentment, considered as a natural passion, neither increased by indulgence, nor corrected by virtue, nor prevailed over by other passions, or particular habits of life.

As to the abuses of anger, which it is to be observed may be in all different degrees,   10 the first which occurs is what is commonly called *passion*; to which some men are liable, in the same way as others are to the *epilepsy*, or any sudden particular disorder. This distemper of the mind seizes them upon the least occasion in the world, and perpetually without any real reason at all: and by means of it they are plainly, every day, every waking hour of their lives, liable and in danger of running into the most extravagant outrages. Of a less boisterous, but not of a less innocent kind,* is *peevishness*; which I mention with pity, with real pity to the unhappy creatures, who, from their inferior station, or other circumstances and relations, are obliged to be in the way of, and to serve for a supply to it. Both these, for aught that I can see, are one and the same principle: but, as it takes root in minds of different makes, it appears differently, and so is come to be distinguished by different names. That which in a more feeble temper is peevishness, and languidly discharges itself upon every thing which comes in its way; the same principle, in a temper of greater force and stronger passions, becomes rage and fury. In one, the humour discharges itself at once; in the other, it is continually discharging. This is the account of *passion* and *peevishness*, as distinct from each other, and appearing in different persons. It is no objection against the truth of it, that they are both to be seen sometimes in one and the same person.

11   With respect to deliberate resentment, the chief instances of abuse are: when, from partiality to ourselves, we imagine an injury done us, when there is none: when this partiality represents it to us greater than it really is: when we fall into that extravagant and monstrous kind of resentment, towards one who has innocently been the occasion of evil to us; that is, resentment upon account of pain or inconvenience, without injury; which is the same absurdity, as settled anger at a thing that is inanimate: when the indignation against injury and injustice rises too high, and is beyond proportion to the particular ill action it is exercised upon: or lastly, when pain or harm of any kind is inflicted merely in consequence of, and to gratify, that resentment, though naturally raised.*

12   It would be endless to descend into and explain all the peculiarities of perverseness, and wayward humour, which might be traced up to this passion. But there is one thing, which so generally belongs to and accompanies all excess and abuse of it, as to require being mentioned: a certain determination, and resolute bent of mind, not to be convinced or set right; though it be ever so plain, that there is no reason for the displeasure, that it was raised merely by error or misunderstanding. In this there is doubtless a great mixture of pride; but there is somewhat more, which I cannot otherwise express than, that resentment has taken possession of the temper and of the mind, and will not quit its hold. It would be too minute, to inquire whether this be any thing more than bare obstinacy: it is sufficient to observe, that it in a very particular manner and degree, belongs to the abuses of this passion.

13   But, notwithstanding all these abuses; "Is not just indignation against cruelty and wrong one of the 'instruments of death' which the Author of our nature hath provided?* Are not cruelty, injustice and wrong, the natural objects of that indignation? Surely then it may one way or other be innocently employed against them."

True. Since therefore it is necessary for the very subsistence of the world, that injury, injustice and cruelty should be punished; and since compassion, which is so natural to mankind, would render that execution of justice exceedingly difficult and uneasy; indignation against vice and wickedness is, and may be allowed to be, a balance to that weakness of pity, and also to anything else which would prevent the necessary methods of severity. Those, who have never thought upon these subjects, may perhaps not see the weight of this: but let us suppose a person guilty of murder, or any other action of cruelty, and that mankind had naturally no indignation against such wickedness and the authors of it; but that every body was affected towards such a criminal in the same way, as towards an innocent man: compassion, amongst other things, would render the execution of justice exceedingly painful and difficult, and would often quite prevent it. And notwithstanding that the principle of benevolence is denied by some, and is really in a very low degree, that men are in great measure insensible to the happiness of their fellow-creatures; yet they are not insensible to their misery, but are very strongly moved with it: insomuch that there plainly is occasion for that feeling which is raised by guilt and demerit, as a balance to that of compassion. Thus much may I think justly be allowed to resentment, in the strictest way of moral consideration.

The good influence which this passion has in fact upon the affairs of the world, is **14** obvious to every one's notice. Men are plainly restrained from injuring their fellow-creatures by fear of their resentment; and it is very happy that they are so, when they would not be restrained by a principle of virtue. And after an injury is done, and there is a necessity that the offender should be brought to justice; the cool consideration of reason, that the security and peace of society requires examples of justice should be made, might indeed be sufficient to procure laws to be enacted, and sentence passed: but is it that cool reflection in the injured person, which, for the most part, brings the offender to justice? Or is it not resentment and indignation against the injury and the author of it? I am afraid there is no doubt, which is commonly the case. This however is to be considered as a good effect, notwithstanding it were much to be wished that men would act from a better principle, reason and cool reflection.

The account now given of the passion of resentment, as distinct from all the abuses **15** of it, may suggest to our thoughts the following reflections.

First, That vice is indeed of ill-desert, and must finally be punished. Why should **16** men dispute concerning the reality of virtue, and whether it be founded in the nature of things,* which yet surely is not matter of question; but why should this, I say, be disputed, when every man carries about him this passion, which affords him demonstration, that the rules of justice and equity are to be the guide of his actions?* For every man naturally feels an indignation upon seeing instances of villainy and baseness, and therefore cannot commit the same without being self-condemned.

Secondly, That we should learn to be cautious lest we 'charge God foolishly',[2] by **17** ascribing that to him, or the nature he has given us, which is owing wholly to our own abuse of it. Men may speak of the degeneracy and corruption of the world, according to the experience they have had of it; but human nature, considered as the divine workmanship, should methinks be treated as sacred: for 'in the image of God made he man'.[3] That passion, from whence men take occasion to run into the dreadful vices of malice and revenge; even that passion, as implanted in our nature by God, is not only innocent, but a generous movement of mind. It is in itself, and in its original, no more than indignation against injury and wickedness: that which is the only deformity in the creation, and the only reasonable object of abhorrence and dislike. How manifold evidence have we of the divine wisdom and goodness, when even pain in the natural world, and the passion, we have been now considering in the moral, come out instances of it!

Notes

1. *Ephes.* iv.26.
2. [*Job* i.22.]
3. [*Gen.* ix.6.]

Sermon 9

Upon Forgiveness of Injuries

Ye have heard that it hath been said, Thou shalt love thy neighbour, and hate
thine enemy. But I say unto you, Love your enemies, bless them that curse you,
do good to them that hate you, and pray for them which despitefully use you, and
persecute you.

(*Matt.* v.43, 44)

As God Almighty foresaw the irregularities and disorders, both natural and moral, 1
which would happen in this state of things; he hath graciously made some provision
against them, by giving us several passions and affections, which arise from, or whose
objects are those disorders. Of this sort are fear, resentment, compassion and others;
of which there could be no occasion or use in a perfect state: but in the present we
should be exposed to greater inconveniences without them; though there are very
considerable ones, which they themselves are the occasions of. They are encumbrances indeed, but such as we are obliged to carry about with us, through this
various journey of life: some of them as a guard against the violent assaults of
others, and in our own defence; some in behalf of others; and all of them to put us
upon, and help to carry us through, a course of behaviour suitable to our condition,
in default of that perfection of wisdom and virtue, which would be in all respects our
better security.

The passion of anger or resentment hath already been largely treated of. It hath 2
been shewn, that mankind naturally feel some emotion of mind against injury and
injustice, whoever are the sufferers by it; and even though the injurious design be
prevented from taking effect. Let this be called anger, indignation, resentment, or
by whatever name anyone shall choose;* the thing itself is understood, and is
plainly natural. It has likewise been observed, that this natural indignation is generally moderate and low enough in mankind,* in each particular man, when the injury
which excites it doth not affect himself, or one whom he considers as himself.
Therefore the precepts to *forgive*, and to *love our enemies*, do not relate to that
general indignation against injury and the authors of it, but to this feeling, or
resentment when raised by private or personal injury. But no man could be thought
in earnest, who should assert, that, though indignation against injury, when others
are the sufferers, is innocent and just; yet the same indignation against it, when we

ourselves are the sufferers, becomes faulty and blameable. These precepts therefore cannot be understood to forbid this in the latter case, more than in the former. Nay they cannot be understood to forbid this feeling in the latter case, though raised to a higher degree, than in the former: because, as was also observed further, from the very constitution of our nature, we cannot but have a greater sensibility to what concerns ourselves. Therefore the precepts in the text, and others of the like import with them, must be understood to forbid only the excess and abuse of this natural feeling, in cases of personal and private injury:* the chief instances of which excess and abuse have likewise been already remarked; and all of them, excepting that of retaliation, do so plainly in the very terms express somewhat unreasonable, dispro-portionate, and absurd, as to admit of no pretence or shadow of justification.

3   But since custom and false honour are on the side of retaliation and revenge, when the resentment is natural and just; and reasons are sometimes offered in justification of revenge in these cases; and since love of our enemies is thought *too hard a saying* to be obeyed: I will shew *the absolute unlawfulness of the former; the obligations we are under to the latter*; and then proceed to *some reflections, which may have a more direct and immediate tendency to beget in us a right temper of mind towards those who have offended us.*

4   In shewing the unlawfulness of revenge, it is not my present design to examine what is alleged in favour of it, from the tyranny of custom and false honour, but only to consider the nature and reason of the thing itself; which ought to have prevented, and ought now to extirpate, every thing of that kind.

5   *First*, Let us begin with the supposition of that being innocent, which is pleaded for, and which shall be shewn to be altogether vicious, the supposition that we were allowed to 'render evil for evil',[1] and see what would be the consequence. Malice or resentment towards any man hath plainly a tendency to beget the same passion in him who is the object of it; and this again increases it in the other. It is of the very nature of this vice to propagate itself, not only by way of example, which it does in common with other vices, but in a peculiar way of its own; for resentment itself, as well as what is done in consequence of it, is the object of resentment: hence it comes to pass that the first offence, even when so slight as presently to be dropped and forgotten, becomes the occasion of entering into a long intercourse of ill offices: neither is at all uncommon to see persons, in this progress of strife and variance, change parts; and him, who was at first the injured person, become more injurious and blameable than the aggressor.* Put the case then, that the law of retaliation was universally received, and allowed, as an innocent rule of life, by all; and the obser-vance of it thought by many (and then it would soon come to be thought by all) a point of honour: this supposes every man in private cases to pass sentence in his own cause; and likewise, that anger or resentment is to be the judge. Thus, from the numberless partialities which we all have for ourselves, every one would often think himself injured when he was not: and in most cases would represent an injury as much greater than it really is; the imagined dignity of the person offended would

scarce ever fail to magnify the offence. And, if bare retaliation, or returning just the mischief received, always begets resentment in the person upon whom we retaliate, what would that excess do? Add to this, that he likewise has his partialities—there is no going on to represent this scene of rage and madness: it is manifest there would be no bounds, nor any end. If the 'beginning of strife is as when one letteth out water',[2] what would it come to when allowed this free and unrestrained course?* 'As coals are to burning coals, or wood to fire'; *so* would these 'contentious men be to kindle strife'.[3] And, since the indulgence of revenge hath manifestly this tendency, and does actually produce these effects in proportion as it is allowed; a passion of so dangerous a nature ought not to be indulged, were there no other reason against it.

Secondly, It hath been shewn* that the passion of resentment was placed in man, **6** upon supposition of, and as a prevention or remedy to irregularity and disorder. Now, whether it be allowed or not, that the passion itself and the gratification of it joined together are painful to the malicious person; it must however be so with respect to the person towards whom it is exercised, and upon whom the revenge is taken. Now, if we consider mankind, according to that fine allusion of St. Paul, as 'one body, and every one members one of another';[4] it must be allowed that resentment is, with respect to society, a painful remedy. Thus then the very notion or idea of this passion, as a remedy or prevention of evil, and as in itself a painful means, plainly shews that it ought never to be made use of, but only in order to produce some greater good.*

It is to be observed, that this argument is not founded upon an illusion or simile; **7** but that it is drawn from the very nature of the passion itself, and the end for which it was given us. We are obliged to make use of words taken from sensible things, to explain what is the most remote from them: and everyone sees from whence the words prevention and remedy are taken. But if you please, let these words be dropped: the thing itself, I suppose, may be expressed without them.

That mankind is a community, that we all stand in a relation to each other, that **8** there is a public end and interest of society which each particular is obliged to promote, is the sum of morals.* Consider then the passion of resentment, as given to this one body, as given to society. Nothing can be more manifest, than that resentment is to be considered as a secondary passion, placed in us upon supposition, upon account of, and with regard to, injury; not, to be sure, to promote and further it, but to render it, and the inconveniences and miseries arising from it, less and fewer than they would be without this passion. It is as manifest, that the indulgence of it is, with regard to society, a painful means of obtaining these ends. Considered in itself, it is very undesirable, and what society must very much wish to be without. It is in every instance absolutely an evil in itself; because it implies producing misery: and consequently must never be indulged or gratified for itself, by any one who considers mankind as a community or family, and himself as a member of it.*

Let us now take this in another view. Every natural appetite, passion and affection, **9** may be gratified in particular instances, without being subservient to the particular chief end, for which these several principles were respectively implanted in our nature. And, if neither this end, nor any other moral obligation be contradicted, such gratification is innocent. Thus, I suppose, there are cases in which each of these principles, this one of resentment excepted, may innocently be gratified, without being subservient to what is the main end of it: that is, though it does not conduce to, yet it may be gratified without contradicting that end, or any other obligation. But the gratification of resentment, if it be not conducive to the end for which it was given us, must necessarily contradict, not only the general obligation to benevolence, but likewise that particular end itself. The end, for which it was given, is to prevent or remedy injury; *i.e.* the misery occasioned by injury; *i.e.* misery itself: and the gratification of it consists in producing misery; *i.e.* in contradicting the end, for which it was implanted in our nature.

10   This whole reasoning is built upon the difference there is between this passion and all others. No other principle, or passion, hath for its end the misery of our fellow-creatures. But malice and revenge meditates evil itself; and to do mischief, to be the author of misery, is the very thing which gratifies the passion: this is what it directly tends towards, as its proper design. Other vices eventually do mischief: this alone aims at it as an end.

11   Nothing can with reason be urged in justification of revenge, from the good effects which the indulgence of it were before mentioned[5]* to have upon the affairs of the world; because, though it be a remarkable instance of the wisdom of Providence to bring good out of evil, yet vice is vice to him who is guilty of it. "But suppose these good effects are foreseen": that is, suppose reason in a particular case leads a man the same way as passion? Why then, to be sure, he should follow his reason, in this as well as in all other cases. So that, turn the matter which way ever you will, no more can be allowed to this passion, than hath been already.[6]

12   As to that love of our enemies, which is commanded; this supposes the general obligation to benevolence or good-will towards mankind: and this being supposed, that precept is no more than to forgive injuries; that is, to keep clear of those abuses before-mentioned: because that we have the habitual temper of benevolence, is taken for granted.

13   Resentment is not inconsistent with good-will:* for we often see both together in very high degree; not only in parents towards their children, but in cases of friendship and dependence, where there is no natural relation. These contrary passions, though they may lessen, do not necessarily destroy each other. We may therefore love our enemy, and yet have resentment against him for his injurious behaviour towards us. But when this resentment entirely destroys our natural benevolence towards him, it is excessive, and becomes malice or revenge. The command to prevent its having this effect, *i.e.* to forgive injuries, is the same as to love our enemies; because that love is always supposed, unless destroyed by resentment.

14   "But though mankind is the natural object of benevolence, yet may it not be lessened upon vice, *i.e.* injury?" Allowed: but if every degree of vice or injury must

destroy that benevolence, then no man is the object of our love; for no man is without faults.

"But if lower instances of injury may lessen our benevolence, why may not higher, or the highest, destroy it?" The answer is obvious. It is not man's being a social creature, much less his being a moral agent, from whence *alone* our obligations to good-will towards him arise. There is an obligation to it prior to either of these, arising from his being a sensible creature; that is, capable of happiness or misery.* Now this obligation cannot be superseded by his moral character. What justifies public executions is, not that the guilt or demerit of the criminal dispenses with the obligation of good-will, neither would this justify any severity; but, that his life is inconsistent with the quiet and happiness of the world: that is, a general and more enlarged obligation necessarily destroys a particular and more confined one of the same kind, inconsistent with it.* Guilt or injury then does not dispense with or supersede the duty of love and good-will.   15

Neither does that peculiar regard to ourselves, which was before allowed to be natural to mankind,[7] dispense with it: because that can no way innocently heighten our resentment against those who have been injurious to ourselves in particular, any otherwise than as it heightens our sense of the injury or guilt; and guilt, though in the highest degree, does not, as hath been shewn, dispense with or supersede the duty of love and good-will.   16

If all this be true, what can a man say, who will dispute the reasonableness, or the possibility, of obeying the divine precept we are now considering? Let him speak out, and it must be thus he will speak. "Mankind, *i.e.* a creature defective and faulty, is the proper object of good-will, whatever his faults are, when they respect others; but not when they respect me myself." That men should be *affected* in this manner, and *act* accordingly, is to be accounted for like other vices; but to *assert* that it *ought*, and *must* be thus, is self-partiality possessed of the very understanding.*   17

Thus love to our enemies, and those who have been injurious to us, is so far from being a *rant*, as it has been profanely called, that it is in truth the law of our nature, and what everyone must see and own, who is not quite blinded with self-love.   18

From hence it is easy to see, what is the degree in which we are commanded to love our enemies, or those who have been injurious to us. It were well if it could as easily be reduced to practice. It cannot be imagined, that we are required to love them with any peculiar kind of affection. But suppose the person injured to have a due, natural sense of the injury, and no more; he ought to be affected towards the injurious person in the same way any good men, uninterested in the case, would be; if they had the same just sense, which we have supposed the injured person to have, of the fault: after which there will yet remain real good-will towards the offender.*   19

Now what is there in all this, which should be thought impracticable? I am sure there is nothing in it unreasonable. It is indeed no more than that we should not indulge a passion, which, if generally indulged, would propagate itself so as almost to lay waste the world: that we should suppress that partial, that false self-love, which is   20 the weakness of our nature: that uneasiness and misery should not be produced, without any good purpose to be served by it: and that we should not be affected towards persons differently from what their nature and character require.

21   But since to be convinced that any temper of mind, and course of behaviour, is our duty, and the contrary vicious, hath but a distant influence upon our temper and actions; let me add some few reflections, which may have a more direct tendency to subdue those vices in the heart, to beget in us this right temper, and lead us to a right behaviour towards those who have offended us: which reflections however shall be such as will further shew the obligations we are under to it.

22   No one, I suppose, would choose to have an indignity put upon him, or to be injuriously treated. If then there be any probability of a misunderstanding in the case, either from our imagining we are injured when we are not, or representing the injury to ourselves as greater than it really is; one would hope an intimation of this sort might be kindly received, and that people would be glad to find the injury not so great as they imagined. Therefore, without knowing particulars, I take upon me to assure all persons who think they have received indignities or injurious treatment, that they may depend upon it, as in a manner certain, that the offence is not so great as they themselves imagine. We are in such a peculiar situation, with respect to injuries done to ourselves, that we can scarce any more see them as they really are, than our eye can see itself. If we could place ourselves at a due distance, i.e. be really unprejudiced, we should frequently discern that to be in reality inadvertence and mistake in our enemy, which we now fancy we see to be malice or scorn. From this proper point of view, we should likewise in all probability see something of these latter in ourselves, and most certainly a great deal of the former. Thus the indignity or injury would almost infinitely lessen, and perhaps at last come out to be nothing at all. Self-love is a medium of a peculiar kind: in these cases it magnifies every thing which is amiss in others, at the same time that it lessens every thing amiss in ourselves.

23   Anger also or hatred may be considered as another false medium of viewing things, which always represents characters and actions much worse than they really are. Ill-will not only never speaks, but never thinks well, of the person towards whom it is exercised. Thus in cases of offence and enmity, the whole character and behaviour is considered with an eye to that particular part which has offended us, and the whole man appears monstrous, without any thing right or human in him: whereas the resentment should surely at least be confined to that particular part of the behaviour which gave offence; since the other parts of a man's life and character stand just the same as they did before.

24   In general, there are very few instances of enmity carried to any length but inadvertency, misunderstanding, some real mistake of the case, on one side however, if not on both, has a great share in it.

25   If these things were attended to, these ill-humours could not be carried to any length amongst good men, and they would be exceedingly abated amongst all. And one would hope they might be attended to: for all that these cautions come to, is

really no more than desiring, that things may be considered and judged of as they are in themselves, that we should have an eye to, and beware of, what would otherwise lead us into mistakes. So that to make allowances for inadvertence, misunderstanding, for the partialities of self-love, and the false light which anger sets things in; I say, to make allowances for these, is not to be spoken of as an instance of humbleness of mind, or meekness and moderation of temper; but as what common sense should suggest, to avoid judging wrong of a matter before us, though virtue and morals were out of the case. And therefore it as much belongs to ill men, who will indulge the vice I have been arguing against; as to good men, who endeavour to subdue it in themselves. In a word, all these cautions, concerning anger and self-love, are no more than desiring a man, who was looking through a glass which either magnified or lessened, to take notice, that the objects are not in themselves what they appear through that medium.

To all these things one might add, that, resentment being out of the case, there is   26 not properly speaking any such thing as direct ill-will in one man towards another:* therefore the first indignity or injury, if it be not owing to inadvertence or misunderstanding, may however be resolved into other particular passions or self-love: principles quite distinct from ill-will, and which we ought all to be disposed to excuse in others, from experiencing so much of them in ourselves. A great man of antiquity is reported to have said, that, as he never was indulgent to any one fault in himself, he could not excuse those of others.* This sentence could scarce with decency come out of the mouth of any human creature. But if we invert the former part, and put it thus: that he was indulgent to many faults in himself, as it is to be feared the best of us are, and yet was implacable; how monstrous would such an assertion appear? And this is the case in respect to every human creature, in proportion as he is without the forgiving spirit I have been recommending.

Further, though injury, injustice, oppression, the baseness of ingratitude, are the   27 natural objects of indignation, or if you please of resentment, as before explained; yet they are likewise the objects of compassion,* as they are their own punishment, and without repentance will for ever be so. No one ever did a designed injury to another, but at the same time he did a much greater to himself.* If therefore we would consider things justly, such an one is, according to the natural course of affections, an object of compassion, as well as of displeasure: and to be affected really in this manner, I say really, in opposition to shew and pretence, argues the true greatness of mind. We have an example of forgiveness in this way in its utmost perfection, and which indeed includes in it all that is good, in that prayer of our blessed Saviour on the cross: 'Father, forgive them; for they know not what they do.'⁸

But *Lastly*, The offences which we are all guilty of against God, and the injuries   28 which men do to each other, are often mentioned together: and, making allowances for the infinite distance between the majesty of heaven, and a frail mortal, and likewise for this, that he cannot possibly be affected or moved as we are; offences committed by others against ourselves, and the manner in which we are apt to be affected with them, give a real occasion for calling to mind our own sins against God. Now there is an apprehension and presentiment, natural to mankind, that we ourselves shall one time or other be dealt with, as we deal with others; and a peculiar acquiescence in, and feeling of the equity and justice of this equal distribution. This natural notion of equity the Son of Sirach has put in the strongest way. 'He that revengeth shall find vengeance from the Lord, and he will surely keep his sins in remembrance. Forgive thy neighbour the hurt he hath done unto thee, so shall thy sins also be forgiven when thou prayest. One man beareth hatred against another, and doth he seek pardon from the Lord? He sheweth no mercy to a man which is like himself; and doth he ask forgiveness of his own sins?'[9] Let anyone read our Saviour's parable of the king who took account of his servants;[10] and the equity and rightness of the sentence, which was passed upon him who was unmerciful to his fellow-servant, will be felt. There is somewhat in human nature, which accords to, and falls in with that method of determination. Let us then place before our eyes the time which is represented in the parable; that of our own death, or the final judgement. Suppose yourselves under the apprehensions of approaching death; that you were just going to appear naked and without disguise before the Judge of all the earth, to give an account of your behaviour towards your fellow-creatures: could any thing raise more dreadful apprehensions of that judgement, than the reflection that you had been implacable, and without mercy towards those who had offended you: without that forgiving spirit towards others, which that it may now be exercised towards yourselves, is your only hope? And these natural apprehensions are authorized by our Saviour's application of the parable: 'So likewise shall my heavenly Father do also unto you, if ye from your hearts forgive not every one his brother their trespasses.'[11] On the other hand, suppose a good man in the same circumstance, in the last part and close of life; conscious of many frailties, as the best are, but conscious too that he had been meek, forgiving and merciful; that he had in simplicity of heart been ready to pass over offences against himself: the having felt this good spirit will give him, not only a full view of the amiableness of it, but the surest hope that he shall meet with it in his Judge. This likewise is confirmed by his own declaration: 'If ye forgive men their trespasses, your heavenly Father will likewise forgive you.'[12] And that we might have a constant sense of it upon our mind, the condition is expressed in our daily prayer. A forgiving spirit is therefore absolutely necessary, as ever we hope for pardon of our own sins; as ever we hope for peace of mind in our dying moments, or for the divine mercy at that day when we shall most stand in need of it.

Notes

1. [*I Thess.* v.15; *I Peter* iii.9.]
2. [*Prov.* xvii.14.]
3. [*Prov.* xxvi.21.]
4. [*Rom.* xii.5.]

5. S 8.14.
6. S 8.13.
7. S 8.7.
8. [*Luke* xxxiii.34.]
9. *Ecclus* xxviii.1–4.
10. *Matt.* xviii.[21–35.]
11. [*Matt.* xviii.35.]
12. [*Matt.* vi.15.]

Sermon 10

Upon Self-Deceit

And Nathan said to David, Thou art the man.

(2 Samuel xii.7)

1   These words are the application of Nathan's parable to David, upon occasion of his adultery with Bathsheba, and the murder of Uriah her husband. The parable, which is related in the most beautiful simplicity, is this.[1] 'There were two men in one city; the one rich, and the other poor. The rich man had exceeding many flocks and herds: but the poor man had nothing save one little ewe-lamb, which he had bought and nourished up: and it grew up together with him, and with his children; it did eat of his own meat, and drank of his own cup, and lay in his bosom, and was unto him as a daughter. And there came a traveller unto the rich man, and he spared to take of his own flock, and of his own herd, to dress for the wayfaring man that was come unto him, but took the poor man's lamb, and dressed it for the man that was come to him. And David's anger was greatly kindled against the man, and he said to Nathan, As the Lord liveth, the man that hath done this thing shall surely die. And he shall restore the lamb four-fold, because he did this thing, and because he had no pity.' David passes sentence, not only that there should be a four-fold restitution made; but he proceeds to the rigor of justice, 'the man that hath done this thing shall die': and this judgement is pronounced with the utmost indignation against such an act of inhumanity; 'As the Lord liveth, he shall surely die: and his anger was greatly kindled against the man.' And the prophet answered, 'Thou art the man.' He had been guilty of much greater inhumanity, with the utmost deliberation, thought and contrivance. Near a year must have passed, between the time of the commission of his crimes, and the time of the prophet's coming to him; and it does not appear from the story, that he had in all this while the least remorse or contrition.

2   There is not any thing, relating to men and characters, more surprising and unaccountable, than this partiality to themselves, which is observable in many; as there is nothing of more melancholy reflection, respecting morality, virtue and religion. Hence it is that many men seem perfect strangers to their own characters. They think, and reason, and judge quite differently upon any matter relating to themselves, from what they do in cases of others where they are not interested. Hence

it is one hears people exposing follies, which they themselves are eminent for; and talking with great severity against particular vices, which, if all the world be not mistaken, they themselves are notoriously guilty of. This self-ignorance and self-partiality may be in all different degrees. It is a lower degree of it, which David himself refers to in these words, 'Who can tell how oft he offendeth? O cleanse thou me from my secret faults.'² This is the ground of that advice of Elihu to Job: 'Surely it is meet to be said unto God, — That which I see not, teach thou me; if I have done iniquity, I will do no more.'³ And Solomon saw this thing in a very strong light, when he said, 'He that trusteth his own heart is a fool.'⁴ This likewise was the reason why that precept, *Know thyself*, was so frequently inculcated by the philosophers of old.* For if it were not for that partial and fond regard to ourselves, it would certainly be no great difficulty to know our own character, what passes within, the bent and bias of our mind; much less would there be any difficulty in judging rightly of our own actions. But from this partiality it frequently comes to pass, that the observation, of many men's being themselves last of all acquainted with what falls out in their own families, may be applied to a nearer home, to what passes within their own breasts.

There is plainly, in the generality of mankind, an absence of doubt or distrust, in a very great measure, as to their moral character and behaviour; and likewise a disposition to take for granted, that all is right and well with them in these respects. The former is owing to their not reflecting, not exercising their judgement upon themselves; the latter, to self-love. I am not speaking of that extravagance, which is sometimes to be met with; instances of persons declaring in words at length, that they never were in the wrong, nor had ever any diffidence of the justness of their conduct, in their whole lives. No, these people are too far gone to have any thing said to them. The thing before us is indeed of this kind, but in a lower degree, and confined to the moral character; somewhat of which we almost all of us have, without reflecting upon it. Now consider how long, and how grossly, a person of the best understanding might be imposed upon by one of whom he had not any suspicion, and in whom he placed an entire confidence; especially if there were friendship and real kindness in the case: surely this holds even stronger with respect to that self we are all so fond of. Hence arises in men a disregard of reproof and instruction, rules of conduct and moral discipline, which occasionally come in their way: a disregard, I say, of these; not in every respect, but in this single one, namely, as what may be of service to them in particular towards mending their own hearts and tempers, and making them better men. It never in earnest comes into their thoughts, whether such admonitions may not relate, and be of service to themselves; and this quite distinct from a positive persuasion to the contrary, a persuasion from reflection that they are innocent and blameless in those respects. Thus we may invert the observation which is somewhere made upon Brutus, that he never read but in order to make himself a better man.* It scarce comes into the thoughts of the generality of mankind, that this use is to be made of moral reflections which they meet with; that this use, I say, is to be made of them by themselves, for every body observes and wonders that it is not done by others.

4   Further, there are instances of persons having so fixed and steady an eye upon their own interest, whatever they place it in, and the interest of those whom they consider as themselves, as in a manner to regard nothing else; their views are almost confined to this alone. Now we cannot be acquainted with, or in any propriety of speech be said to know any thing, but what we attend to. If therefore they attend only to one side, they really will not, cannot see or know what is to be alleged on the other. Though a man hath the best eyes in the world, he cannot see any way but that which he turns them. Thus these persons, without passing over the least, the most minute thing which can possibly be urged in favour of themselves, shall overlook entirely the plainest and most obvious things on the other side. And whilst they are under the power of this temper, thought and consideration upon the matter before them has scarce any tendency to set them right: because they are engaged; and their deliberation concerning an action to be done, or reflection upon it afterwards, is not to see whether it be right, but to find out reasons to justify or palliate it; palliate it, not to others, but to themselves.

5   In some there is to be observed a general ignorance of themselves, and wrong way of thinking and judging in every thing relating to themselves; their fortune, reputation, every thing in which self can come in: and this perhaps attended with the rightest judgement in all other matters. In others this partiality is not so general, has not taken hold of the whole man, but is confined to some particular favourite passion, interest or pursuit; suppose ambition, covetousness, or any other. And these persons may probably judge and determine what is perfectly just and proper, even in things in which they themselves are concerned, if these things have no relation to their particular favourite passion or pursuit. Hence arises that amazing incongruity, and seeming inconsistency of character, from whence slight observers take it for granted, that the whole is hypocritical and false; not being able otherwise to reconcile the several parts: whereas in truth there is real honesty, so far as it goes. There is such a thing as men's being honest to such a degree, and in such respects, but no further. And this, as it is true, so it is absolutely necessary to be taken notice of, and allowed them; such general and undistinguishing censure of their whole character, as designing and false, being one main thing which confirms them in their self-deceit. They know that the whole censure is not true; and so take for granted that no part of it is.

6   But to go on with the explanation of the thing itself: vice in general consists in having an unreasonable and too great regard to ourselves, in comparison of others. Robbery and murder is never from the love of injustice or cruelty, but to gratify some other passion, to gain some supposed advantage: and it is false selfishness alone, whether cool or passionate, which makes a man resolutely pursue that end, be it ever so much to the injury of another. But whereas, in common and ordinary wickedness, this unreasonableness, this partiality and selfishness relates only, or chiefly, to the temper and passions; in the characters we are now considering, it reaches to

the understanding, and influences the very judgement.[5] And, besides that general want of distrust and diffidence concerning our own character, there are, you see, two things which may thus prejudice and darken the understanding itself: that over-fondness for ourselves, which we are all so liable to; and also being under the power of any particular passion or appetite, or engaged in any particular pursuit. And these, especially the last of the two, may be in so great a degree, as to influence our judgement, even of other persons and their behaviour. Thus a man, whose temper is formed to ambition or covetousness, shall even approve of them sometimes in others.*

This seems to be in a good measure the account of self-partiality and self-deceit,   7 when traced up to its original. Whether it be, or be not thought satisfactory, that there is such a thing is manifest; and that it is the occasion of great part of the unreasonable behaviour of men towards each other: that by means of it they palliate their vices and follies to themselves: and that it prevents their applying to themselves those reproofs and instructions, which they meet with either in Scripture or in moral and religious discourses, though exactly suitable to the state of their own mind, and the course of their behaviour. There is one thing further to be added here, that the temper we distinguish by hardness of heart with respect to others, joined with this self-partiality, will carry a man almost any lengths of wickedness, in the way of oppression, hard usage of others, and even to plain injustice; without his having, from what appears, any real sense at all of it. This indeed was not the general character of David: for he plainly gave scope to the affections of compassion and good-will, as well as to his passions of another kind.

But as some occasions and circumstances lie more open to this self-deceit, and give   8 it greater scope and opportunities than others, these require to be particularly mentioned.

It is to be observed then, that as there are express determinate acts of wickedness,   9 such as murder, adultery, theft: so on the other hand, there are numberless cases in which the vice and wickedness cannot be exactly defined; but consists in a certain general temper and course of action, or in the neglect of some duty, suppose charity or any other, whose bounds and degrees are not fixed. This is the very province of self-deceit and self-partiality: here it governs without check or control. "For what commandment is there broken? Is there a transgression where there is no law? a vice which cannot be defined?"

Whoever will consider the whole commerce of human life, will see that a great   10 part, perhaps the greatest part, of the intercourse amongst mankind, cannot be reduced to fixed determinate rules.* Yet in these cases there is a right and a wrong: a merciful, a liberal, a kind and compassionate behaviour, which surely is our duty; and an unmerciful contracted spirit, an hard and oppressive course of behaviour, which is most certainly immoral and vicious. But who can define precisely, wherein that contracted spirit and hard usage of others consist, as murder and theft may be defined? There is not a word in our language, which expresses more detestable wickedness than *oppression*: yet the nature of this vice cannot be so exactly stated, nor the bounds of it so determinately marked, as that we shall be able to say in all instances, where rigid right and justice ends, and oppression begins. In these cases there is great latitude left, for everyone to determine for, and consequently to deceive himself. It is chiefly in these cases that self-deceit comes in; as everyone must see that there is much larger scope for it here, than in express, single, determinate acts of wickedness. However it comes in with respect to the *circumstances* attending the most gross and determinate acts of wickedness. Of this, the story of David, now before us, affords the most astonishing instance. It is really prodigious, to see a man, before so remarkable for virtue and piety, going on deliberately from adultery to murder, with the same cool contrivance, and, from what appears, with as little disturbance, as a man would endeavour to prevent the ill consequences of a mistake he had made in any common matter. That total insensibility of mind with respect to those horrid crimes, after the commission of them, manifestly shews that he did some way or other delude himself: and this could not be with respect to the crimes themselves, they were so manifestly of the grossest kind. What the particular circumstances were, with which he extenuated them, and quieted and deceived himself, is not related.

11   Having thus explained the nature of internal hypocrisy and self-deceit,* and remarked the occasions upon which it exerts itself; there are several things further to be observed concerning it: that all of the sources, to which it was traced up, are sometimes observable together in one and the same person: but that one of them is more remarkable, and to a higher degree, in some, and others of them are so in others: that in general it is a complicated thing; and may be in all different degrees and kinds: that the temper itself is essentially in its own nature vicious and immoral. It is unfairness; it is dishonesty; it is falseness of heart: and is therefore so far from extenuating guilt, that it is itself the greatest of all guilt in proportion to the degree it prevails; for it is a corruption of the whole moral character in its principle. Our understanding, and sense of good and evil, is the light and guide of life: 'If therefore' this 'light that is in thee be darkness, how great is that darkness?'[6] For this reason our Saviour puts an 'evil eye' as the direct opposite to a 'single eye'; the absence of that simplicity, which these last words imply, being itself evil and vicious.* And whilst men are under the power of this temper, in proportion still to the degree they are so, they are fortified on every side against conviction: and when they hear the vice and folly of what is in truth their own course of life, exposed in the justest and strongest manner, they will often assent to it, and even carry the matter further; persuading themselves, one does not know how, but some way or other persuading themselves, that they are out of the case, and that it hath no relation to them. Yet, notwithstanding this, there *frequently appears* a suspicion, that all is not right, or as it should be; and perhaps there *is always* at bottom somewhat of this sort. There are doubtless many instances of the ambitious, the revengeful, the covetous, and those whom with too great indulgence we only call the men of pleasure, who will not allow themselves to think how guilty they are, who explain and argue away their guilt to themselves:

and though they do really impose upon themselves, in some measure, yet there are none of them but have, if not a proper knowledge, yet at least an implicit suspicion, where the weakness lies, and what part of their behaviour they have reason to wish unknown or forgotten for ever. Truth, and real good sense, and thorough integrity, carry along with them a peculiar consciousness of their own genuineness: there is a feeling belonging to them, which does not accompany their counterfeits, error, folly, half-honesty, partial and slight regards to virtue and right, so far only as they are consistent with that course of gratification which men happen to be set upon. And, if this be the case, it is much the same as if we should suppose a man to have had a general view of some scene, enough to satisfy him that it was very disagreeable, and then to shut his eyes, that he might not have particular or distinct view of its several deformities. It is as easy to close the eyes of the mind, as those of the body: and the former is more frequently done with wilfulness, and yet not attended to, than the latter; the actions of the mind being more quick and transient, than those of the senses. This may be further illustrated by another thing observable in ordinary life. It is not uncommon for persons, who run out their fortunes, entirely to neglect looking into the state of their affairs, and this from a general knowledge, that the condition of them is bad.* These extravagant people are perpetually ruined before they themselves expect it: and they tell you for an excuse, and tell you truly, that they did not think they were so much in debt, or that their expenses so far exceeded their income. And yet no one will take this for an excuse, who is sensible that their ignorance of their particular circumstances was owing to their general knowledge of them; that is, their general knowledge, that matters were not well with them, prevented their looking into particulars. There is somewhat of the like kind with this in respect to morals, virtue, and religion. Men find that the survey of themselves, their own heart and temper, their own life and behaviour, doth not afford them satisfaction: things are not as they should be: therefore they turn away, will not go over particulars, or look deeper, lest they should find more amiss. For who would choose to be put out of humour with himself? No one, surely, if it were not in order to amend, and to be more thoroughly and better pleased with himself for the future.

If this sincere self-enjoyment and home-satisfaction be thought desirable, and 12 worth some pains and diligence; the following reflections will, I suppose, deserve your attention; as what may be of service and assistance to all who are in any measure honestly disposed, for avoiding that fatal self-deceit, and towards getting acquainted with themselves.

The *first* is, that those who have never had any suspicion of, who have never made 13 allowances for this weakness in themselves, who have never (if I may be allowed such a manner of speaking) caught themselves in it, may almost take for granted that they have been very much misled by it. For consider: nothing is more manifest, than that affection and passion of all kinds influence the judgement. Now as we have naturally a greater regard to ourselves than to others,* as the private affection is more prevalent than the public; the former will have proportionally a greater influence upon the judgement, upon our way of considering things. People are not backward in owning this partiality of judgement, in cases of friendship and natural relation. The reason is obvious, why it is not so readily acknowledged, when the interest which misleads us is more confined, confined to ourselves: but we all take notice of it in each other in these cases. There is not any observation more common, than that there is no judging of a matter from hearing only one side. This is not founded upon supposition, at least it is not always, of a formed design in the relater to deceive: for it holds in cases, where he expects that the whole will be told over again by the other side. But the supposition, which this observation is founded upon, is the very thing now before us; namely, that men are exceedingly prone to deceive themselves, and judge too favourably in every respect, where themselves, and their own interest are concerned. Thus, though we have not the least reason to suspect that such an interested person hath any intention to deceive us, yet we of course make great allowances for his having deceived himself. If this be general, almost universal, it is prodigious that every man can think himself an exception, and that he is free from this self-partiality. The direct contrary is the truth. Every man may take for granted that he has a great deal of it, till, from the strictest observation upon himself, he finds particular reason to think otherwise.

14   *Secondly,* There is one easy and almost sure way to avoid being misled by this self-partiality, and to get acquainted with our real character: to have regard to the suspicious part of it, and keep a steady eye over ourselves in that respect. Suppose then a man fully satisfied with himself, and his own behaviour; such an one, if you please, as the Pharisee in the Gospel,* or a better man.—Well, but allowing this good opinion you have of yourself to be true, yet everyone is liable to be misrepresented. Suppose then an enemy were to set about defaming you, what part of your character would he single out? What particular scandal, think you, would he be most likely to fix upon you? And what would the world be most ready to believe? There is scarce a man living, but could, from the most transient superficial view of himself, answer this question. What is that ill thing, that faulty behaviour, which I am apprehensive an enemy, who was thoroughly acquainted with me, would be most likely to lay to my charge, and which the world would be most apt to believe? It is indeed possible that a man may not be guilty in that respect. All that I say is, let him in plainness and honesty fix upon that part of his character for a particular survey and reflection; and by this he will come to be acquainted, whether he be guilty or innocent in that respect, and how far he is one or the other.

15   *Thirdly,* It would very much prevent our being misled by this self-partiality, to reduce that practical rule of our Saviour, 'Whatsoever ye would that men should do to you, even so do unto them',⁷ to our judgement, and way of thinking. This rule, you see, consists of two parts. One is, to substitute another for yourself, when you take a survey of any part of your behaviour, or consider what is proper and fit and reasonable for you to do upon any occasion: the other part is, that you substitute yourself in the room of another; consider yourself as the person affected by such a behaviour, or towards whom such an action is done: and then you would not only

see, but likewise feel, the reasonableness or unreasonableness of such an action or behaviour. But alas, the rule itself may be dishonestly applied: there are persons who have not impartiality enough with respect to themselves, nor regard enough for others, to be able to make a just application of it. This just application, if men would honestly make it, is in effect all that I have been recommending; it is the whole thing, the direct contrary to that inward dishonesty as respecting our intercourse with our fellow-creatures. And even the bearing this rule in their thoughts, may be of some service; the attempt thus to apply it, is an attempt towards being fair and impartial, and may chance unawares to shew them to themselves, to shew them the truth of the case they are considering.

Upon the whole it is manifest, that there is such a thing as this self-partiality and   16
self-deceit: that in some persons it is to a degree which would be thought incredible, were not the instances before our eyes; of which the behaviour of David is perhaps the highest possible one, in a single particular case; for there is not the least appearance, that it reached his general character: that we are almost all of us influenced by it in some degree, and in some respects: that therefore everyone ought to have an eye to and beware of it. And all that I have further to add upon this subject is, that either there is a difference between right and wrong, or there is not: religion is true, or it is not. If it be not, there is no reason for any concern about it: but if it be true, it requires real fairness of mind and honesty of heart. And, if people will be wicked, they had better of the two be so from the common vicious passions without such refinements, than from this deep and calm source of delusion; which undermines the whole principle of good; darkens that light, that 'candle of the Lord within',[8] which is to direct our steps; and corrupts conscience, which is the guide of life.

Notes

1. *2 Sam.* xii.1–6.
2. [*Ps.* xix.12.]
3. [*Job* xxxiv.32.]
4. [*Prov.* xxviii.26.]
5. That peculiar regard for ourselves, which frequently produces this partiality of judgement in our own favour, may have a quite contrary effect, and occasion the utmost diffidence and distrust of ourselves; were it only, as it may set us upon a more frequent and strict survey and review of our own character and behaviour. This search or recollection itself implies somewhat of diffidence; and the discoveries we make, what is brought to our view, may possibly increase it. Good-will to another may either blind our judgement, so as to make us overlook his faults; or it may put us upon exercising that judgement with greater strictness, to see whether he is so faultless and perfect as we wish him. If that peculiar regard to ourselves leads us to examine our own character with this greater severity, in order really to improve and grow better, it is the most commendable turn of mind possible, and can scarce be to excess. But if, as every thing hath its counterfeit, we are so much employed about

ourselves in order to disguise what is amiss, and to make a better appearance; or if our attention to ourselves has chiefly this effect; it is liable to run up into the greatest weakness and excess, and is like all other excesses its own disappointment: for scarce any shew themselves to advantage, who are over solicitous of doing so.

6. [*Matt.* vi.23.]
7. [*Matt.* vii.12.]
8. [*Prov.* xx.27.]

Sermon 11

Upon the Love of Our Neighbour

Preached on Advent Sunday

And if there be any other commandment, it is briefly comprehended in this
saying, namely, Thou shalt love thy neighbour as thyself.

(Romans xiii.9)

It is commonly observed, that there is a disposition in men to complain of the   1
viciousness and corruption of the age in which they live, as greater than that of
former ones; which is usually followed with this further observation, that mankind
has been in that respect much the same in all times. Now not to determine whether
this last be not contradicted by the accounts of history; thus much can scarce be
doubted, that vice and folly takes different turns, and some particular kinds of it are
more open and avowed in some ages than in others: and, I suppose, it may be spoken
of as very much the distinction of the present, to profess a contracted spirit, and
greater regards to self-interest, than appears to have been done formerly.* Upon this
account it seems worth while to inquire, whether private interest is likely to be
promoted in proportion to the degree in which self-love engrosses us, and prevails
over all other principles; *or whether the contracted affection may not possibly be so
prevalent as to disappoint itself, and even contradict its own end, private good.*

And since further, there is generally thought to be some peculiar kind of contra-   2
riety between self-love and the love of our neighbour, between the pursuit of public
good and of private good; insomuch that when you are recommending one of these,
you are supposed to be speaking against the other; and from hence arises a secret
prejudice against, and frequently open scorn of all talk of public spirit, and real good-
will to our fellow-creatures; it will be necessary to *inquire what respect benevolence
hath to self-love, and the pursuit of private interest, to the pursuit of public*: or whether
there be any thing of that peculiar inconsistence and contrariety between them, over
and above what there is between self-love and other passions and particular affections, and their respective pursuits.

These inquiries, it is hoped, may be favourably attended to: for there shall be all   3
possible concessions made to the favourite passion, which hath so much allowed to it,

and whose cause is so universally pleaded: it shall be treated with the utmost tenderness, and concern for its interests.

4   In order to this, as well as to determine the forementioned questions, it will be necessary to *consider the nature, the object and end of that self-love, as distinguished from other principles or affections in the mind, and their respective objects.*

5   Every man hath a general desire of his own happiness; and likewise a variety of particular affections, passions and appetites to particular external objects. The former proceeds from, or is self-love; and seems inseparable from all sensible creatures, who can reflect upon themselves and their own interest or happiness, so as to have that interest and object to their minds: what is to be said of the latter is, that they proceed from, or together make up that particular nature, according to which man is made. The object the former pursues is somewhat internal, our own happiness, enjoyment, satisfaction; whether we have, or have not a distinct particular perception what it is, or wherein it consists: the objects of the latter are this or that particular external thing, which the affections tend towards, and of which it hath always a particular idea or perception. The principle we call self-love never seeks any thing external for the sake of the thing, but only as a means of happiness or good: particular affections rest in the external things themselves. One belongs to man as a reasonable creature reflecting upon his own interest or happiness. The other, though quite distinct from reason, are as much a part of human nature.

6   That all particular appetites and passions are towards *external things themselves,* distinct from the *pleasure arising from them,* is manifested from hence; that there could not be this pleasure, were it not for that prior suitableness between the object and the passion: there could be no enjoyment or delight for one thing more than another, from eating food more than from swallowing a stone, if there were not an affection or appetite to one thing more than another.

7   Every particular affection, even the love of our neighbour, is as really our own affection, as self-love; and the pleasure arising from its gratification is as much my own pleasure, as the pleasure self-love would have, from knowing I myself should be happy some time hence, would be my own pleasure. And if, because every particular affection is a man's own, and the pleasure arising from its gratification his own pleasure, or pleasure to himself, such particular affection must be called self-love; according to this way of speaking, no creature whatever can possibly act but merely from self-love; and every action and every affection whatever is to be resolved up into this one principle. But then this is not the language of mankind: or if it were, we should want words to express the difference, between the principle of an action, proceeding from cool consideration that it will be to my own advantage; and an action, suppose of revenge, or of friendship, by which a man runs upon certain ruin, to do evil or good to another. It is manifest the principles of these actions are totally different, and so want different words to be distinguished by: all that they agree in is, that they both proceed from, and are done to gratify an inclination in a man's self. But the principle or inclination in one case is self-love; in the other, hatred or love of

another. There is then a distinction between the cool principle of self-love, or general desire of our own happiness, as one part of our nature, and one principle of action; and the particular affections towards particular external objects, as another part of our nature, and another principle of action. How much soever therefore is to be allowed for self-love, yet it cannot be allowed to be the whole of our inward constitution; because, you see, there are other parts or principles which come into it.

Further, private happiness or good is all which self-love can make us desire, or be concerned about: in having this consists its gratification: it is an affection to ourselves; a regard to our own interest, happiness, and private good: and in the proportion a man hath this, he is interested, or a lover of himself. Let this be kept in mind; because there is commonly, as I shall presently have occasion to observe, another sense put upon these words.* On the other hand, particular affections tend towards particular external things: these are their objects: having these is their end: in this consists their gratification: no matter whether it be, or be not, upon the whole, our interest or happiness. An action done from the former of these principles is called an interested action. An action proceeding from any of the latter has its denomination of passionate, ambitious, friendly, revengeful, or any other, from the particular appetite or affection from which it proceeds. Thus self-love as one part of human nature, and the several particular principles as the other part, are, themselves, their objects and ends, stated and shewn.   8

From hence it will be easy to see, how far, and in what ways, each of these can contribute and be subservient to the private good of the individual. Happiness does not consist in self-love. The desire of happiness is no more the thing itself, than the desire of riches is the possession or enjoyment of them. People may love themselves with the most entire and unbounded affection, and yet be extremely miserable. Neither can self-love any way help them out, but by setting them on work to get rid of the causes of their misery, to gain or make use of those objects which are by nature adapted to afford satisfaction. Happiness or satisfaction consists only in the enjoyment of those objects, which are by nature suited to our several particular appetites, passions and affections. So that if self-love wholly engrosses us, and leaves no room for any other principle, there can be absolutely no such thing at all as happiness, or enjoyment of any kind whatever; since happiness consists in the gratification of particular passions, which supposes the having of them. Self-love then does not constitute *this* or *that* to be our interest or good; but, our interest or good being constituted by nature and supposed, self-love only puts us upon obtaining and securing it. Therefore, if it be possible, that self-love may prevail and exert itself in a degree or manner which is not subservient to this end; then it will not follow, that our interest will be promoted in proportion to the degree in which that principle engrosses us, and prevails over others. Nay further, the private and contracted affection, when it is not subservient to this end private good, may, for any thing that appears, have a direct contrary tendency and effect. And if we will consider the matter, we shall see that it often really has. *Disengagement* is absolutely necessary to   9 enjoyment; and a person may have so steady and fixed an eye upon his own interest, whatever he places it in, as may hinder him from *attending* to many gratifications within his reach, which others have their minds *free* and *open* to. Over-fondness for a child is not generally thought to be for its advantage: and, if there be any guess to be made from appearances, surely that character we call selfish is not the most promising for happiness. Such a temper may plainly be, and exert itself in a degree and manner which may give unnecessary and useless solicitude and anxiety, in a degree and manner which may prevent obtaining the means and materials of enjoyment, as well as the making use of them. Immoderate self-love does very ill consult its own interest: and, how much soever a paradox it may appear, it is certainly true, that even from self-love we should endeavour to get over all inordinate regard to, and consideration of ourselves. Every one of our passions and affections hath its natural stint and bound, which may easily be exceeded; whereas our enjoyments can possibly be but in a determinate measure and degree. Therefore such excess of the affection, since it cannot procure any enjoyment, must in all cases be useless; but is generally attended with inconveniences, and often is downright pain and misery. This holds as much with regard to self-love as to all other affections. The natural degree of it, so far as it sets us on work to gain and make use of the materials of satisfaction, may be to our real advantage; but beyond or besides this, it is in several respects an inconvenience and disadvantage. Thus it appears, that private interest is so far from being likely to be promoted in proportion to the degree in which self-love engrosses us, and prevails over all other principles; that *the contracted affection may be so prevalent as to disappoint itself, and even contradict its own end, private good.**

10   "But who, except the most sordidly covetous, ever thought there was any rivalship between the love of greatness, honour, power, or between sensual appetites and self-love? No, there is a perfect harmony between them. It is by means of these particular appetites and affections that self-love is gratified in enjoyment, happiness and satisfaction. The competition and rivalship is between self-love, and the love of our neighbour: that affection which leads us out of ourselves, makes us regardless of our own interest, and substitute that of another in its stead." Whether then there be any peculiar competition and contrariety in this case, shall now be considered.

11   Self-love and interestedness was stated to consist in or be an affection to ourselves, a regard to our own private good: it is therefore distinct from benevolence, which is an affection to the good of our fellow-creatures. But that benevolence is distinct from, that is, not the same thing with self-love, is no reason for its being looked upon with any peculiar suspicion; because every principle whatever, by means of which self-love is gratified, is distinct from it; and all things which are distinct from each other are equally so. A man has an affection or aversion to another: that one of these tends to and is gratified by doing good, that the other tends to and is gratified by doing harm, does not in the least alter the respect which either one or the other of these inward feelings has to self-love. We use the word *property* so as to exclude any other person's having an interest in that of which we say a particular man has the property. And we

often use the word *selfish* so as to exclude in the same manner all regards to the good of others. But the cases are not parallel: for though that exclusion is really part of the idea of property; yet such positive exclusion, or bringing this peculiar disregard to the good of others into the idea of self-love, is in reality adding to the idea, or changing it from what it was before stated to consist in, namely, in an affection to ourselves.[1] This being the whole idea of self-love, it can no otherwise exclude good-will or love of others, than merely by not including it, no otherwise, than it excludes love of arts or reputation, or of any thing else. Neither on the other hand does benevolence, any more than love of arts or of reputation, exclude self-love. Love of our neighbour then* has just the same respect to, is no more distant from self-love, than hatred of our neighbour, or than love or hatred of any thing else. Thus the principles, from which men rush upon certain ruin for the destruction of an enemy, and for the preservation of a friend, have the same respect to the private affection, and are equally interested, or equally disinterested: and it is of no avail, whether they are said to be one or the other. Therefore to those who are shocked to hear virtue spoken of as disinterested, it may be allowed that it is indeed absurd to speak thus of it; unless hatred, several particular instances of vice, and all the common affections and aversions in mankind, are acknowledged to be disinterested too. Is there any less inconsistence, between the love of inanimate things, or of creatures merely sensitive, and self-love; than between self-love and the love of our neighbour? Is desire of and delight in the happiness of another any more a diminution of self-love, than desire of and delight in the esteem of another? They are both equally desire of and delight in somewhat external to ourselves: either both or neither are so. The object of self-love is expressed in the term, self: and every appetite of sense, and every particular affection of the heart, are equally interested or disinterested, because the objects of them all are equally self or somewhat else. Whatever ridicule therefore the mention of a disinterested principle or action may be supposed to lie open to, must, upon the matter being thus stated, relate to ambition, and every appetite and particular affection, as much as to benevolence. And indeed all the ridicule, and all the grave perplexity, of which this subject hath had its full share, is merely from words. The most intelligible way of speaking of it seems to be this: that self-love, and the actions done in consequence of it (for these will presently appear to be the same as to this question) are interested; that particular affections towards external objects, and the actions done in consequence of those affections, are not so. But everyone is at liberty to use words as he pleases. All that is here insisted upon is, that ambition, revenge, benevolence, all particular passions whatever, and the actions they produce, are equally interested or disinterested.

Thus it appears that there is no peculiar contrariety between self-love and benevolence; no greater competition between these, than between any other particular affections and self-love. This relates to the affections themselves. Let us now see whether there be any peculiar contrariety between the respective courses of life which these affections lead to; whether there be any greater competition between the pursuit 12 of private and of public good, than between any other particular pursuits and that of private good.

13   There seems no other reason to suspect that there is any such peculiar contrariety, but only that the course of action which benevolence leads to, has a more direct tendency to promote the good of others, than that course of action which love of reputation, suppose, or any other particular affection leads to. But that any affection tends to the happiness of another, does not hinder its tending to one's own happiness too. That others enjoy the benefit of the air and the light of the sun, does not hinder but that these are as much one's own private advantage now, as they would be if we had the property of them exclusive of all others. So a pursuit which tends to promote the good of another, yet may have as great tendency to promote private interest, as a pursuit which does not tend to the good of another at all, or which is mischievous to him. All particular affections whatever, resentment, benevolence, love of arts, equally lead to a course of action for their own gratification, *i.e.* the gratification of ourselves; and the gratification of each gives delight: so far then it is manifest they have all the same respect to private interest. Now take into consideration further concerning these three pursuits, that the end of the first is the harm, of the second, the good of another, of the last, somewhat indifferent; and is there any necessity, that these additional considerations should alter the respect, which we before saw these three pursuits had to private interest; or render any one of them less conducive to it, than any other?* Thus one man's affection is to honour as his end; in order to obtain which, he thinks no pains too great. Suppose another with such a singularity of mind, as to have the same affection to public good as his end, which he endeavours with the same labour to obtain. In case of success, surely the man of benevolence hath as great enjoyment as the man of ambition; they both equally having the end their affections, in the same degree, tended to: but in case of disappointment, the benevolent man has clearly the advantage; since endeavouring to do good considered as a virtuous pursuit, is gratified by its own consciousness, *i.e.* is in a degree its own reward.*

14   And as to these two, or benevolence and any other particular passions whatever, considered in a further view, as forming a general temper, which more or less disposes us for enjoyment of all the common blessings of life, distinct from their own gratification: is benevolence less the temper of tranquillity and freedom than ambition or covetousness? Does the benevolent man appear less easy with himself, from his love to his neighbour? Does he less relish his being? Is there any peculiar gloom seated on his face? Is his mind less open to entertainment, to any particular gratification? Nothing is more manifest, than that being in good-humour, which is benevolence whilst it lasts, is itself the temper of satisfaction and enjoyment.

15   Suppose then a man sitting down to consider how he might become most easy to himself, and attain the greatest pleasure he could; all that which is his real natural happiness. This can only consist in the enjoyment of those objects, which are by nature adapted to our several faculties. These particular enjoyments make up the sum total of our happiness: and they are supposed to arise from riches, honours, and the

gratification of sensual appetites: be it so: yet none profess themselves so completely happy in these enjoyments, but that there is room left in the mind for others, if they were presented to them: nay these, as much as they engage us, are not thought so high, but that human nature is capable even of greater. Now there have been persons in all ages, who have professed that they found satisfaction in the exercise of charity, in the love of their neighbour, in endeavouring to promote the happiness of all they had to do with, and in the pursuit of what is just and right and good, as the general bent of their mind, and end of their life; and that doing an action of baseness or cruelty, would be as great violence to *their* self, as much breaking in upon their nature, as any external force. Persons of this character would add, if they might be heard, that they consider themselves as acting in the view of an infinite Being, who is in a much higher sense the object of reverence and of love, than all the world besides; and therefore they could have no more enjoyment from a wicked action done under his eye, than the persons to whom they are making their apology could, if all mankind were the spectators of it; and that the satisfaction of approving themselves to his unerring judgement, to whom they thus refer all their actions, is a more continued settled satisfaction than any this world can afford; as also that they have, no less than others, a mind free and open to all the common innocent gratifications of it, such as they are. And if we go no further, does there appear any absurdity in this? Will anyone take upon him to say, that a man cannot find his account in this general course of life, as much as in the most unbounded ambition, and the excesses of pleasure? Or that such a person has not consulted so well for himself, for the satisfaction and peace of his own mind, as the ambitious or dissolute man? And though the consideration, that God himself will in the end justify their taste, and support their cause, is not formally to be insisted upon here; yet thus much comes in, that all enjoyments whatever are much more clear and unmixed from the assurance that they will end well.* Is it certain then that there is nothing in these pretensions to happiness? especially when there are not wanting persons, who have supported themselves with satisfactions of this kind in sickness, poverty, disgrace, and in the very pangs of death; whereas it is manifest all other enjoyments fail in these circumstances. This surely looks suspicious of having somewhat in it. Self-love methinks should be alarmed. May she not possibly pass over greater pleasures, than those she is so wholly taken up with?

The short of the matter is no more than this. Happiness consists in the gratification   16 of certain affections, appetites, passions, with objects which are by nature adapted to them. Self-love may indeed set us on work to gratify these: but happiness or enjoyment has no immediate connection with self-love, but arises from such gratifications alone. Love of our neighbour is one of those affections. This, considered as a *virtuous principle*, is gratified by a consciousness of *endeavouring* to promote the good of others; but considered as a natural affection, its gratification consists in the actual accomplishment of this endeavour.* Now indulgence or gratification of this affection, whether in that consciousness, or this accomplishment, has the same respect to interest, as indulgence of any other affection; they equally proceed from or do not proceed from self-love, they equally include or equally exclude this principle. Thus it appears, that *benevolence and the pursuit of public good hath at least as great respect to self-love and the pursuit of private good, as any other particular passions, and their respective pursuits.*

17   Neither is covetousness, whether as a temper or pursuit, any exception to this. For if by covetousness is meant the desire and pursuit of riches for their own sake, without any regard to, or consideration of the uses of them; this hath as little to do with self-love, as benevolence hath. But by this word is usually meant, not such madness and total distraction of mind, but immoderate affection to and pursuit of riches as possessions in order to some further end: namely, satisfaction, interest, or good. This therefore is not a particular affection, or particular pursuit, but it is the general principle of self-love, and the general pursuit of our own interest: for which reason, the word, selfish, is by everyone appropriated to this temper and pursuit. Now as it is ridiculous to assert, that self-love and the love of our neighbour are the same; so neither is it asserted, that following these different affections hath the same tendency and respect to our own interest. The comparison is not between self-love and the love of our neighbour; between pursuit of our own interest, and the interest of others: but between the several particular affections in human nature towards external objects, as one part of the comparison; and the one particular affection to the good of our neighbour, as the other part of it: and it has been shewn, that all these have the same respect to self-love and private interest.

18   There is indeed frequently an inconsistence or interfering between self-love or private interest, and the several particular appetites, passions, affections, or the pursuits they lead to. But this competition or interfering is merely accidental; and happens much oftener between pride, revenge, sensual gratifications, and private interest, than between private interest and benevolence. For nothing is more common, than to see men give themselves up to a passion or an affection to their known prejudice and ruin, and in direct contradiction to manifest and real interest, and the loudest calls of self-love:* whereas the seeming competitions and interfering, between benevolence and private interest, relate much more to the materials or means of enjoyment, than to enjoyment itself. There is often an interfering in the former, when there is none in the latter. Thus as to riches: so much money as a man gives away, so much less will remain in his possession. Here is a real interfering. But though a man cannot possibly give without less lessening his fortune, yet there are multitudes might give without lessening their own enjoyment; because they may have more than they can turn to any real use or advantage to themselves. Thus the more thought and time any one employs about the interests and good of others, he must necessarily have less to attend his own; but he may have so ready and large a supply of his own wants, that such thought might be really useless to himself, though of great service and assistance to others.

19   The general mistake, that there is some greater inconsistence between endeavouring to promote the good of another and self-interest, than between self-interest and

pursuing any thing else seems, as hath already been hinted, to arise from our notions of property; and to be carried on by this property's being supposed to be itself our happiness or good. People are so very much taken up with this one subject, that they seem from it to have formed a general way of thinking, which they apply to other things that they have nothing to do with. Hence, in a confused and slight way, it might well be taken for granted, that another's having no interest in an affection (*i.e.* his good not being the object of it) renders, as one may speak, the proprietor's interest in it greater; and that if another had an interest in it, this would render his less, or occasion that such affection could not be so friendly to self-love, or conducive to private good, as an affection or pursuit which has not a regard to the good of another. This I say, might be taken for granted, whilst it was not attended to, that the object of every particular affection is equally somewhat external to ourselves; and whether it be the good of another person, or whether it be any other external thing, makes no alteration with regard to its being one's own affection, and the gratification of it one's own private enjoyment. And so far as it is taken for granted, that barely having the means and materials of enjoyment is what constitutes interest and happiness; that our interest or good consists in possessions themselves, in having the property of riches, houses, lands, gardens, not in the enjoyment of them; so far it will even more strongly be taken for granted, in the way already explained, that an affection's conducing to the good of another, must even necessarily occasion it to conduce less to private good, if not to be positively detrimental to it. For, if property and happiness are one and the same thing, as by increasing the property of another, you lessen your own property, so by promoting the happiness of another you must lessen your own happiness.* But whatever occasioned the mistake, I hope it has been fully proved to be one;* as it has been proved, that there is no peculiar rivalship or competition between self-love and benevolence; that as there may be a competition between these two, so there may also between any particular affection whatever and self-love; that every particular affection, benevolence among the rest, is subservient to self-love by being the instrument of private enjoyment; and that in one respect benevolence contributes more to private interest, *i.e.* enjoyment or satisfaction, than any other of the particular common affections, as it is in a degree its own gratification.

And to all these things may be added, that religion, from whence arises our   20 strongest obligation to benevolence, is so far from disowning the principle of self-love,* that it often addresses itself to that very principle, and always to the mind in that state when reason presides; and there can no access be had to the understanding, but by convincing men, that the course of life we would persuade them to is not contrary to their interest. It may be allowed, without any prejudice to the cause of virtue and religion, that our ideas of happiness and misery are of all our ideas the nearest and most important to us; that they will, nay, if you please, that they ought to prevail over those of order, and beauty, and harmony, and proportion, if there should ever be, as it is impossible there ever should be, any inconsistence between them: though these last too, as expressing the fitness of actions, are real as truth itself.* Let it be allowed, though virtue or moral rectitude does indeed consist in affection to and pursuit of what is right and good, as such; yet, that when we sit down in a cool hour, we can neither justify to ourselves this or any other pursuit, till we are convinced that it will be for our happiness, or at least not contrary to it.*

21   Common reason and humanity will have some influence upon mankind, whatever becomes of speculations; but, so far as the interests of virtue depend upon the theory of it being secured from open scorn, so far its very being in the world depends upon its appearing to have no contrariety to private interest and self-love.* The foregoing observations therefore, it is hoped, may have gained a little ground in favour of the precept before us; the particular explanation of which, shall be the subject of the next discourse.

22   I will conclude at present, with observing the peculiar obligation which we are under to virtue and religion, as enforced in the verses following the text, in the epistle for the day,* from our Saviour's coming into the world. 'The night is far spent, the day is at hand; let us therefore cast off the works of darkness, and let us put on the armour of light,' etc.[2] The meaning and force of which exhortation is, that Christianity lays us under new obligations to a good life, as by it the will of God is more clearly revealed, and as it affords additional motives to the practice of it, over and above those which arise out of the nature of virtue and vice; I might add, as our Saviour has set us a perfect example of goodness in our own nature. Now love and charity is plainly the thing in which he hath placed his religion; in which therefore, as we have any pretence to the name of Christians, we must place ours. He hath at once enjoined it upon us by way of command with peculiar force; and by his example, as having undertaken the work of our salvation out of pure love and good-will to mankind. The endeavour to set home this example upon our minds is a very proper employment of this season, which is bringing on the festival of his birth: which as it may teach us many excellent lessons of humility, resignation, and obedience to the will of God; so there is none it recommends with greater authority, force and advantage, than this of love and charity; since it was 'for us men, and for our salvation', that 'he came down from heaven, and was incarnate, and was made man';* that he might teach us our duty, and more especially that he might enforce the practice of it, reform mankind, and finally bring us to that 'eternal salvation', of which 'he is the Author to all those that obey him'.[3]

Notes

1. S 11.8.
2. [*Rom.* xiii.12.]
3. [*Heb.* v.9.]

Sermon 12

Upon the Love of Our Neighbour

And if there be any other commandment, it is briefly comprehended in this saying, namely, Thou shalt love thy neighbour as thyself.

(*Romans* xiii.9)

Having already removed the prejudices against public spirit, or the love of our 1 neighbour, on the side of private interest and self-love; I proceed to the particular explanation of the precept before us, by shewing, *who is our neighbour: in what sense we are required to love him as ourselves: the influence such love would have upon our behaviour in life:* and lastly, *how this commandment comprehends in it all others.*

I. The objects and due extent of this affection will be understood by attending to 2 the nature of it, and to the nature and circumstances of mankind in this world. The love of our neighbour is the same with charity, benevolence, or good-will: it is an affection to the good and happiness of our fellow-creatures. This implies in it a disposition to produce happiness: and this is the simple notion of goodness, which appears so amiable wherever we meet with it. From hence it is easy to see, that the perfection of goodness consists in love to the whole universe.* This is the perfection of Almighty God.*

But as man is so much limited in his capacity, as so small a part of the creation 3 comes under his notice and influence, and as we are not used to consider things in so general a way; it is not to be thought of, that the universe should be the object of benevolence to such creatures as we are. Thus in that precept of our Saviour, 'Be ye perfect even as your Father which is in heaven is perfect,'[1] the perfection of the divine goodness is proposed to our imitation as it is promiscuous, and extends to the evil as well as the good; not as it is absolutely universal, imitation of it in this respect being plainly beyond us. The object is too vast. For this reason moral writers also have substituted a less general object for our benevolence, mankind. But this likewise is an object too general, and very much out of our view. Therefore persons more practical have, instead of mankind, put our country; and made the principle of virtue, of human virtue, to consist in the entire uniform love of our country: and this is what we call a public spirit; which in men of public stations is the character of a patriot. But this is speaking to the upper part of the world. Kingdoms and governments are large; and the sphere of action of far the greatest part of mankind is much narrower than the government they live under: or however, common men do not consider their actions as affecting the whole community of which they are members. There plainly is wanting a less general and nearer object of benevolence for the bulk of men, than that of their country. Therefore the Scripture, not being a book of theory and speculation, but a plain rule of life for mankind, has with the utmost possible propriety put the principle of virtue upon the love of our neighbour; which is that part of the universe, that part of mankind, that part of our country, which comes under our immediate notice, acquaintance and influence, and with which we have to do.

4   This is plainly the true account or reason, why our Saviour places the principle of virtue in the love of our *neighbour*; and the account itself shews who are comprehended under that relation.

5   II. Let us now consider in what sense we are commanded to love our neighbour *as ourselves*.

6   This precept, in its first delivery by our Saviour, is thus introduced: 'Thou shalt love the Lord thy God with all thine heart, with all thy soul, and with all thy strength; and thy neighbour as thyself.'[2] These very different manners of expression do not lead our thoughts to the same measure or degree of love, common to both objects; but to one, peculiar to each. Supposing then, which is to be supposed, a distinct meaning and propriety in the words, *as thyself*; the precept we are considering will admit of any of these senses: that we bear the *same kind* of affection to our neighbour, as we do to ourselves: or, that the love we bear to our neighbour should have *some certain proportion or other* to self-love: or, lastly, that it should bear the particular proportion of *equality*, that *it be in the same degree*.

7   *First*, The precept may be understood as requiring only, that we have the *same kind* of affection to our fellow-creatures, as to ourselves: that, as every man has the principle of self-love, which disposes him to avoid misery, and consult his own happiness; so we should cultivate the affection of good-will to our neighbour, and that it should influence us to have the same kind of regard to him. This at least must be commanded: and this will not only prevent our being injurious to him, but will also put us upon promoting his good. There are blessings in life, which we share in common with others; peace, plenty, freedom, healthful seasons. But real benevolence to our fellow-creatures would give us the notion of a common interest in a stricter sense: for in the degree we love one another, his interest, his joys and sorrows, are our own. It is from self-love that we form the notion of private good, and consider it as our own: love of our neighbour would teach us thus to appropriate to ourselves his good and welfare; to consider ourselves as having a real share in his happiness. Thus the principle of benevolence would be an advocate within our own breasts, to take care of the interests of our fellow-creatures in all the interfering and competitions which cannot but be, from the imperfection of our nature, and the state we are in. It would likewise, in some measure, lessen that interfering; and hinder men from forming so strong a notion of private good, exclusive of the good of others, as we

commonly do. Thus, as the private affection makes us in a peculiar manner sensible of humanity, justice, or injustice, when exercised towards ourselves; love of our neighbour would give us the same kind of sensibility in his behalf. This would be the greatest security of our uniform obedience to that most equitable rule; 'Whatsoever ye would that men should do unto you, do ye even so unto them.'[3]

All this is indeed no more than that we should have a real love to our neighbour: but then, which is to he observed, the words, *as thyself*, express this in the most distinct manner, and determine the precept to relate to the affection itself. The advantage, which this principle of benevolence has over other remote considerations, is that it is itself the temper of virtue; and likewise, that it is the chief, nay the only effectual security of our performing the several offices of kindness, we owe to our fellow-creatures. When from distant considerations men resolve upon any thing to which they have no liking, or perhaps an averseness, they are perpetually finding out evasions and excuses; which need never be wanting, if people look for them: and they equivocate with themselves in the plainest cases in the world. This may be in respect to single determinate acts of virtue: but it comes in much more, where the obligation is to a general course of behaviour; and most of all, if it be such as cannot be reduced to fixed determinate rules. This observation may account for the diversity of the expression, in that known passage of the prophet Micah: 'to do justly, and to love mercy'.[4] A man's heart must be formed to humanity and benevolence, he must *love mercy*, otherwise he will not act mercifully in any settled course of behaviour. As consideration of the future sanctions of religion is our only security of persevering in our duty, in cases of great temptations: so to get our heart and temper formed to a love and liking of what is good, is absolutely necessary in order to our behaving rightly in the familiar and daily intercourses amongst mankind. **8**

Secondly, The precept before us may be understood to require, that we love our neighbour in some certain *proportion* or other, *according as* we love ourselves. And indeed a man's character cannot be determined by the love he bears to his neighbour, considered absolutely: but the proportion which this bears to self-love, whether it be attended to or not, is the chief thing which forms the character, and influences the actions. For, as the form of the body is a composition of various parts; so likewise our inward structure is not simple or uniform, but a composition of various passions, appetites, affections, together with rationality; including in this last both the discernment of what is right, and a disposition to regulate ourselves by it.* There is greater variety of parts in what we call a character, than there are features in a face: and the morality of that is no more determined by one part, than the beauty or deformity of this is by one single feature: each is to be judged of by all the parts or features, not taken singly but together. In the inward frame the various passions, appetites, affections, stand in different respects to each other. The principles in our mind may be contradictory, or checks and allays only, or incentives and assistants to each other. And principles, which in their nature have no kind of contrariety or affinity, may yet accidentally be each other's allays or incentives. **9**

10   From hence it comes to pass, that though we were able to look into the inward contexture of the heart, and see with the greatest exactness in what degree any one principle is in a particular man; we could not from thence determine, how far that principle would go towards forming the character, or what influence it would have upon the actions, unless we could likewise discern what other principles prevailed in him, and see the proportion which that one bears to the others. Thus, though two men should have the affection of compassion in the same degree exactly; yet one may have the principle of resentment, or of ambition so strong in him, is to prevail over that of compassion, and prevent its having any influence upon his actions; so that he may deserve the character of an hard or cruel man: whereas the other, having compassion in just the same degree only, yet having resentment or ambition in a lower degree, his compassion may prevail over them, so as to influence his actions, and to denominate his temper compassionate. So that, how strange soever it may appear to people who do not attend to the thing, yet it is quite manifest, that, when we say one man is more resenting or compassionate than another, this does not necessarily imply that one has the principle of resentment or of compassion stronger than the other. For if the proportion, which resentment or compassion bears to other inward principles, is greater in one than in the other; this is itself sufficient to denominate one more resenting or compassionate than the other.

11   Further, the whole system as I may speak, of affections, (including rationality) which constitute the heart, as this word is used in Scripture and on moral subjects, are each and all of them stronger in some than in others. Now the proportion which the two general affections, benevolence and self-love, bear to each other, according to this interpretation of the text, denominates men's character as to virtue. Suppose then one man to have the principle of benevolence in an higher degree than another: it will not follow from hence, that his general temper or character or actions will be more benevolent than the other's. For he may have self-love in such a degree as quite to prevail over benevolence; so that it may have no influence at all upon his actions; whereas benevolence in the other person, though in a lower degree, may yet be the strongest principle in his heart; and strong enough to be the guide of his actions, so as to denominate him a good and virtuous man. The case is here as in scales: it is not one weight, considered in itself, which determines whether the scale shall ascend or descend; but this depends upon the proportion, which that one weight hath to the other.

12   It being thus manifest that the influence which benevolence has upon our actions, and how far it goes towards forming our character, is not determined by the degree itself of this principle in our mind; but by the proportion it has to self-love and other principles: a comparison also being made in the text between self-love and the love of our neighbour; these joint considerations afforded suffi-cient occasion for treating here of that proportion: it plainly is implied in the precept, though it should be questioned whether it be the exact meaning of the words, *as thyself.*

Love of our neighbour then must bear some proportion to self-love, and virtue to **13** be sure consists in the due proportion.* What this due proportion is, whether as a principle in the mind, or as exerted in actions, can be judged of only from our nature and condition in this world. Of the degree in which affections and the principles of action, considered in themselves, prevail, we have no measure: let us then proceed to the course of behaviour, the actions they produce.

Both our nature and condition require, that each particular man should make **14** particular provision for himself: and the inquiry, what proportion benevolence should have to self-love, when brought down to practice, will be, what is a competent care and provision for ourselves. And how certain soever it be, that each man must determine this for himself; and how ridiculous soever it would be, for any to attempt to determine it for another: yet it is to be observed, that the proportion is real; and that a competent provision has a bound; and that it cannot be all which we can possibly get and keep within our grasp, without legal injustice. Mankind almost universally bring in, vanity, supplies for what is called a life of pleasure, covetousness, or imaginary notions of superiority over others, to determine this question: but every one, who desires to act a proper part in society, would do well to consider, how far any of them come in to determine it, in the way of moral consideration. All that can be said is, supposing, what, as the world goes, is so much to be supposed that it is scarce to be mentioned, that persons do not neglect what they really owe to themselves; the more of their care and thought, and of their fortune they employ in doing good to their fellow-creatures, the nearer they come up to the law of perfection 'Thou shalt love thy neighbour as thyself.'*

Thirdly, If the words, *as thyself*, were to be understood of an equality of affection; **15** it would not be attended with those consequences, which perhaps may be thought to follow from it. Suppose a person to have the same settled regard to others, as to himself; that in every deliberate scheme or pursuit he took their interest into the account in the same degree as his own, so far as an equality of affection would produce this: yet he would in fact, and ought to be, much more taken up and employed about himself, and his own concerns; than about others, and their interests.* For, besides the one common affection toward himself and his neighbour, he would have several other particular affections, passions, appetites, which he could not possibly feel in common both for himself and others: now these sensations themselves very much employ us; and have perhaps as great influence as self-love. So far indeed as self-love, and cool reflection upon what is for our interest, would set us on work to gain a supply of our own several wants; so far the love of our neighbour would make us do the same for him: but the degree in which we are put upon seeking and making use of the means of gratification, by the feeling of those affections, appetites, and passions, must necessarily be peculiar to ourselves.

That there are particular passions, (suppose shame, resentment) which men seem **16** to have, and feel in common both for themselves and others, makes no alteration in respect to those passions and appetites which cannot possibly be thus felt in common.* From hence, (and perhaps more things of the like kind might be mentioned), it follows, that though there were an equality of affection to both, yet regards to ourselves would be more prevalent than attention to the concerns of others.

17   And from moral considerations it ought to be so, supposing still the equality of affection commanded: because we are in a peculiar manner, as I may speak, intrusted with ourselves; and therefore care of our own interests, as well as of our conduct, particularly belongs to us.*

18   To these things must be added, that moral obligations can extend no further than to natural possibilities. Now we have a perception of our own interests, like consciousness of our own existence, which we always carry about with us; and which, in its continuation, kind, and degree, seems impossible to be felt in respect to the interests of others.

19   From all these things it fully appears, that though we were to love our neighbour in the same degree as we love ourselves, so far as this is possible; yet the care of ourselves, of the individual, would not be neglected; the apprehended danger of which seems to be the only objection against understanding the precept in this strict sense.

20   III. The general temper of mind which the due love of our neighbour would form us to, and the influence it would have upon our behaviour in life, is now to be considered.

21   The temper and behaviour of charity is explained at large, in that known passage of St. Paul: [5] 'Charity suffereth long, and is kind; charity envieth not, doth not behave itself unseemly, seeketh not her own, thinketh no evil, beareth all things, believeth all things, hopeth all things.' As to the meaning of the expressions, *seeketh not her own, thinketh no evil, believeth all things*; however those expressions may be explained away, this meekness, and in some degree, easiness of temper, readiness to forego our right for the sake of peace as well as in the way of compassion, freedom from mistrust, and disposition to believe well of our neighbour, this general temper, I say, accompanies and is plainly the effect of love and good-will. And, though such is the world in which we live, that experience and knowledge of it, not only may, but must beget in us greater regard to ourselves, and doubtfulness of the characters of others, than is natural to mankind;* yet these ought not to be carried further than the nature and course of things make necessary. It is still true, even in the present state of things, bad as it is, that a real good man had rather be deceived, than be suspicious; had rather forego his known right, than run the venture of doing even a hard thing. This is the general temper of that charity, of which the apostle asserts, that if he had it not, giving his 'body to be burned would avail him nothing'; and which, he says, 'shall never fail'.[6]

22   The happy influence of this temper extends to every different relation and circumstance in human life. It plainly renders a man better, more to be desired, as to all the respects and relations we can stand in to each other. The benevolent man is disposed to make use of all external advantages in such a manner as shall contribute to the good of others, as well as to his own satisfaction. His own satisfaction consists

in this. He will be easy and kind to his dependants, compassionate to the poor and distressed, friendly to all with whom he has to do. This includes the good neighbour, parent, master, magistrate: and such a behaviour would plainly make dependence, inferiority, and even servitude, easy. So that a good or charitable man of superior rank in wisdom, fortune, authority, is a common blessing to the place he lives in; happiness grows under his influence. This good principle in inferiors would discover itself in paying respect, gratitude, obedience, as due. It were therefore methinks one just way of trying one's own character, to ask ourselves, Am I in reality a better master or servant, a better friend, a better neighbour, than such and such persons; whom, perhaps, I may think not to deserve the character of virtue and religion so much as myself?

And as to the spirit of party, which unhappily prevails amongst mankind, what-   23 ever are the distinctions which serve for a supply to it, some or other of which have obtained in all ages and countries: one, who is thus friendly to his kind, will immediately make due allowances for it, as what cannot but be amongst such creatures as men, in such a world as this. And as wrath and fury and overbearing upon these occasions proceed, as I may speak, from men's feeling only on their own side: so a common feeling, for others as well as for ourselves, would render us sensible to this truth, which it is strange can have so little influence; that we ourselves differ from others, just as much as they do from us. I put the matter in this way, because it can scarce be expected that the generality of men should see, that those things, which are made the occasions of dissension and fomenting the party-spirit, are really nothing at all: but it may be expected from all people, how much soever they are in earnest about their respective peculiarities, that humanity, and common good-will to their fellow-creatures, should moderate and restrain that wretched spirit.

This good temper of charity likewise would prevent strife and enmity arising from   24 other occasions: it would prevent our giving just cause of offence, and our taking it without cause. And in cases of real injury, a good man will make all the allowances which are to be made; and, without any attempts of retaliation, he will only consult his own and other men's security for the future, against injustice and wrong.

IV. I proceed to consider lastly, what is affirmed of the precept now explained,   25 that it comprehends in it all others; *i.e.* that to love our neighbour as ourselves includes in it all virtues.

Now the way in which every maxim of conduct, or general speculative assertion,   26 when it is to be explained at large, should be treated, is, to shew what are the particular truths which were designed to be comprehended under such a general observation, how far it is strictly true; and then the limitations, restrictions, and exceptions, if there be exceptions, with which it is to be understood. But it is only the former of these, namely, how far the assertion in the text holds, and the ground of the pre-eminence assigned to the precept of it, which in strictness comes into our present consideration.

However, in almost every thing that is said, there is somewhat to be understood   27 beyond what is explicitly laid down, and which we of course supply; somewhat,

I mean, which would not be commonly called a restriction or limitation. Thus, when benevolence is said to be the sum of virtue, it is not spoken of as a blind propension, but as a principle in reasonable creatures, and so to be directed by their reason:* for reason and reflection comes into our notion of a moral agent. And that will lead us to consider distant consequences, as well as the immediate tendency of an action: it will teach us, that the care of some persons, suppose children and families, is particularly committed to our charge by Nature and Providence; as also that there are other circumstances, suppose friendship or former obligations, which require that we do good to some, preferably to others. Reason, considered merely as subservient to benevolence, as assisting to produce the greatest good, will teach us to have particular regard to these relations and circumstances; because it is plainly for the good of the world that they should be regarded. And as there are numberless cases, in which, notwithstanding appearances, we are not competent judges, whether a particular action will upon the whole do good or harm; reason in the same way will teach us to be cautious how we act in these cases of uncertainty. It will suggest to our consideration, which is the safer side; how liable we are to be led wrong by passion and private interest; and what regard is due to laws, and the judgement of mankind. All these things must come into consideration, were it only in order to determine which way of acting is likely to produce the greatest good. Thus, upon supposition that it were in the strictest sense true, without limitation, that benevolence includes in it all virtues; yet reason must come in as its guide and director, in order to attain its own end, the end of benevolence, the greatest public good. Reason then being thus included, let us now consider the truth of the assertion itself.

28   *First*, It is manifest that nothing can be of consequence to mankind or any creature, but happiness. This then is all which any person can, in strictness of speaking, be said to have a right to. We can therefore 'owe no man any thing',[7] but only to further and promote his happiness, according to our abilities. And therefore a disposition and endeavour to do good to all with whom we have to do, in the degree and manner which the different relations we stand in to them require, is a discharge of all the obligations we are under to them.

29   As human nature is not one simple uniform thing, but a composition of various parts; body, spirit, appetites, particular passions and affections; for each of which reasonable self-love would lead men to have due regard, and make suitable provision: so society consists of various parts, to which we stand in different respects and relations; and just benevolence would as surely lead us to have due regard to each of these, and behave as the respective relations require. Reasonable good-will, and right behaviour towards our fellow-creatures, are in a manner the same: only that the former expresseth the principle as it is in the mind; the latter, the principle as it were, become external, *i.e.* exerted in actions.

30   And so far as temperance, sobriety, and moderation in sensual pleasures, and the contrary vices, have any respect to our fellow-creatures, any influence upon their quiet, welfare, and happiness; as they always have a real, and often a near influence

upon it; so far it is manifest those virtues may be produced by the love of our neighbour, and that the contrary vices would be prevented by it. Indeed, if men's regard to themselves will not restrain them from excess; it may be thought little probable, that their love to others will be sufficient: but the reason is, that their love to others is not, any more than their regard to themselves, just, and in its due degree. There are however manifest instances of persons kept sober and temperate from regard to their affairs, and the welfare of those who depend upon them. And it is obvious to every one, that habitual excess, a dissolute course of life, implies a general neglect of the duties we owe towards our friends, our families and our country.

From hence it is manifest that the common virtues, and the common vices of **31** mankind, may be traced up to benevolence, or the want of it. And this entitles the precept, 'Thou shalt love thy neighbour as thyself', to the pre-eminence given to it; and is a justification of the apostle's assertion, that all other commandments are comprehended in it; whatever cautions and restrictions[8] there are, which might require to be considered, if we were to state particularly and at length, what is virtue and right behaviour in mankind. But,

Secondly, It might be added, that in a higher and more general way of consider- **32** ation, leaving out the particular nature of creatures, and the particular circumstances in which they are placed, benevolence seems in the strictest sense to include in it all that is good and worthy; all that is good, which we have any distinct particular notion of. We have no clear conception of any positive moral attribute in the Supreme Being, but what may be resolved up into goodness.* And, if we consider a reasonable creature or moral agent, without regard to the particular relations and circumstances in which he is placed; we cannot conceive any thing else to come in towards determining whether he is to be ranked in an higher or lower class of virtuous beings, but the higher or lower degree in which that principle, and what is manifestly connected with it, prevail in him.

That which we more strictly call piety, or the love of God, and which is an essential **33** part of a right temper, some may perhaps imagine no way connected with benevolence: yet surely they must be connected, if there be indeed in being an object infinitely good. Human nature is so constituted, that every good affection implies the love of itself; *i.e.* becomes the object of a new affection in the same person.* Thus, to be righteous implies in it the love of righteousness; to be benevolent the love of benevolence; to be good the love of goodness; whether this righteousness, benevolence, or goodness, be viewed as in our own mind, or in another's: and the love of God as a being perfectly good, is the love of perfect goodness contemplated in a being or person. Thus morality and religion, virtue and piety, will at last necessarily coincide, run up into one and the same point, and *love* will be in all senses 'the end of the commandment'.[9]

O Almighty God, inspire us with this divine principle; kill in us all the seeds of envy and ill-will; and help us, by cultivating within ourselves the love of our neighbour, to improve in the love of

thee. Thou hast placed us in various kindreds, friendships, and relations, as the school of discipline for our affections: help us, by the due exercise of them, to improve to perfection; till all partial affection be lost in that entire universal one, and thou, O God, shalt be all in all.

Notes

1. *Matt.* v.48.
2. [*Matt.* xii.37.]
3. [*Matt.* vii.12.]
4. [*Micah* vi.8.]
5. *I Cor.* xiii.4–7.
6. [*I Cor.* xiii.3, 8.]
7. [*Rom.* xiii.8.]
8. For instance: as we are not competent judges, what is upon the whole for the good of the world; there may be other immediate ends appointed us to pursue, besides that one of doing good, or producing happiness. Though the good of the creation be the only end of the Author of it, yet he may have laid us under particular obligations, which we may discern and feel ourselves under, quite distinct from a perception, that the observance or violation of them is for the happiness or misery of our fellow-creatures. And this is in fact the case. For there are certain dispositions of mind, and certain actions, which are in themselves approved or disapproved by mankind, abstracted from the consideration of their tendency to the happiness or misery of the world; approved or disapproved by reflection, by that principle within, which is the guide of life, the judge of right and wrong. Numberless instances of this kind might be mentioned. There are pieces of treachery, which in themselves appear base and detestable to every one. There are actions, which perhaps can scarce have any other general name given them than indecencies, which yet are odious and shocking to human nature. There is such a thing as meanness, a little mind; which, as it is quite distinct from incapacity, so it raises a dislike and disapprobation quite different from that contempt, which men are too apt to have, of mere folly. On the other hand; what we call greatness of mind, is the object of another sort of approbation, than superior understanding. Fidelity, honour, strict justice, are themselves approved in the highest degree, abstracted from the consideration of their tendency. Now, whether it be thought that each of these are connected with benevolence in our nature, and so may be considered as the same thing with it; or whether some of them be thought an inferior kind of virtues and vices, somewhat like natural beauties and deformities; or lastly, plain exceptions to the general rule; thus much however is certain, that the things now instanced in, and numberless others, are approved or disapproved by mankind in general, in quite another view than as conducive to the happiness or misery of the world.*
9. [*I Tim.* i.5.]

Sermon 13

Upon the Love of God*

Thou shalt love the Lord thy God with all thy heart, and with all thy soul, and with all thy mind.

(St. Matt. xxii.37)

Every body knows, you therefore need only just be put in mind, that there is such a thing, as having so great horror of one extreme, as to run insensibly and of course into the contrary; and that a doctrine's having been a shelter for enthusiasm, or made to serve the purposes of superstition, is no proof of the falsity of it: truth or right being somewhat real in itself, and so not to be judged of by its liableness to abuse, or by its supposed distance from or nearness to error. It may be sufficient to have mentioned this in general, without taking notice of the particular extravagancies, which have been vented under the pretence or endeavour of explaining the love of God: or how manifestly we are got into the contrary extreme, under the notion of a reasonable religion; so very reasonable, as to have nothing to do with the heart and affections, if these words signify any thing but the faculty by which we discern speculative truth.* 1

By the love of God, I would understand all those regards, all those affections of mind, which are due immediately to him from such a creature as man, and which rest in him as their end. As this does not include servile fear; so neither will any other regards, how reasonable soever, which respect any thing out of or besides the perfection of the divine nature, come into consideration here. But all fear is not excluded, because his displeasure is itself the natural proper object of fear. Reverence, ambition of his love and approbation, delight in the hope or consciousness of it, come likewise into this definition of the love of God; because he is the natural object of all those affections or movements of mind, as really as he is the object of the affection, which is in the strictest sense called love; and all of them equally rest in him, as their end. And they may all be understood to be implied in these words of our Saviour, without putting any force upon them: for he is speaking of the love of God and our neighbour, as containing the whole of piety and virtue. 2

It is plain that the nature of man is so constituted, as to feel certain affections upon the sight or contemplation of certain objects. Now the very notion of affection 3 implies resting in its object as an end. And the particular affection to good characters, reverence and moral love of them, is natural to all those who have any degree of real goodness in themselves. This will be illustrated by the description of a perfect character in a creature; and by considering the manner, in which a good man in his presence would be affected towards such a character. He would of course feel the affections of love, reverence, desire of his approbation, delight in the hope or consciousness of it. And surely all this is applicable, and may be brought up to that Being, who is infinitely more than an adequate object of all those affections; whom we are commanded to 'love with all our heart, with all our soul, and with all our mind'. And of these regards towards Almighty God, some are more particularly suitable to and becoming so imperfect a creature as man, in this mortal state we are passing through; and some of them, and perhaps other exercises of the mind, will be the employment and happiness of good men in a state of perfection.*

4   This is a general view of what the following discourse will contain. And it is manifest the subject is a real one: there is nothing in it enthusiastical or unreasonable. And if it be indeed at all a subject, it is one of the utmost importance.

5   As mankind have a faculty by which they discern speculative truth; so we have various affections towards external objects. Understanding and temper, reason and affection, are as distinct ideas, as reason and hunger; and one would think could no more be confounded. It is by reason that we get the ideas of several objects of our affections: but in these cases reason and affection are no more the same, than sight of a particular object, and the pleasure or uneasiness consequent thereupon, are the same. Now, as reason tends to and rests in the discernment of truth, the object of it; so the very nature of affection consists in tending towards, and resting in, its objects as an end. We do indeed often in common language say, that things are loved, desired, esteemed, not for themselves, but for somewhat further, somewhat out of and beyond them: yet, in these cases, whoever will attend, will see, that these things are not in reality the objects of the affections, *i.e.* are not loved, desired, esteemed, but the somewhat further and beyond them. If we have no affections which rest in what are called their objects, then what is called affection, love, desire, hope, in human nature, is only an uneasiness in being at rest; an unquiet disposition to action, progress, pursuit, without end or meaning. But if there be any such thing as delight in the company of one person, rather than of another; whether in the way of friendship, or mirth and entertainment, it is all one, if it be without respect to fortune, honour, or increasing our stores of knowledge, or any thing beyond the present time; here is an instance of an affection absolutely resting in its object as its end, and being gratified, in the same way as the appetite of hunger is satisfied with food. Yet nothing is more common than to hear it asked, what advantage a man hath in such a course, suppose of study, particular friendships, or in any other; nothing, I say, is more common than to hear such a question put in a way which supposes no gain, advantage or interest, but as a means to somewhat further: and if so, then there is no such thing at all as real interest, gain or advantage. This is the same absurdity

with respect to life, as an infinite series of effects without a cause is in speculation.* The gain, advantage or interest consists in the delight itself, arising from such a faculty's having its object: neither is there any such thing as happiness or enjoyment, but what arises from hence. The pleasures of hope and of reflection are not exceptions: the former being only this happiness anticipated; the latter, the same happiness enjoyed over again after its time. And even the general expectation of future happiness can afford satisfaction, only as it is a present object to the principle of self-love.

It was doubtless intended, that life should be very much a pursuit to the gross of 6 mankind. But this is carried so much farther than is reasonable, that what gives immediate satisfaction, *i.e.* our present interest, is scarce considered as our interest at all. It is inventions which have only a remote tendency towards enjoyment, perhaps but a remote tendency towards gaining the means only of enjoyment, which are chiefly spoken of as useful to the world. And though this way of thinking were just with respect to the imperfect state we are now in, where we know so little of satisfaction without satiety; yet it must be guarded against, when we are considering the happiness of a state of perfection; which happiness being enjoyment and not hope, must necessarily consist in this, that our affections have their objects, and rest in those objects as an end, *i.e.* be satisfied with them. This will further appear in the sequel of this discourse.

Of the several affections, or inward sensations, which particular objects excite in 7 man, there are some, the having of which implies the love of them, when they are reflected upon.[1] This cannot be said of all our affections, principles, and motives of action. It were ridiculous to assert, that a man upon reflection hath the same kind of approbation of the appetite of hunger, or the passion of fear, as he hath of good-will to his fellow-creatures. To be a just, a good, a righteous man, plainly carries with it a peculiar affection to or love of justice, goodness, righteousness, when these principles are the objects of contemplation.* Now if a man approves of, or hath an affection to, any principle in and for itself; incidental things allowed for, it will be the same whether he views it in his own mind or in another; in himself, or in his neighbour. This is the account of our approbation of, our moral love and affection to good characters; which cannot but be in those who have any degrees of real goodness in themselves, and who discern and take notice of the same principle in others.

From observation of what passes within ourselves, our own actions, and the 8 behaviour of others, the mind may carry on its reflections as far as it pleases; much beyond what we experience in ourselves, or discern in our fellow-creatures. It may go on, and consider goodness as become an uniform continued principle of action, as conducted by reason, and forming a temper and character absolutely good and perfect, which is in a higher sense excellent, and proportionably the object of love and approbation.

Let us then suppose a creature perfect according to his created nature: let his 9 form be human, and his capacities no more than equal to those of the chief of men: goodness shall be his proper character; with wisdom to direct it, and power within some certain determined sphere of action to exert it: but goodness must be the simple actuating principle within him; this being the moral quality which is amiable, or the immediate object of love as distinct from other affections of approbation. Here then is a finite object for our mind to tend towards, to exercise itself upon: a creature, perfect according to his capacity, fixed, steady, equally unmoved by weak pity or more weak fury and resentment; forming the justest scheme of conduct; going on undisturbed in the execution of it, through the several methods of severity and reward, towards his end, namely, the general happiness of all with whom he hath to do, as in itself right and valuable. This character, though uniform in itself, in its principle, yet exerting itself in different ways, or considered in different views, may by its appearing variety move different affections. Thus, the severity of justice would not affect us in the same way as an act of mercy: the adventitious qualities of wisdom and power may be considered in themselves: and even the strength of mind, which this immoveable goodness supposes, may likewise be viewed as an object of contemplation, distinct from the goodness itself. Superior excellence of any kind, as well as superior wisdom and power, is the object of awe and reverence to all creatures, whatever their moral character be: but so far as creatures of the lowest rank were good, so far the view of this character, as simply good, must appear amiable to them, be the object of, or beget love. Further, suppose we were conscious, that this superior person so far approved of us, that we had nothing servilely to fear from him; that he was really our friend, and kind and good to us in particular, as he had occasionally intercourse with us: we must be other creatures than we are, or we could not but feel the same kind of satisfaction and enjoyment (whatever would be the degree of it) from this higher acquaintance and friendship, as we feel from common ones; the intercourse being real, and the persons equally present, in both cases. We should have a more ardent desire to be approved by his better judgement, and a satisfaction in that approbation of the same sort with what would be felt in respect to common persons, or be wrought in us by their presence.

10   Let us now raise the character, and suppose this creature, for we are still going on with the supposition of a creature, our proper guardian and governor; that we were in a progress of being towards somewhat further; and that his scheme of government was too vast for our capacities to comprehend; remembering still that he is perfectly good, and our friend as well as our governor. Wisdom, power, goodness, accidentally viewed any where, would inspire reverence, awe, love: and as these affections would be raised in higher or lower degrees, in proportion as we had occasionally more or less intercourse with the creature endued with those qualities; so this further consideration and knowledge, that he was our proper guardian and governor, would much more bring these objects and qualities home to ourselves; teach us they had a greater respect to us in particular, that we had an higher interest in that wisdom and power and goodness. We should, with joy, gratitude, reverence, love, trust, and dependence, appropriate the character, as what we had a right in; and make our boast in such our

relation to it. And the conclusion of the whole would be, that we should refer ourselves implicitly to him, and cast ourselves entirely upon him. As the whole attention of life should be to obey his commands; so the highest enjoyment of it must arise from the contemplation of this character, and our relation to it, from a consciousness of his favour and approbation, and from the exercise of those affections towards him which could not but be raised from his presence. A being who hath these attributes, who stands in this relation, and is thus sensibly present to the mind, must necessarily be the object of these affections: there is as real a correspondence between them, as between the lowest appetite of sense and its object.

That this being is not a creature, but the Almighty God; that he is of infinite power   11 and wisdom and goodness, does not render him less the object of reverence and love, than he would be if he had those attributes only in a limited degree. The Being who made us, and upon whom we entirely depend, is the object of some regards. He hath given us certain affections of mind, which correspond to wisdom, power, goodness; *i.e.* which are raised upon view of those qualities. If then he be really wise, powerful, good; he is the natural object of those affections, which he hath endued us with, and which correspond to those attributes. That he is infinite in power, perfect in wisdom and goodness, makes no alteration, but only that he is the object of those affections raised to the highest pitch.* He is not indeed to be discerned by any of our senses. 'I go forward, but he is not there; and backward, but I cannot perceive him: on the left hand where he doth work, but I cannot behold him: he hideth himself on the right hand, that I cannot see him. Oh that I knew where I might find him! that I might come even to his seat!'[2] But is he then afar off: does he not fill heaven and earth with his presence? The presence of our fellow-creatures affects our senses, and our senses give us the knowledge of their presence; which hath different kinds of influence upon us; love, joy, sorrow, restraint, encouragement, reverence. However this influence is not immediately from our senses, but from that knowledge. Thus suppose a person neither to see nor hear another, not to know by any of his senses, but yet certainly to know, that another was with him; this knowledge might, and in many cases would, have one or more of the effects before mentioned. It is therefore not only reasonable, but also natural, to be affected with a presence, though it be not the object of our senses: whether it be, or be not, is merely an accidental circumstance, which needs not come into consideration: it is the certainty that he is with us, and we with him, which hath the influence. We consider persons then as present, not only when they are within reach of our senses, but also when we are assured by any other means that they are within such a nearness; nay, if they are not, we can recall them to our mind, and be moved towards them as present: and must he, who is so much more intimately with us, that 'in him we live, and move and have our being',[3] be thought too distant to be the object of our affections? We own and feel the force of amiable and worthy qualities in our fellow-creatures: and can we be insensible to the contemplation of perfect goodness? Do we reverence the shadows of greatness here below, are we solicitous about honour and esteem and the opinion of the world: and shall we not feel the same with respect to him, whose are wisdom and power in their original, who 'is the God of judgement by whom actions are weighed'?[4] Thus love, reverence, desire of esteem, every faculty, every affection, tends towards, and is employed about its respective object in common cases: and must the exercise of them be suspended with regard to him alone, who is an object, an infinitely more than adequate object, to our most exalted faculties; him, 'of whom, and through whom, and to whom are all things'?[5]

12   As we cannot remove from this earth, or change our general business on it; so neither can we alter our real nature. Therefore no exercise of the mind can be recommended, but only the exercise of those faculties you are conscious of. Religion does not demand new affections, but only claims the direction of those you already have, those affections you daily feel; though unhappily confined to objects, not altogether unsuitable, but altogether unequal to them. We only represent to you the higher, the adequate objects of those very faculties and affections. Let the man of ambition go on still to consider disgrace as the greatest evil; honour, as his chief good. But disgrace, in whose estimation? Honour, in whose judgement? This is the only question. If shame, and delight in esteem be spoken of as real, as any settled ground of pain or pleasure; both these must be in proportion to the supposed wisdom and worth of him, by whom we are contemned or esteemed. Must it then be thought enthusiastical, to speak of a sensibility of this sort, which shall have respect to an unerring judgement, to infinite wisdom; when we are assured this unerring judgement, this infinite wisdom does observe upon our actions?

13   It is the same with respect to the love of God in the strictest and most confined sense. We only offer and represent the highest object of an affection, supposed already in your mind. Some degree of goodness must be previously supposed: this always implies the love of itself, an affection to goodness: the highest, the adequate object of this affection, is perfect goodness; which therefore we are to 'love with all our heart, with all our soul, and with all our strength'. "Must we then, forgetting our own interest, as it were go out of ourselves, and love God for his own sake?" No more forget your own interest, no more go out of yourselves than when you prefer one place, one prospect, the conversation of one man to that of another. Does not every affection necessarily imply, that the object of it be itself loved? If it be not, it is not the object of the affection.* You may and ought if you can, but it is a great mistake to think you can, love or fear or hate any thing, from consideration that such love or fear or hatred may be a means of obtaining good or avoiding evil. But the question, whether we ought to love God for his sake or for our own, being a mere mistake in language; the real question, which this is mistaken for, will, I suppose, be answered by observing, that the goodness of God already exercised towards us, our present dependence upon him, and our expectation of future benefits, ought, and have a natural tendency, to beget in us the affection of gratitude, and greater love towards him, than the same goodness exercised towards others: were it only for this reason, that every affection is moved in proportion to the sense we have of the object of it;

and we cannot but have a more lively sense of goodness, when exercised towards ourselves, than when exercised towards others. I added expectation of future benefits, because the ground of that expectation is present goodness.

Thus Almighty God is the natural object of the several affections, love, reverence, fear, desire of approbation. For though he is simply one, yet we cannot but consider him in partial and different views. He is in himself one uniform being, and for ever the same without 'variableness or shadow of turning':[6] but his infinite greatness, his goodness, his wisdom, are different objects to our mind. To which is to be added, that from the changes in our own characters, together with his unchangeableness, we cannot but consider ourselves as more or less the objects of his approbation, and really be so. For if he approves what is good; he cannot, merely from the unchangeableness of his nature, approve what is evil. Hence must arise more various movements of mind, more different kinds of affections. And this greater variety also is just and reasonable in such creatures as we are, though it respects a Being simply one, good and perfect. As some of these affections are most particularly suitable to so imperfect a creature as man, in this mortal state we are passing through; so there may be other exercises of mind, or some of these in higher degrees, our employment and happiness in a state of perfection.

14

Notes

1. St. Austin observes, 'Amor ipse ordinate amandus est, quo bene amatur quod amandum est, ut sit in nobis virtus qua vivitur bene.' *i.e.* 'The affection which we rightly have for what is lovely, must *ordinate* justly, in due manner, and proportion, become the object of a new affection, or be itself beloved, in order to our being endued with that virtue which is the principle of a good life' (*Civ. Dei.* I. 15. Ch. 22).*
2. *Job* xxiii.[8, 9, 3].
3. [*Acts* xvii.28.]
4. [*I Sam.* Ii.3.]
5. [*Rom.* xi.36.]
6. [*James* i.17.]

Sermon 14

Upon the Love of God

Thou shalt love the Lord thy God with all thy heart, and with all thy soul, and with all thy mind.

(St. Matt. xxii.37)

1   Consider then our ignorance, the imperfection of our nature, our virtue and our condition in this world, with respect to an infinitely good and just Being, our Creator and Governor; and you will see what religious affections of mind are most particularly suitable to this mortal state we are passing through.

2   Though we are not affected with any thing so strongly, as what we discern with our senses; and though our nature and condition require, that we be much taken up about sensible things; yet our reason convinces us that God is present with us, and we see and feel the effects of his goodness: he is therefore the object of some regards. The imperfection of our virtue, joined with the consideration of his absolute rectitude or holiness, will scarce permit that perfection of love, which entirely casts out all fear: yet goodness is the object of love to all creatures who have any degree of it themselves; and consciousness of a real endeavour to approve ourselves to him, joined with the consideration of his goodness, as it quite excludes servile dread and horror, so it is plainly a reasonable ground for hope of his favour. Neither fear, nor hope, nor love then are excluded: and one or another of these will prevail, according to the different views we have of God; and ought to prevail, according to the changes we find in our own character. There is a temper of mind made up of, or which follows from all three, fear, hope, love; namely, resignation to the divine will, which is the general temper belonging to this state; which ought to be the habitual frame of our mind and heart, and to be exercised at proper seasons more distinctly, in acts of devotion.

3   Resignation to the will of God is the whole of piety: it includes in it all that is good, and is a source of the most settled quiet and composure of mind. There is the general principle of submission in our nature. Man is not so constituted as to desire things, and be uneasy in the want of them, in proportion to their known value: many other considerations come in to determine the degrees of desire; particularly, whether the advantage we take a view of, be within the sphere of our rank. Who ever felt uneasiness, upon observing any of the advantages brute creatures have over us?

And yet it is plain they have several.* It is the same with respect to advantages belonging to creatures of a superior order. Thus, though we see a thing to be highly valuable yet that it does not belong to our condition of being, is sufficient to suspend our desires after it, to make us rest satisfied without such advantage. Now there is just the same reason for quiet resignation in the want of every thing equally unattainable, and out of our reach in particular, though others of our species be possessed of it. All this may be applied to the whole of life; to positive inconveniences as well as wants; not indeed to the sensations of pain and sorrow, but to all the uneasinesses of reflection, murmuring and discontent. Thus is human nature formed to compliance, yielding, submission of temper. We find the principles of it within us; and every one exercises it towards some objects or other; *i.e.* feels it with regard to some persons, and some circumstances. Now this is an excellent foundation of a reasonable and religious resignation. Nature teaches and inclines us to take up with our lot: the consideration, that the course of things is unalterable, hath a tendency to quiet the mind under it, to beget a submission of temper to it. But when we can add, that this unalterable course is appointed and continued by infinite wisdom and goodness; how absolute should be our submission, how entire our trust and dependence?

This would reconcile us to our condition; prevent all the supernumerary troubles   4
arising from imagination, distant fears, impatience; all uneasiness, except that which necessarily arises from the calamities themselves we may be under. How many of our cares should we by this means be disburdened of? Cares not properly our own, how apt soever they may be to intrude upon us, and we to admit them; the anxieties of expectation, solicitude about success and disappointment, which in truth are none of our concern. How open to every gratification would that mind be, which was clear of these encumbrances?

Our resignation to the will of God may be said to be perfect, when our will is lost   5
and resolved up into his; when we rest in his will as our end, as being itself most just, and right, and good. And where is the impossibility of such an affection to what is just, and right, and good, such a loyalty of heart to the Governor of the Universe, as shall prevail over all sinister indirect desires of our own? Neither is this at bottom any thing more than faith, and honesty, and fairness of mind; in a more enlarged sense indeed, than those words are commonly used. And as, in common cases, fear and hope and other passions are raised in us by their respective objects: so this submission of heart and soul and mind, this religious resignation, would be as naturally produced by our having just conceptions of Almighty God, and a real sense of his presence with us. In how low a degree soever this temper usually prevails amongst men, yet it is a temper right in itself: it is what we owe to our Creator: it is particularly suitable to our mortal condition, and what we should endeavour after for our own sakes in our passage through such a world as this; where is nothing upon which we can rest or depend; nothing, but what we are liable to be deceived and disappointed in. Thus we might *acquaint ourselves with God, and be at peace.** This is piety and religion in the strictest sense, considered as an habit of mind: an habitual sense of

God's presence with us; being affected towards him, as present, in the manner his superior nature requires from such a creature as man: this is to *walk with God*.*

6   Little more need be said of devotion or religious worship, than that it is this temper exerted into act. The nature of it consists in the actual exercise of those affections towards God, which are supposed habitual in good men. He is always equally present with us: but we are so much taken up with sensible things, that, 'lo, he goeth by us, and we see him not: he passeth on also, but we perceive him not'.[1] Devotion is retirement, from the world he has made, to him alone: it is to withdraw from the avocations of sense, to employ our attention wholly upon him as upon an object actually present, to yield ourselves up to the influence of the divine presence, and to give full scope to the affections of gratitude, love, reverence, trust and dependence; of which infinite power, wisdom and goodness, is the natural and only adequate object. We may apply to the whole of devotion those words of the son of Sirach: 'When you glorify the Lord, exalt him as much as you can; for even yet will he far exceed: and when you exalt him, put forth all your strength, and be not weary; for you can never go far enough.'[2] Our most raised affections of every kind cannot but fall short and be disproportionate, when an infinite Being is the object of them. This is the highest exercise and employment of mind, that a creature is capable of. As this divine service and worship is itself absolutely due to God, so also is it necessary in order to a further end, to keep alive upon our minds a sense of his authority, a sense that in our ordinary behaviour amongst men we act under him as our Governor and Judge.*

7   Thus you see the temper of mind respecting God, which is particularly suitable to a state of imperfection; to creatures in a progress of being towards somewhat further.

8   Suppose now this something further attained; that we were arrived at it: what a perception will it be, to see and know and feel that our trust was not vain, our dependence not groundless? That the issue, event, and consummation came out such as fully to justify and answer that resignation? If the obscure view of the divine perfection, which we have in this world, ought in just consequence to beget an entire resignation; what will this resignation be exalted into, when 'we shall see face to face, and know as we are known'?[3] If we cannot form any distinct notion of that perfection of the love of God, which 'casts out all fear';[4] of that enjoyment of him, which will be the happiness of good men hereafter; the consideration of our wants and capacities of happiness, and that he will be an adequate supply to them, must serve us instead of such distinct conception of the particular happiness itself.

9   Let us then suppose a man entirely disengaged from business and pleasure, sitting down alone and at leisure, to reflect upon himself and his own condition of being. He would immediately feel that he was by no means complete of himself, but totally insufficient for his own happiness. One may venture to affirm that every man hath felt this, whether he hath again reflected upon it or not. It is feeling this deficiency, that they are unsatisfied with themselves, which makes men look out for assistance from abroad; and which has given rise to various kinds of amusements, altogether needless any otherwise than as they serve to fill up the blank spaces of time, and so

hinder their feeling this deficiency, and being uneasy with themselves. Now, if these external things we take up with, were really an adequate supply to this deficiency of human nature, if by their means our capacities and desires were all satisfied and filled up; then it might be truly said, that we had found out the proper happiness of man; and so might sit down satisfied, and be at rest in the enjoyment of it. But if it appears, that the amusements, which men usually pass their time in, are so far from coming up to, or answering our notions and desires of happiness or good, that they are really no more than what they are commonly called, somewhat to pass away the time; *i.e.* somewhat which serves to turn us aside from, and prevent our attending to this our internal poverty and want; if they serve only, or chiefly, to suspend, instead of satisfying our conceptions and desires of happiness; if the want remains, and we have found out little more than barely the means of making it less sensible; then are we still to seek for somewhat to be an adequate supply to it. It is plain that there is a capacity in the nature of man, which neither riches, nor honours, nor sensual gratifications, nor any thing in this world can perfectly fill up, or satisfy: there is a deeper and more essential want, than any of these things can be the supply of.* Yet surely there is a possibility of somewhat, which may fill up all our capacities of happiness; somewhat, in which our souls may find rest; somewhat, which may be to us that satisfactory good we are inquiring after. But it cannot be any thing which is valuable only as it tends to some further end. Those therefore who have got this world so much into their hearts, as not to be able to consider happiness as consisting in any thing but property and possessions, which are only valuable as the means to somewhat else, cannot have the least glimpse of the subject before us; which is the end, not the means; the thing itself, not somewhat in order to it. But if you can lay aside that general, confused, undeterminate notion of happiness, as consisting in such possessions; and fix in your thoughts, that it really can consist in nothing but in a faculty's having its proper object; you will clearly see, that in the coolest way of consideration, without either the heat of fanciful enthusiasm, or the warmth of real devotion, nothing is more certain, than that an infinite Being may himself be, if he pleases, the supply to all the capacities of our nature. All the common enjoyments of life are from the faculties he hath endued us with, and the objects he hath made suitable to them. He may himself be to us infinitely more than all these: he may be to us all that we want. As our understanding can contemplate itself, and our affections be exercised upon themselves by reflection, so may each be employed in the same manner upon any other mind: and since the Supreme Mind, the Author and Cause of all things, is the highest possible object to himself, he may be an adequate supply to all the faculties of our souls; a subject to our understanding, and an object to our affections.

Consider then: when we shall have put off this mortal body, when we shall be **10** divested of sensual appetites, and those possessions which are now the means of gratification shall be of no avail; when this restless scene of business and vain pleasures, which now diverts us from ourselves, shall be all over; we, our proper self, shall still remain: we shall still continue the same creatures we are, with wants to be supplied, and capacities of happiness. We must have faculties of perception, though not sensitive ones; and pleasure or uneasiness from our perceptions, as now we have.*

11   There are certain ideas, which we express by the words, order, harmony, proportion, beauty, the furthest removed from any thing sensual. Now what is there in those intellectual images, forms, or ideas, which begets that approbation, love, delight, and even rapture, which is seen in some person's faces upon having those objects present to their minds?—"Mere enthusiasm!"—Be it what it will: there are objects, works of nature and of art, which all mankind have delight from, quite distinct from their affording gratification to sensual appetites; and from quite another view of them, than as being for their interest and further advantage. The faculties from which we are capable of these pleasures, and the pleasures themselves, are as natural, and as much to be accounted for, as any sensual appetite whatever, and the pleasure from its gratification. Words to be sure are wanting upon this subject: to say, that every thing of grace and beauty throughout the whole of nature, every thing excellent and amiable shared in differently lower degrees by the whole creation, meet in the Author and Cause of all things; this is an inadequate, and perhaps improper way of speaking of the divine nature: but it is manifest that absolute rectitude, the perfection of being, must be in all senses, and in every respect the highest object to the mind.

12   In this world it is only the effects of wisdom and power and greatness, which we discern:* it is not impossible, that hereafter the qualities themselves in the Supreme Being may be the immediate object of contemplation. What amazing wonders are opened to view by late improvements! What an object is the universe to a creature, if there be a creature who can comprehend its system! But it must be an infinitely higher exercise of the understanding, to view the scheme of it in that Mind, which projected it, before its foundations were laid. And surely we have meaning to the words, when we speak of going further; and viewing, not only this system in his mind, but the wisdom and intelligence itself from whence it proceeded. The same may be said of power. But since wisdom and power are not God, he is a wise, a powerful Being; the divine nature may therefore be a further object to the understanding. It is nothing to observe that our senses give us but an imperfect knowledge of things: effects themselves, if we knew them thoroughly, would give us but imperfect notions of wisdom and power; much less of his Being, in whom they reside. I am not speaking of any fanciful notion of seeing all things in God;* but only representing to you, how much an higher object to the understanding an infinite Being himself is, than the things which he has made: and this is no more than saying, that the Creator is superior to the works of his hands.

13   This may be illustrated by a low example. Suppose a machine, the sight of which would raise, and discoveries in its contrivance gratify, our curiosity: the real delight, in this case, would arise from its being the effect of skill and contrivance. The skill in the mind of the artificer would be an higher object, if we had any senses or ways to discern it. For, observe, the contemplation of that principle, faculty or power which

produced any effect, must be an higher exercise of the understanding, than the contemplation of the effect itself. The cause must be an higher object to the mind than the effect.

But whoever considers distinctly what the delight of knowledge is, will see reason   14
to be satisfied that it cannot be the chief good of man:* all this, as it is applicable, so it was mentioned with regard to the attribute of goodness. I say, goodness. Our being and all our enjoyments are the effects of it: just men bear its resemblance: but how little do we know of the original, of what it is in itself? Recall what was before observed concerning the affection to moral characters; which, in how low a degree soever, yet is plainly natural to man, and the most excellent part of his nature: suppose this improved, as it may be improved to any degree whatever, in the 'spirits of just men made perfect';[5] and then suppose that they had a real view of that 'righteousness, which is an everlasting righteousness';[6] of the conformity of the divine will to the *law of truth*, in which the moral attributes of God consist;* of that goodness in the Sovereign Mind, which gave birth to the universe: add, what will be true of all good men hereafter, a consciousness of having an interest in what they are contemplating; suppose them able to say, 'This God is our God for ever and ever':[7] would they be any longer to seek for what was their chief happiness, their final good? Could the utmost stretch of their capacities look further? Would not infinite perfect goodness be their very end, the last end and object of their affections; beyond which they could neither have, nor desire; beyond which they could not form a wish or thought?

Consider wherein that presence of a friend consists, which has often so strong an   15
effect, as wholly to possess the mind, and entirely suspend all other affections and regards; and which itself affords the highest satisfaction and enjoyment. He is within reach of the senses. Now, as our capacities of perception improve, we shall have, perhaps by some faculty entirely new, a perception of God's presence with us in a nearer and stricter way; since it is certain he is more intimately present with us than any thing else can be. Proof of the existence and presence of any being, is quite different from the immediate perception, the consciousness of it. What then will be the joy of heart, which his presence, and 'the light of his countenance',[8] who is the life of the universe, will inspire good men with, when they shall have a sensation, that he is the sustainer of their being, that they exist in him; when they shall feel his influence to cheer and enliven and support their frame, in a manner of which we have now no conception? He will be in a literal sense 'their strength and their portion for ever'.[9]

When we speak of things so much above our comprehension, as the employment   16
and happiness of a future state, doubtless it behoves us to speak with all modesty and distrust of ourselves. But the Scripture represents the happiness of that state under the notions of 'seeing God, seeing him as he is',[10] 'knowing as we are known', and 'seeing face to face'.[11] These words are not general or undetermined, but express a particular determinate happiness. And I will be bold to say, that nothing can account for, or come up to these expressions, but only this, that God himself will be an object to our faculties, that he himself will be our happiness; as distinguished from the

enjoyments of the present state, which seem to arise, not immediately from him, but from the objects he has adapted to give us delight.*

17   To conclude: let us suppose a person tired with care and sorrow, and the repetition of vain delights which fill up the round of life; sensible that every thing here below in its best estate is altogether vanity. Suppose him to feel that deficiency of human nature, before taken notice of; and to be convinced that God alone was the adequate supply to it. What could be more applicable to a good man, in this state of mind; or better express his present wants and distant hopes, his passage through this world as a progress towards a state of perfection, than the following passages in the devotions of the royal prophet? They are plainly in an higher and more proper sense applicable to this, than they could be to any thing else. 'I have seen an end of all perfection. Whom have I in heaven but thee? and there is none upon earth that I desire in comparison of thee. My flesh and my heart faileth: but God is the strength of my heart, and my portion for ever. Like as the hart desireth the water-brooks: so longeth my soul after thee, O God. My soul is athirst for God, yea, even for the living God: when shall I come to appear before him? How excellent is thy loving-kindness, O God! and the children of men shall put their trust under the shadow of thy wings. They shall be satisfied with the plenteousness of thy house: and thou shalt give them drink of thy pleasures, as out of the river. For with thee is the well of life: and in thy light shall we see light. Blessed is the man whom thou choosest, and receivest unto thee: he shall dwell in thy court, and shall be satisfied with the pleasures of thy house, even of thy holy temple. Blessed is the people, O Lord, that can rejoice in thee: they shall walk in the light of thy countenance. Their delight shall be daily in thy name, and in thy righteousness shall they make their boast. For thou art the glory of their strength: and in thy loving-kindness they shall be exalted. As for me, I will behold thy presence in righteousness: and when I awake up after thy likeness, I shall be satisfied with it. Thou shalt shew me the path of life; in thy presence is the fullness of joy, and at thy right hand there is pleasure for evermore.'[12]

Notes

1. *Job* ix.11.
2. *Ecclus.* xliii.30.
3. [*I Cor.* xiii.12.]
4. [*I John* iv.18.]
5. [*Heb.* xii.23.]
6. [*Ps.* cxix.142.]
7. [*Ps.* xlviii.14.]
8. [*Ps.* iv.6.]
9. [*Ps.* lxxiii.26.]
10. [*I John* iii.2.]
11. [*I Cor.* xiii.12.]
12. [*Ps.* cxix.96; lxxiii.25, 26; xlii.1, 2; xxxvi.7–9; lxv.4; lxxix.15, 16; xvii.15; xvi.11.]

Sermon 15

Upon the Ignorance of Man

When I applied mine heart to know wisdom, and to see the business that is done upon the earth: then I beheld all the work of God, that a man cannot find out the work that is done under the sun: because though a man labour to seek it out, yet he shall not find it; yea farther, though a wise man think to know it, yet shall he not be able to find it.

(Eccles. viii.16, 17)

The writings of Solomon are very much taken up with reflections upon human 1
nature and human life; to which he hath added, in this book, reflections upon the
constitution of things. And it is not improbable, that the little satisfaction, and the
great difficulties he met with in his researches into the general constitution of nature,
might be the occasion of his confining himself, so much as he hath done, to life and
conduct. However, upon that joint review he expresses great ignorance of the works
of God, and the method of his providence in the government of the world; great
labour and weariness in the search and observation he had employed himself about;
and great disappointment, pain, and even vexation of mind, upon that which he had
remarked of the appearances of things, and of what was going forward upon this
earth. This whole review and inspection, and the result of it, sorrow, perplexity, a
sense of his necessary ignorance, suggests various reflections to his mind. But,
notwithstanding all this ignorance and dissatisfaction, there is somewhat, upon
which he assuredly rests and depends; somewhat, which is the conclusion of the
whole matter, and the only concern of man. Following this his method and train of
reflection, let us consider,

I. The assertion of the text, the ignorance of man; that the wisest and most 2
knowing cannot comprehend the ways and works of God: and then,

II. What are the just consequences of this observation and knowledge of our own 3
ignorance, and the reflections which it leads us to.

I. The wisest and most knowing cannot comprehend the works of God, the 4
methods and designs of his providence in the creation and government of the world.

Creation is absolutely and entirely out of our depth, and beyond the extent of our 5
utmost reach. And yet it is as certain that God made the world, as it is certain that
effects must have a cause. It is indeed in general no more than effects, that the most

knowing are acquainted with: for as to causes, they are as entirely in the dark as the most ignorant. What are the laws by which matter acts upon matter, but certain effects; which some, having observed to be frequently repeated, have reduced to general rules? The real nature and essence of beings likewise is what we are altogether ignorant of. All these things are so entirely out of our reach, that we have not the least glimpse of them. And we know little more of ourselves, than we do of the world about us: how we were made, how our being is continued and preserved, what the faculties of our minds are, and upon what the power of exercising them depends.* 'I am fearfully and wonderfully made: marvellous are thy works, and that my soul knoweth right well.'[1] Our own nature, and the objects we are surrounded with, serve to raise our curiosity; but we are quite out of a condition of satisfying it. Every secret which is disclosed, every discovery which is made, every new effect which is brought to view, serves to convince us of numberless more which remain concealed, and which we had before no suspicion of. And what if we were acquainted with the whole creation, in the same way and as thoroughly as we are with any single object in it? What would all this natural knowledge amount to? It must be a low curiosity indeed which such superficial knowledge could satisfy. On the contrary, would it not serve to convince us of our ignorance still; and to raise our desire of knowing the nature of things themselves, the Author, the Cause, and the End of them?

6   As to the government of the world: though from consideration of the final causes which come within our knowledge; of characters, personal merit and demerit; of the favour and disapprobation, which respectively are due and belong to the righteous and the wicked, and which therefore must necessarily be in a mind which sees things as they really are; though, I say, from hence we may know somewhat concerning the designs of Providence in the government of the world, enough to enforce upon us religion and the practice of virtue: yet, since the monarchy of the universe is a dominion unlimited in extent, and everlasting in duration; the general system of it must necessarily be quite beyond our comprehension. And, since there appears such a subordination and reference of the several parts to each other, as to constitute it properly one administration or government; we cannot have a thorough knowledge of any part, without knowing the whole. This surely should convince us, that we are much less competent judges of the very small part which comes under our notice in this world, than we are apt to imagine. 'No heart can think upon these things worthily: and who is able to conceive his way? It is a tempest which no man can see: for the most part of his works are hid. Who can declare the works of his justice? for his covenant is afar off, and the trial of all things is in the end':[2] i.e. the dealings of God with the children of men are not yet completed, and cannot be judged of by that part which is before us. 'So that a man cannot say, This is worse than that: for in time they shall be well approved.'[3] 'Thy faithfulness, O Lord, reacheth unto the clouds: thy righteousness standeth like the strong mountains: thy judgement are like the great deep.'[4] 'He hath made every thing beautiful in his time: also he hath set the world in their heart; so that no man can find out the work that God maketh from the

beginning to the end.'[5] And thus St. Paul concludes a long argument upon the various dispensations of Providence: 'O the depth of the riches, both of the wisdom and knowledge of God! How unsearchable are his judgement, and his ways past finding out! For who hath known the mind of the Lord?'[6]

Thus the scheme of Providence, the ways and works of God, are too vast, of too large extent for our capacities. There is, as I may speak, such an expanse of power, and wisdom, and goodness, in the formation and government of the world, as is too much for us to take in or comprehend. Power, and wisdom, and goodness are manifest to us in all those works of God, which come within our view: but there are likewise infinite stores of each poured forth throughout the immensity of the creation; no part of which can be thoroughly understood, without taking in its reference and respect to the whole: and this is what we have not faculties for. **7**

And as the works of God, and his scheme of government, are above our capacities thoroughly to comprehend: so there possibly may be reasons which originally made it fit that many things should be concealed from us, which we have perhaps natural capacities of understanding; many things concerning the designs, methods and ends of divine providence in the government of the world. There is no manner of absurdity in supposing a veil on purpose drawn over some scenes of infinite power, wisdom, and goodness, the sight of which might some way or other strike us too strongly; or that better ends are designed and served by their being concealed, than could be by their being exposed to our knowledge. The Almighty may cast 'clouds and darkness round about him',[7] for reasons and purposes of which we have not the least glimpse or conception. **8**

However, it is surely reasonable, and what might have been expected, that creatures in some stage of their being, suppose in the infancy of it, should be placed in a state of discipline and improvement, where their patience and submission is to be tried by afflictions, where temptations are to be resisted, and difficulties gone through in the discharge of their duty. Now if the greatest pleasures and pains of the present life may be overcome and suspended, as they manifestly may, by hope and fear, and other passions and affections; then the evidence of religion, and the sense of the consequences of virtue and vice, might have been such, as entirely in all cases to prevail over those afflictions, difficulties and temptations; prevail over them so, as to render them absolutely none at all. But the very notion itself, now mentioned, of a state of discipline and improvement, necessarily excludes such sensible evidence and conviction of religion, and of the consequences of virtue and vice. Religion consists in submission and resignation to the divine will.* Our condition in this world is a school of exercise for this temper: and our ignorance, the shallowness of our reason, the temptations, difficulties, afflictions, which we are exposed to, all equally contribute to make it so. The general observation may be carried on; and whoever will attend to the thing will plainly see, that less sensible evidence, with less difficulty in practice, is the same, as more sensible evidence, with greater difficulty in practice. Therefore difficulties in speculation as much come into the notion of a state of discipline, as difficulties **9** in practice: and so the same reason or account is to be given of both. Thus, though it is indeed absurd to talk of the greater merit of assent, upon little or no evidence, than upon demonstration; yet the strict discharge of our duty, with less sensible evidence, does imply in it a better character, than the same diligence in the discharge of it, upon more sensible evidence. This fully accounts for and explains that assertion of our Saviour, 'Blessed are they that have not seen, and yet have believed';[8] have become Christians and obeyed the gospel, upon less sensible evidence, than that which Thomas, to whom he is speaking, insisted upon.*

10   But after all, the same account is to be given, why we were placed in these circumstances of ignorance, as why nature has not furnished us with wings; namely, that we were designed to be inhabitants of this earth. I am afraid we think too highly of ourselves; of our rank in the creation, and of what is due to us. What sphere of action, what business is assigned to man, that he has not capacities and knowledge fully equal to? It is manifest he has reason, and knowledge, and faculties superior to the business of the present world: faculties which appear superfluous, if we do not take in the respect which they have to somewhat further, and beyond it. If to acquire knowledge were our proper end, we should indeed be but poorly provided:* but if somewhat else be our business and duty, we may, notwithstanding our ignorance, be well enough furnished for it; and the observation of our ignorance may be of assistance to us in the discharge of it.

11   II. Let us then consider, what are the consequences of this knowledge and observation of our own ignorance, and the reflection it leads us to.

12   *First*, We may learn from it, with what temper of mind a man ought to inquire into the subject of religion; namely, with expectation of finding difficulties, and with a disposition to take up and rest satisfied with any evidence whatever, which is real.

13   He should beforehand expect things mysterious, and such as he will not be able thoroughly to comprehend, or go to the bottom of. To expect a distinct comprehensive view of the whole subject, clear of difficulties and objections, is to forget our nature and condition; neither of which admit of such knowledge, with respect to any science whatever. And to inquire with this expectation, is not to inquire as a man, but as one of another order of creatures.

14   Due sense of the general ignorance of man would also beget in us a disposition to take up and rest satisfied with any evidence whatever, which is real. I mention this as the contrary to a disposition, of which there are not wanting instances, to find fault with and reject evidence, because it is not such as was desired. If a man were to walk by twilight, must he not follow his eyes as much as if it were broad day and clear sunshine? Or if he were obliged to take a journey by night, would he not 'give heed to' any 'light shining in the darkness, till the day should break and the day-star arise?'[9] It would not be altogether unnatural for him to reflect how much better it were to have daylight; he might perhaps have great curiosity to see the country round about him; he might lament that the darkness concealed many extended prospects from his eyes, and wish for the sun to draw away the veil: but how ridiculous would it be, to

reject with scorn and disdain the guidance and direction which that lesser light might afford him, because it was not the sun itself? If the make and constitution of man, the circumstances he is placed in, or the reason of things affords the least hint or intimation, that virtue is the law he is born under; scepticism itself should lead him to the most strict and inviolable practice of it;* that he may not make the dreadful experiment, of leaving the course of life marked out for him by nature, whatever that nature be, and entering paths of his own, of which he can know neither the dangers nor the end. For though no danger be seen, yet darkness, ignorance and blindness are no manner of security.

Secondly, Our ignorance is the proper answer to many things, which are called **15** objections against religion; particularly, to those which arise from the appearances of evil and irregularity in the constitution of nature and the government of the world. In all other cases it is thought necessary to be thoroughly acquainted with the whole of a scheme, even one of so narrow a compass as those which are formed by men, in order to judge of the goodness or badness of it: and the most slight and superficial view of any human contrivance comes abundantly nearer to a thorough knowledge of it, than that part, which we know of the government of the world, does to the general scheme and system of it; to the whole set of laws by which it is governed. From our ignorance of the constitution of things, and the scheme of Providence in the government of the world; from the reference the several parts have to each other, and to the whole; and from our not being able to see the end and the whole; it follows, that however perfect things are, they must even necessarily appear to us otherwise, less perfect than they are.[10]

Thirdly, Since the constitution of nature, and the methods and designs of Provi- **16** dence in the government of the world, are above our comprehension, we should acquiesce in, and rest satisfied with our ignorance; turn our thoughts from that which is above and beyond us, and apply ourselves to that which is level to our capacities, and which is our real business and concern. Knowledge is not our proper happiness. Whoever will in the least attend to the thing will see, that it is the gaining, not the having of it, which is the entertainment of the mind. Indeed, if the proper happiness of man consisted in knowledge considered as a possession or treasure, men who are possessed of the largest share would have a very ill time of it; as they would be infinitely more sensible than others, of their poverty in this respect. Thus *he who increases knowledge would* eminently *increase sorrow*.[11] Men of deep research and curious inquiry should just be put in mind, not to mistake what they are doing. If their discoveries serve the cause of virtue and religion, in the way of proof, motive to practice, or assistance in it; or if they tend to render life less unhappy, and promote its satisfactions; then they are most usefully employed: but bringing things to light, alone and of itself, is of no manner of use, any otherwise than as an entertainment or diversion. Neither is this at all amiss, if it does not take up the time which should be employed in better work. But it is evident that there is another mark set up for us to aim at; another end appointed us to direct our lives to: an end, which the most knowing may fail of, and the most ignorant arrive at. 'The secret things belong unto the Lord our God; but those things which are revealed belong unto us, and to our children for ever, that we may do all the words of this law.'[12] Which reflection of Moses, put in general terms, is, that the only knowledge, which is of any avail to us, is that which teaches us our duty, or assists us in the discharge of it. The economy of the universe, the course of nature, almighty power exerted in the creation and government in the world, is out of our reach. What would be the consequence, if we could really get an insight into these things, is very uncertain; whether it would assist us in, or divert us from what we have to do in this present state. If then there be a sphere of knowledge, of contemplation and employment, level to our capacities, and of the utmost importance to us; we ought surely to apply ourselves with all diligence to this our proper business, and esteem every thing else nothing, nothing as to us, in comparison of it. Thus Job, discoursing of natural knowledge, how much it is above us, and of wisdom in general, says, 'God understandeth the way thereof, and he knoweth the place thereof. And unto man he said, Behold, the fear of the Lord, that is wisdom, and to depart from evil is understanding.'[13] Other orders of creatures may perhaps be let into the secret counsels of heaven; and have the designs and methods of Providence, in the creation and government of the world, communicated to them: but this does not belong to our rank or condition. 'The fear of the Lord', and 'to depart from evil', is the only wisdom which man should aspire after, as his work and business. The same is said, and with the same connection and context, in the conclusion of the book of Ecclesiastes. Our ignorance, and the little we can know of other things, affords a reason why we should not perplex ourselves about them: but no way invalidates that which is the 'conclusion of the whole matter, Fear God, and keep his commandments; for this is the whole concern of man.'[14] So that Socrates was not the first who endeavoured to draw men off from labouring after, and laying stress upon other knowledge, in comparison of that which related to morals.* Our province is virtue and religion, life and manners; the science of improving the temper, and making the heart better. This is the field assigned us to cultivate: how much it has lain neglected is indeed astonishing. Virtue is demonstrably the happiness of man: it consists in good actions, proceeding from a good principle, temper or heart. Overt acts are entirely in our power. What remains is, that we learn to 'keep our heart';[15] to govern and regulate our passions, mind, affections: that so we may be free from the impotencies of fear, envy, malice, covetousness, ambition; that we may be clear of these, considered as vices seated in the heart, considered as constituting a general wrong temper; from which general wrong frame of mind, all the mistaken pursuits, and far the greatest part of the unhappiness of life, proceed. He, who should find out one rule to assist us in this work, would deserve infinitely better of mankind, than all the improvers of other knowledge put together.

17   *Lastly*, Let us adore that infinite wisdom and power and goodness, which is above our comprehension. 'To whom hath the root of wisdom been revealed? Or who hath known her wise counsels? There is One wise and greatly to be feared; the Lord sitting

upon his throne. He created her, and saw her, and numbered her, and poured her out upon all his works.'[16] If It be thought a considerable thing, to be acquainted with a few, a very few, of the effects of infinite power and wisdom; the situation, bigness, and revolution of some of the heavenly bodies; what sentiments should our minds be filled with concerning him, who appointed to each its place and measure and sphere of motion, all which are kept with the most uniform constancy? 'Who stretched out the heavens, and telleth the number of the stars, and calleth them all by their names. Who laid the foundations of the earth, who comprehendeth the dust of it in a measure, and weigheth the mountains in scales, and the hills in a balance.'[17] And, when we have recounted all the appearances which come within our view, we must add, 'Lo, these are part of his ways; but how little a portion is heard of him?'[18] 'Canst thou by searching find out God? Canst thou find out the Almighty unto perfection? It is as high as heaven; what canst thou do? deeper than hell; what canst thou know?'[19]

The conclusion is, that in all lowliness of mind we set lightly by ourselves: that we   **18** form our temper to an implicit submission to the Divine Majesty; beget within ourselves an absolute resignation to all the methods of his providence, in his dealings with the children of men: that, in the deepest humility of our souls, we prostrate ourselves before him, and join in that celestial song; 'Great and marvellous are thy works, Lord God Almighty; just and true are thy ways, thou King of saints: who shall not fear thee, O Lord, and glorify thy name?'[20]

Notes

1. [*Ps.* cxxxix.14.]
2. [*Ecclus.* xvi.20–2.]
3. [*Ecclus.* xxxix.34.]
4. [*Ps.* xxxvi.5, 6.]
5. [*Ecclus.* iii.11.]
6. [*Rom.* xi.33, 34.]
7. [*Ps.* xcvii.2.]
8. *John* xx.29.
9. [*2 Pet.* i.19.]
10. Suppose some very *complicated piece of work*, some *system* or *constitution*, formed for some *general end*, to which each of the *parts* had a *reference*. The perfection or justness of this work or constitution would consist in the reference and respect, which the several parts have to the general design. This reference of parts to the general design may be infinitely various, both in degree and kind. Thus one part may only contribute and be subservient to another; this to a third; and so on through a long series, the last part of which alone may contribute immediately and directly to the general design. Or a part may have this distant reference to the general design, and may also contribute immediately to it. For instance: if the general design or end, for which the complicated frame of nature was brought into being, is happiness; whatever affords present satisfaction, and likewise tends to carry on the course of things, hath this double respect to the general design. Now

suppose a spectator of that work or constitution was in a great measure ignorant of such various reference to the general end, whatever that end be; and that, upon a very slight and partial view which he had of the work, several things appeared to his eye as disproportionate and wrong; others, just and beautiful: what would he gather from these appearances? He would immediately conclude there was a probability, if he could see the whole reference of the parts appearing wrong to the general design, that this would destroy the appearance of wrongness and disproportion: but there is no probability, that the reference would destroy the particular right appearances, though that reference might shew the things already appearing just, to be so likewise in an higher degree or another manner. There is a probability, that the right appearances were intended: there is no probability, that the wrong appearances were. We cannot suspect irregularity and disorder to be designed. The pillars of a building appear beautiful; but their being likewise its support does not destroy that beauty: there still remains a reason to believe that the architect intended the beautiful appearance, after we have found out the reference, support. It would be reasonable for a man of himself to think thus, upon the first piece of architecture he ever saw.*

11. [Eccles. i.18.]*
12. [Deut. xxix.29.]
13. [Job xxviii.23, 28.]
14. [Eccles. xii.13.]*
15. [Prov. iv.23.]*
16. [Ecclus. i.6, 8, 9.]
17. [Isa. xl.12, 22, 26.]
18. [Job xxvi.14.]
19. [Job xi.7, 8.]
20. [Rev. xv.3, 4.]

A Dissertation of the Nature of Virtue

That which renders beings capable of moral government, is their having a moral nature, and moral faculties of perception and of action. Brute creatures are impressed and actuated by various instincts and propensions: so also are we. But additional to this, we have a capacity of reflecting upon actions and characters, and making them an object to our thought: and on doing this, we naturally and unavoidably approve some actions, under the peculiar view of their being virtuous and of good-desert; and disapprove others, as vicious and of ill-desert. That we have this moral approving and disapproving[1] faculty, is certain from our experiencing it in ourselves, and recognizing it in each other. It appears from our exercising it unavoidably, in the approbation and disapprobation even of feigned characters: from the words, right and wrong, odious and amiable, base and worthy, with many others of like signification in all languages, applied to actions and characters: from the many written systems of morals which suppose it; since it cannot be imagined, that all these authors, throughout all these treatises, had absolutely no meaning at all to their words, or a meaning merely chimerical: from our natural sense of gratitude, which implies a distinction between merely being the instrument of good, and intending it: from the like distinction, every one makes, between injury and mere harm, which, Hobbes says,* is peculiar to mankind; and between injury and just punishment, a distinction plainly natural, prior to the consideration of human laws. It is manifest great part of common language, and of common behaviour over the world, is formed upon supposition of such a moral faculty; whether called conscience, moral reason, moral sense, or divine reason; whether considered as a sentiment of the understanding, or as a perception of the heart, or, which seems the truth, as including both.* Nor is it at all doubtful in the general, what course of action this faculty, or practical discerning power within us, approves, and what it disapproves. For, as much as it has been disputed wherein virtue consists, or whatever ground for doubt there may be about particulars; yet, in general, there is in reality an universally acknowledged standard of it. It is that, which all ages and all countries have made profession of in public: it is that, which every man you meet, puts on the show of: it is that, which the primary and fundamental laws of all civil constitutions, over the face of the earth, make it their business and endeavour to enforce the practice of upon mankind: namely, justice, veracity, and regard to common good. It being manifest then, in general, that we have such a faculty or discernment as this; it may be of use to remark some things, more distinctly, concerning it.

2   *First*, It ought to be observed, that the object of this faculty is actions,[2] compre-hending under that name active or practical principles: those principles from which men would act, if occasions and circumstances gave them power; and which, when fixed and habitual in any person, we call, his character. It does not appear, that brutes have the least reflex sense of actions, as distinguished from events: or that will and design, which constitute the very nature of actions as such, are at all an object to their perception. But to ours they are: and they are the object, and the only one, of the approving and disapproving faculty. Acting, conduct, behaviour, abstracted from all regard to what is, in fact and event, the consequence of it, is itself the natural object of the moral discernment; as speculative truth and falsehood is, of speculative reason. Intention of such and such consequences, indeed, is always included; for it is part of the action itself: but though the intended good or bad consequences do not follow, we have exactly the same sense of the action as if they did. In like manner we think well or ill of characters, abstracted from all consideration of the good or the evil, which persons of such characters have it actually in their power to do. We never, in the moral way, applaud or blame either ourselves or others, for what we enjoy or what we suffer, or for having impressions made upon us which we consider as altogether out of our power: but only for what we do, or would have done, had it been in our power; or for what we leave undone which we might have done, or would have left undone though we could have done it.

3   *Secondly*, Our sense or discernment of actions as morally good or evil, implies in it a sense or discernment of them as of good or ill desert. It may be difficult to explain this perception, so as to answer all the questions which may be asked concerning it: but every one speaks of such and such actions as deserving punishment; and it is not, I suppose, pretended that they have absolutely no meaning at all to the expression. Now the meaning plainly is not, that we conceive it for the good of society, that the doer of such actions should be made to suffer. For if unhappily it were resolved, that a man who, by some innocent action, was infected with the plague, should be left to perish, lest, by other people's coming near him, the infection should spread; no one would say he deserved this treatment. Innocence and ill-desert are inconsistent ideas.* Ill-desert always supposes guilt: and if one be no part of the other, yet they are evidently and naturally connected in our mind. The sight of a man in misery raises our compassion towards him; and, if this misery be inflicted on him by another, our indignation against the author of it. But when we are informed, that the sufferer is a villain, and is punished only for his treachery or cruelty; our compassion exceedingly lessens, and, in many instances, our indignation wholly subsides. Now what produces this effect, is the conception of that in the sufferer, which we call ill-desert. Upon considering then, or viewing together, our notion of vice and that of misery, there results a third, that of ill-desert. And thus there is in human creatures an association

of the two ideas, natural and moral evil, wickedness and punishment. If this association were merely artificial or accidental, it were nothing: but being most unquestionably natural, it greatly concerns us to attend to it, instead of endeavouring to explain it away.

It may be observed further, concerning our perception of good and of ill desert,   4
that the former is very weak with respect to common instances of virtue. One reason of which may be, that it does not appear to a spectator, how far such instances of virtue proceed from a virtuous principle, or in what degree this principle is prevalent: since a very weak regard to virtue may be sufficient to make men act well in many common instances. And on the other hand, our perception of ill-desert in vicious actions lessens, in proportion to the temptations men are thought to have had to such vices. For, vice in human creatures consisting chiefly in the absence or want of the virtuous principle; though a man be overcome, suppose, by tortures, it does not from thence appear, to what degree the virtuous principle was wanting. All that appears is, that he had it not in such a degree, as to prevail over the temptation: but possibly he had it in a degree, which would have rendered him proof against common temptations.

Thirdly, Our perception of vice and ill-desert arises from, and is the result of, a   5
comparison of actions with the nature and capacities of the agent.* For the mere neglect of doing what we ought to do, would, in many cases, be determined by all men to be in the highest degree vicious. And this determination must arise from such comparison, and be the result of it; because such neglect would not be vicious in creatures of other natures and capacities, as brutes. And it is the same also with respect to positive vices, or such as consist in doing what we ought not. For, every one has a different sense of harm done by an idiot, madman or child, and by one of mature and common understanding; though the action of both, including the intention which is part of the action, be the same: as it may be, since idiots and madmen, as well as children, are capable not only of doing mischief, but also of intending it. Now this difference must arise from somewhat discerned in the nature or capacities of one, which renders the action vicious; and the want of which in the other, renders the same action innocent or less vicious: and this plainly supposes a comparison, whether reflected upon or not, between the action and capacities of the agent, previous to our determining an action to be vicious. And hence arises a proper application of the epithets, incongruous, unsuitable, disproportionate, unfit, to actions which our moral faculty determines to be vicious.*

Fourthly, It deserves to be considered, whether men are more at liberty, in point of   6
morals, to make themselves miserable without reason, than to make other people so: or dissolutely to neglect their own greater good, for the sake of a present lesser gratification, than they are to neglect the good of others, whom nature has committed to their care. It should seem, that a due concern about our own interest or happiness, and a reasonable endeavour to secure and promote it, which is, I think, very much the meaning of the word, prudence, in our language; it should seem, that this is

virtue, and the contrary behaviour faulty and blamable: since, in the calmest way of reflection, we approve of the first, and condemn the other conduct, both in ourselves and others.* This approbation and disapprobation are altogether different from mere desire of our own or of their happiness, and from sorrow upon missing it. For the object or occasion of this last kind of perception, is satisfaction, or uneasiness: whereas the object of the first is active behaviour. In one case, what our thoughts fix upon, is our condition: in the other, our conduct. It is true indeed, that nature has not given us so sensible a disapprobation of imprudence and folly, either in *ourselves* or *others*, as of falsehood, injustice and cruelty: I suppose, because that constant habitual sense of private interest and good, which we always carry about with us, renders such sensible disapprobation less necessary, less wanting, to keep us from imprudently neglecting our own happiness, and foolishly injuring ourselves, than it is necessary and wanting to keep us from injuring others, to whose good we cannot have so strong and constant a regard: and also because imprudence and folly, appearing to bring its own punishment more immediately and constantly than injurious behaviour, it less needs the additional punishment, which would be inflicted upon it by others, had they the same sensible indignation against it, as against injustice and fraud and cruelty. Besides, unhappiness being in itself the natural object of compassion; the unhappiness which people bring upon themselves, though it be wilfully, excites in us some pity for them: and this of course lessens our displeasure against them. But still it is matter of experience, that we are formed so, as to reflect very severely upon the greater instances of imprudent neglect and foolish rashness, both in ourselves and others. In instances of this kind, men often say of themselves with remorse, and of others with some indignation, that they deserved to suffer such calamities, because they brought them upon themselves, and would not take warning. Particularly when persons come to poverty and distress by a long course of extravagance, and after frequent admonitions, though without falsehood or injustice; we plainly do not regard such people as alike objects of compassion with those, who are brought into the same condition by unavoidable accidents. From these things it appears, that prudence is a species of virtue, and folly of vice: meaning by *folly*, somewhat quite different from mere incapacity; a thoughtless want of that regard and attention to our own happiness, which we had capacity for. And this the word properly includes; and, as it seems, in its usual acceptation: for we scarcely apply it to brute creatures.

7   However, if any person be disposed to dispute the matter, I shall very willingly give him up the words virtue and vice, as not applicable to prudence and folly: but must beg leave to insist, that the faculty within us, which is the judge of actions, approves of prudent actions, and disapproves imprudent ones; I say prudent and imprudent *actions* as such, and considered distinctly from the happiness or misery which they occasion.* And by the way, this observation may help to determine, what justness there is in that objection against religion, that it teaches us to be interested and selfish.

Fifthly, Without inquiring how far, and in what sense, virtue is resolvable into 8 benevolence, and vice into the want of it; it may be proper to observe, that benevolence and the want of it, singly considered, are in no sort the whole of virtue and vice.* For if this were the case, in the review of one's own character or that of others, our moral understanding and moral sense would be indifferent to every thing, but the degrees in which benevolence prevailed, and the degrees in which it was wanting. That is, we should neither approve of benevolence to some persons rather than to others, nor disapprove injustice and falsehood upon any other account, than merely as an overbalance of happiness was foreseen likely to be produced by the first, and of misery by the second. But now on the contrary, suppose two men competitors for any thing whatever, which would be of equal advantage to each of them: though nothing indeed would be more impertinent, than for a stranger to busy himself to get one of them preferred to the other; yet such endeavour would be virtue, in behalf of a friend or benefactor, abstracted from all consideration of distant consequences:* as that examples of gratitude, and the cultivation of friendship, would be of general good to the world. Again, suppose one man should, by fraud or violence, take from another the fruit of his labour, with intent to give it to a third, who, he thought, would have as much pleasure from it, as would balance the pleasure which the first possessor would have had in the enjoyment, and his vexation in the loss of it; suppose also that no bad consequences would follow: yet such an action would surely be vicious. Nay further, were treachery, violence and injustice, no otherwise vicious, than as foreseen likely to produce an overbalance of misery to society; then, if in any case a man could procure to himself as great advantage by an act of injustice,* as the whole foreseen inconvenience, likely to be brought upon others by it, would amount to; such a piece of injustice would not be faulty or vicious at all: because it would be no more than, in any other case, for a man to prefer his own satisfaction to another's in equal degrees. The fact then appears to be, that we are constituted so, as to condemn falsehood, unprovoked violence, injustice, and to approve of benevolence to some preferably to others, abstracted from all consideration, which conduct is likeliest to produce an overbalance of happiness or misery. And therefore, were the Author of Nature to propose nothing to himself as an end but the production of happiness, were his moral character merely that of benevolence; yet ours is not so. Upon that supposition indeed, the only reason of his giving us the above-mentioned approbation of benevolence to some persons rather than others, and disapprobation of falsehood, unprovoked violence, and injustice, must be, that he foresaw, this constitution of our nature would produce more happiness, than forming us with a temper of mere general benevolence.* But still, since this is our constitution; falsehood, violence, injustice, must be vice in us, and benevolence to some preferably to others, virtue; abstracted from all consideration of the overbalance of evil or good, which they may appear likely to produce.

Now if human creatures are endued with such a moral nature as we have been 9 explaining, or with a moral faculty, the natural object of which is actions: moral government must consist, in rendering them happy and unhappy, in rewarding and punishing them, as they follow, neglect, or depart from, the moral rule of action interwoven in their nature, or suggested and enforced by this moral faculty;[3] in rewarding and punishing them upon account of their so doing.

10   I am not sensible, that I have, in this fifth observation, contradicted what any author designed to assert. But some of great and distinguished merit,* have, I think, expressed themselves in a manner, which may occasion some danger, to careless readers, of imagining the whole of virtue to consist in singly aiming, according to the best of their judgement, at promoting the happiness of mankind in the present state; and the whole of vice, in doing what they foresee, or might foresee, is likely to produce an overbalance of unhappiness in it: than which mistakes, none can be conceived more terrible. For it is certain, that some of the most shocking instances of injustice, adultery, murder, perjury, and even of persecution, may, in many supposable cases, not have the appearance of being likely to produce an overbalance of misery in the present state; perhaps sometimes may have the contrary appearance. For this reflection might easily be carried on, but I forbear—the happiness of the world is the concern of him, who is the Lord and the Proprietor of it: nor do we know what we are about, when we endeavour to promote the good of mankind in any ways, but those which he has directed; that is indeed in all ways, not contrary to veracity and justice. I speak thus upon supposition of persons really endeavouring, in some sort, to do good without regard to these. But the truth seems to be, that such supposed endeavours proceed, almost always, from ambition, the spirit of party, or some indirect principle, concealed perhaps in great measure from persons themselves. And though it is our business and our duty to endeavour, within the bounds of veracity and justice, to contribute to the ease, convenience, and even cheerfulness and diversion of our fellow-creatures: yet from our short views, it is greatly uncertain, whether this endeavour will in particular instances, produce an overbalance of happiness upon the whole; since so many and distant things must come into the account. And that which makes it our duty, is, that there is some appearance that it will, and no positive appearance sufficient to balance this, on the contrary side; and also, that such benevolent endeavour is a cultivation of that most excellent of all virtuous principles, the active principle of benevolence.

11   However, though veracity, as well as justice, is to be our rule of life; it must be added, otherwise a snare will be laid in the way of some plain men, that the use of common forms of speech generally understood, cannot be falsehood; and, in general, that there can be no designed falsehood without designing to deceive. It must likewise be observed, that in numberless cases, a man may be under the strictest obligations to what he foresees will deceive, without his intending it. For it is impossible not to foresee, that the words and actions of men in different ranks and employments, and of different educations, will perpetually be mistaken by each other: and it cannot but be so, whilst they will judge with the utmost carelessness, as they daily do, of what

they are not, perhaps, enough informed to be competent judges of, even though they considered it with great attention.

Notes

1. This way of speaking is taken from Epictetus (Arr. Epict. L. I. c. 1.),* and is made use of as seeming the most full, and least liable to cavil. And the moral faculty may be understood to have these two epithets, δοκιμαστική and ἀποδοκιμαστική, upon a double account: because, upon a survey of actions, whether before or after they are done, it determines them to be good or evil; and also because it determines itself to be the guide of action and of life, in contradistinction from all other faculties, or natural principles of action: in the very same manner, as speculative reason *directly* and naturally judges of speculative truth and false-hood; and, at the same time, is attended with a consciousness upon *reflection*, that the natural right to judge of them belongs to it.
2. Οὐδὲ ἡ ἀρετὴ καὶ κακία—ἐν πείσει ἀλλὰ ἐνεργεία. M. Anton. L. 9. 16. Virtutis laus omnis in actione consistit. Cic. Off. l. i. c. 6.*
3. A I. vi. 14.

A Sermon Preached Before the House of Lords

in the *Abbey Church* of *Westminster*, on Friday, January 30, 1740–41. Being the day appointed to be observed as the day of the Martyrdom of King Charles I.*

And not using your liberty for a cloak of maliciousness, but as the servants of God.

(*I Peter* ii.16)

1   An history so full of important and interesting events as that which this day recalls annually to our thoughts, cannot but afford them very different subjects for their most serious and useful employment. But there seems none which it more naturally leads us to consider than that of hypocrisy, as it sets before us so many examples of it; or which will yield us more practical instruction, as these examples so forcibly admonish us, not only to be upon our guard against the pernicious effects of this vice in others, but also to watch over our own hearts, against every thing of the like kind in ourselves: for hypocrisy, in the moral and religious consideration of things, is of much larger extent than every one may imagine.

2   In common language, which is formed upon the common intercourses amongst men, hypocrisy signifies little more than their pretending what they really do not mean, in order to delude one another. But in Scripture, which treats chiefly of our behaviour towards God and our own consciences, it signifies not only the endeavour to delude our fellow-creatures, but likewise insincerity towards him, and towards ourselves. And therefore, according to the whole analogy of Scripture language,[1] 'to use liberty as a cloak of maliciousness', must be understood to mean, not only endeavouring to impose upon others, by indulging wayward passions, or carrying on indirect designs, under pretences of it; but also excusing and palliating such things to ourselves; serving ourselves of such pretences to quiet our own minds in any thing which is wrong.

Liberty in the writings of the New Testament, for the most part, signifies, being delivered from the bondage of the ceremonial law; or of sin and the devil, which St. Paul calls 'the glorious liberty of the children of God'.[2] This last is a progressive state: and the perfection of it, whether attainable in this world or not, consists in that 'perfect love',[3] which St. John speaks of; and which, as it implies an entire coincidence of our wills with the will of God, must be a state of the most absolute freedom, in the most literal and proper sense. But whatever St. Peter distinctly meant by this word, *liberty*, the text gives occasion to consider any kind of it, which is liable to the abuse he here warns us against. However, it appears that he meant to comprehend that liberty, were it more or less, which they to whom he was writing enjoyed under civil government: for of civil government he is speaking just before and afterwards: 'Submit yourselves to every ordinance of man for the Lord's sake: whether it be to the king, as supreme; or unto governors, as unto them that are sent by him. For so is the will of God, that with well-doing', of which dutiful behaviour towards authority is a very material instance, 'ye may put to silence the ignorance of foolish men':[4] *as free*, perhaps in distinction from the servile state, of which he speaks afterwards, 'and not using your liberty for a cloak of maliciousness',[5] of anything wrong, for so the word signifies; and therefore comprehends petulance, affectation of popularity, with any other like frivolous turn of mind, as well as the more hateful and dangerous passions, such as malice, or ambition; for all of which *liberty* may equally be 'used as a cloak'. The apostle adds, 'but as the servants of God': *as free—but as his servants*, who requires dutiful submission to 'every ordinance of man', to magistracy; and to whom we are accountable for our manner of using the liberty we enjoy under it; as well as for all other parts of our behaviour. 'Not using your liberty as a cloak of maliciousness, but as the servants of God'.

Here are three things offered to our consideration:

First, A general supposition, that what is wrong cannot be avowed in its proper colours, but stands in need of some *cloak* to be thrown over it: *Secondly*, A particular one, that there is danger, some singular danger, of liberty's being made use of for this purpose: *Lastly*, An admonition not to make this ill use of our liberty, *but* to use it 'as the servants of God.'

I. Here is a general supposition, that what is wrong cannot be avowed in its proper colours, but stands in need of some *cloak* to be thrown over it. God has constituted our nature, and the nature of society after such a manner, that, generally speaking, men cannot encourage or support themselves in wickedness upon the foot of there being no difference between right and wrong, or by a direct avowal of wrong; but by disguising it, and endeavouring to spread over it some colours of right. And they do this in every capacity and every respect, in which there is a right or a wrong. They do it, not only as social creatures under civil government, but also as moral agents under the government of God; in one case to make a proper figure in the world, and delude their fellow-creatures; in the other to keep peace within themselves, and delude their own consciences. And the delusion in both cases being voluntary,* is, in Scripture, called by one name, and spoken against in the same manner: though doubtless they are much more explicit with themselves, and more distinctly conscious of what they are about, in one case than in the other.

7   The fundamental laws of all governments are virtuous ones, prohibiting treachery, injustice, cruelty: and the law of reputation enforces those civil laws, by rendering these vices everywhere infamous, and the contrary virtues honourable and of good report. Thus far the constitution of society is visibly moral: and hence it is, that men cannot live in it without taking care to cover those vices when they have them, and make some profession of the opposite virtues, fidelity, justice, kind regard to others when they have them not: but especially is this necessary in order to disguise and colour over indirect purposes, which require the concurrence of several persons.

8   Now all false pretences of this kind are to be called hypocritical, as being contrary to simplicity; though not always designed, properly speaking, to beget a false belief.* For it is to be observed, that they are often made without any formal intention to have them believed, or to have it thought that there is any reality under these pretences. Many examples occur of verbal professions of fidelity, justice, public regards, in cases where there could be no imagination of their being believed. And what other account can be given of these merely verbal professions, but that they were thought the proper language for the public ear; and made in business, for the very same kind of reasons as civility is kept up in conversation?

9   These false professions of virtue, which men have, in all ages, found it necessary to make their appearance with abroad, must have been originally taken up in order to deceive in the proper sense: then they became habitual, and often intended merely by way of form: yet often still, to serve their original purpose of deceiving.

10   There is doubtless amongst mankind a great deal of this hypocrisy towards each other: but not so much as may sometimes be supposed. For part which has, at first sight, this appearance, is in reality that other hypocrisy before mentioned; that self-deceit, of which the Scripture so remarkably takes notice. There are indeed persons who live 'without God in the world':[6] and some appear so hardened as to keep no measures with themselves. But as very ill men may have a real and strong sense of virtue and religion, in proportion as this is the case with any, they cannot be easy within themselves but by deluding their consciences. And though they should, in great measure, get over their religion, yet this will not do. For as long as they carry about with them any such sense of things, as makes them condemn what is wrong in others, they could not but condemn the same in themselves, and dislike and be disgusted with their own character and conduct, if they would consider them distinctly, and in a full light. But this sometimes they carelessly neglect to do, and sometimes carefully avoid doing. And as 'the integrity of the upright guides him',[7] guides even a man's judgement; so wickedness may distort it to such a degree, as that he may 'call evil good, and good evil; put darkness for light, and light for darkness';[8] and 'think wickedly, that God is such an one as himself'.[9] Even the better sort of men are, in some degree, liable to disguise and palliate their failings to themselves: but

perhaps there are few men who go on calmly in a course of very bad things, without somewhat of the kind now described in a very high degree. They try appearances upon themselves as well as upon the world, and with at least as much success; and choose to manage so as to make their own minds easy with their faults, which can scarce be without management, rather than to mend them.*

But whether from men's deluding themselves, or from their intending to delude   11 the world, it is evident scarce anything wrong in public has ever been accomplished, or even attempted, but under false colours: either by pretending one thing, which was right, to be designed, when it was really another thing, which was wrong; or if that which was wrong was avowed, by endeavouring to give it some appearance of right. For tyranny, and faction so friendly to it, and which is indeed tyranny out of power, and unjust wars, and persecution, by which the earth has been laid waste; all this has all along been carried on with pretences of truth, right, general good. So it is, men cannot find in their heart to join in such things, without such honest words to be the bond of the union, though they know among themselves, that they are only words, and often though they know, that everybody else knows it too.

These observations might be exemplified by numerous instances in the history   12 which led to them: and without them it is impossible to understand in any sort the general character of the chief actors in it, who were engaged in the black design of subverting the constitution of their country. This they completed with the most enormous act of mere power, in defiance of all laws of God and man, and in express contradiction to the real design and public votes of that assembly, whose commission, they professed, was their only warrant for anything they did throughout the whole rebellion. Yet with unheard-of hypocrisy towards men, towards God and their own consciences, for without such a complication of it their conduct is inexplicable; even this action, which so little admitted of any cloak, was, we know, contrived and carried into execution, under pretences of authority, religion, liberty, and by profaning the forms of justice in an arraignment and trial, like to what is used in regular legal procedures. No age indeed can shew an example of hypocrisy parallel to this. But the history of all ages, and all countries will shew, what has been really going forward over the face of the earth, to be very different from what has been always pretended; and that virtue has been everywhere professed much more than it has been any where practised: nor could society, from the very nature of its constitution, subsist without some general public profession of it. Thus the face, and appearance which the world has in all times put on, for the ease and ornament of life, and in pursuit of further ends, is the justest satire upon what has in all times been carrying on under it: and ill men are destined, by the condition of their being as social creatures, always to bear about with them, and, in different degrees, to profess, that law of virtue, by which they shall finally be judged and condemned.

II. As fair pretences, of one sort or other, have thus always been made use of by   13 mankind to colour over indirect and wrong designs from the world, and to palliate and excuse them to their own minds; liberty, in common with all other good things, is liable to be made this use of, and is also liable to it in a way more peculiar to itself: which was the second thing to be considered.

14   In the history which this day refers us to, we find our constitution, in Church and State, destroyed under pretences, not only of religion, but of securing liberty, and carrying it to a greater height. The destruction of the former was with zeal of such a kind, as would not have been warrantable, though it had been employed in the destruction of heathenism. And the confusions, the persecuting spirit, and incredible fanaticism, which grew up upon its ruins, cannot but teach sober-minded men to reverence so mild and reasonable an establishment, now it is restored; for the preservation of Christianity and keeping up a sense of it amongst us, and for the instruction and guide of the ignorant; nay were it only for guarding religion from such extravagancies: especially as these important purposes are served by it without bearing hard in the least upon any.

15   And the concurrent course of things, which brought on the ruin of our civil constitution, and what followed upon it, are no less instructive. The opposition, by legal and parliamentary methods, to prerogatives unknown to the constitution, was doubtless formed upon the justest fears in behalf of it. But new distrusts arose: new causes were given for them: these were most unreasonably aggravated. The better part gradually gave way to the more violent: and the better part themselves seem to have insisted upon impracticable securities against that one danger to liberty, of which they had too great cause to be apprehensive; and wonderfully overlooked all other dangers to it, which yet were, and ever will be many and great. Thus they joined in the current measures, till they were utterly unable to stop the mischiefs, to which, with too much distrust on one side, and too little on the other, they had contributed. Never was a more remarkable example of the Wise Man's observation, that 'the beginning of strife is as when one letteth out water'.[10]* For this opposition, thus begun, surely without intent of proceeding to violence; yet as it went on, like an overflowing stream in its progress, it collected all sorts of impurities, and grew more outrageous as it grew more corrupted; till at length it bore down everything good before it. This naturally brought on arbitrary power in one shape, which was odious to every body, and which could not be accommodated to the forms of our constitution; and put us in the utmost danger of having it entailed upon us under another, which might. For at the king's return, such was the just indignation of the public at what it had seen, and fear of feeling again what it had felt, from the popular side; such the depression and compliance, not only of the more guilty, but also of those, who with better meaning had gone on with them; and a great deal too far many of this character had gone; and such the undistinguishing distrust the people had of them all, that the chief security of our liberties seems to have been, their not being attempted at that time.

16   But though persons contributed to all this mischief and danger with different degrees of guilt, none could contribute to them with innocence, who at all knew what they were about. Indeed the destruction of a free constitution of government, though

men see or fancy many defects in it, and whatever they design or pretend, ought not to be thought of without horror. For the design is in itself unjust, since it is romantic to suppose it legal: it cannot be prosecuted without the most wicked means: nor accomplished but with the present ruin of liberty, religious as well as civil; for it must be the ruin of its present security. Whereas the restoration of it must depend upon a thousand future contingencies, the integrity, understanding, power of the persons, into whose hands anarchy and confusion should throw things: and who they will be, the history before us may surely serve to shew, no human foresight can determine; even though such a terrible crisis were to happen in an age, not distinguished for the want of principle and public spirit, and when nothing particular were to be apprehended from abroad. It would be partiality to say, that no constitution of government can possibly be imagined more perfect than our own. And ingenuous youth may be warmed with the idea of one, against which nothing can be objected. But it is the strongest objection against attempting to put in practice the most perfect theory, that it is impracticable, or too dangerous to be attempted. And whoever will thoroughly consider, in what degree mankind are really influenced by reason, and in what degree by custom, may, I think, be convinced, that the state of human affairs does not even admit of an equivalent, for the mischief of setting things afloat; and the danger of parting with those securities of liberty, which arise from regulations of long prescription and ancient usage: especially at a time when the directors are so very numerous, and the obedient so few. Reasonable men therefore will look upon the general plan of our constitution, transmitted down to us by our ancestors, as sacred; and content themselves with calmly doing what their station requires, towards rectifying the particular things which they think amiss, and supplying the particular things which they think deficient in it, so far as is practicable without endangering the whole.*

But liberty is in many other dangers from itself besides those which arise from formed designs of destroying it, under hypocritical pretences, or romantic schemes of restoring it upon a more perfect plan. It is particularly liable to become excessive, and to degenerate insensibly into licentiousness; in the same manner as liberality, for example, is apt to degenerate into extravagance. And as men cloak their extravagance to themselves under the notion of liberality, and to the world under the name of it, so licentiousness passes under the name and notion of liberty. Now it is to be observed, that there is, in some respects or other, a very peculiar contrariety between those vices which consist in excess, and the virtues of which they are said to be the excess, and the resemblance, and whose names they affect to bear; the excess of any thing being always to its hurt, and tending to its destruction. In this manner licentiousness is, in its very nature, a present infringement upon liberty, and dangerous to it for the future.* Yet it is treated by many persons with peculiar indulgence under this very notion, as being an excess of liberty. And an excess of liberty it is to the licentious themselves: but what is it to those who suffer by them, and who do not think, that amends is at all made them by having it left in their power to retaliate safely? When by popular insurrections, or defamatory libels, or in any like way, the needy and the

17

turbulent securely injure quiet people in their fortune or good name, so far quiet people are no more free than if a single tyrant used them thus. A particular man may be licentious without being less free: but a community cannot; since the licentiousness of one will unavoidably break in upon the liberty of another. Civil liberty, the liberty of a community, is a severe and a restrained thing; implies in the notion of it, authority, settled subordinations, subjection and obedience; and is altogether as much hurt by too little of this kind as by too much of it. And the love of liberty, when it is indeed the love of liberty, which carries us to withstand tyranny, will as much carry us to reverence authority, and support it; for this most obvious reason, that one is as necessary to the very being of liberty, as the other is destructive of it. And therefore the love of liberty, which does not produce this effect; the love of liberty, which is not a real principle of dutiful behaviour towards authority; is as hypocritical, as the religion which is not productive of a good life. Licentiousness is in truth, such an excess of liberty as is of the same nature with tyranny. For what is the difference between them, but that one is lawless power exercised under pretence of authority, or by persons invested with it; the other lawless power exercised under pretence of liberty, or without any pretence at all? A people then must always be less free in proportion as they are more licentious; licentiousness being, not only different from liberty, but directly contrary to it; a direct breach upon it.

18   It is moreover of a growing nature; and of speedy growth too; and, with the culture which it has amongst us, needs no great length of time to get to such an height as no legal government will be able to restrain, or subsist under: which is the condition the historian describes in saying, they could neither bear their vices, nor the remedies of them.[11] I said legal government: for, in the present state of the world, there is no danger of our becoming savages. Had licentiousness finished its work, and destroyed our constitution, power would not be wanting, from one quarter or another, sufficient to subdue us, and keep us in subjection. But government, as distinguished from mere power, free government, necessarily implies reverence in the subjects of it, for authority, or power regulated by laws; and an habit of submission to the subordinations in civil life, throughout its several ranks: nor is a people capable of liberty without somewhat of this kind. But it must be observed, and less surely cannot be observed, this reverence and submission will at best be very precarious, if it be not founded upon a sense of authority being God's ordinance, and the subordinations in life a providential appointment of things. Now let it be considered, for surely it is not duly considered, what is really the short amount of those representations, which persons of superior rank give, and encourage to be given of each other, and which are spread over the nation? Is it not somewhat, in itself, and in its circumstances, beyond any thing in any other age or country of the world? And what effect must the continuance of this extravagant licentiousness in them, not to mention other kinds of it, have upon the people in those respects just mentioned? Must it not necessarily tend to wear out of their minds all reverence for authority, and respect for superiors of every sort; and, joined with the irreligious principles we find so industriously

propagated, to introduce a total profligateness amongst them; since, let them be as bad as they will, it is scarce possible they can be so bad as they are instructed they may be, or worse than they are told their superiors are? And is there no danger that all this, to mention only one supposable course of it, may raise somewhat like that levelling spirit, upon atheistical principles, which, in the last age, prevailed upon enthusiastic ones? not to speak of the possibility, that different sorts of people may unite, in it, upon these contrary principles. And may not this spirit, together with a concurrence of ill humours, and of persons who hope to find their account in confusion, soon prevail to such a degree, as will require more of the good old principles of loyalty and of religion to withstand it, than appear to be left amongst us?

What legal remedies can be provided against these mischiefs, or whether any at all,   **19** are considerations the furthest from my thoughts. No government can be free, which is not administered by general stated laws: and these cannot comprehend every case, which wants to be provided against:* nor can new ones be made for every particular case, as it arises: and more particular laws, as well as more general ones, admit of infinite evasions: and legal government forbids any but legal methods of redress; which cannot but be liable to the same sort of imperfections: besides the additional one of delay; and whilst redress is delayed, however unavoidably, wrong subsists. Then there are very bad things, which human authority can scarce provide against at all, but by methods dangerous to liberty; nor fully, but by such as would be fatal to it. These things shew, that liberty, in the very nature of it, absolutely requires, and even supposes, that people be able to govern themselves in those respects in which they are free; otherwise their wickedness will be in proportion to their liberty, and this greatest of blessings will become a curse.

III. These things shew likewise, that there is but one adequate remedy to the   **20** forementioned evils, even that which the apostle prescribes in the last words of the text, to consider ourselves 'as the servants of God', who enjoins dutiful submission to civil authority, as his ordinance; and to whom we are accountable for the use we make of the liberty which we enjoy under it. Since men cannot live out of society, nor in it without government, government is plainly a divine appointment; and consequently submission to it, a most evident duty of the law of nature. And we all know in how forcible a manner it is put upon our consciences in Scripture. Nor can this obligation be denied formally upon any principles, but such as subvert all other obligations. Yet many amongst us seem not to consider it as any obligation at all. This doubtless is, in a great measure, owing to dissoluteness and corruption of manners: but I think it is partly owing to their having reduced it to nothing in theory. Whereas this obligation ought to be put upon the same foot with all other general ones, which are not absolute and without exception: and our submission is due in all cases but those, which we really discern to be exceptions to the general rule. And they, who are perpetually displaying the exceptions, though they do not indeed contradict the meaning of any particular texts of Scripture, which surely intended to make no alteration in men's civil rights; yet they go against the general tenor of Scripture.

For the Scripture, throughout the whole of it, commands submission; supposing men apt enough of themselves to make the exceptions, and not to need being continually reminded of them. Now if we are really under any obligations of duty at all to magistrates, honour and respect, in our behaviour towards them, must doubtless be their due. And they who refuse to pay them this small and easy regard, who 'despise dominion, and speak evil of dignities',[12] should seriously ask themselves, what restrains them from any other instance whatever of undutifulness? And if it be principle, why not from this? Indeed free government supposes, that the conduct of affairs may be inquired into, and spoken of with freedom. Yet surely this should be done with decency, for the sake of liberty itself; for its honour, and its security. But be it done as it will, it is a very different thing from libelling, and endeavouring to vilify the persons of such as are in authority. It will be hard to find an instance, in which a serious man could calmly satisfy himself in doing this. It is in no case necessary, and in every case of very pernicious tendency. But the immorality of it increases in proportion to the integrity, and superior rank of the persons thus treated. It is therefore in the highest degree immoral, when it extends to the supreme authority in the person of a prince, from whom our liberties are in no imaginable danger, whatever they may be from ourselves; and whose mild, and strictly legal government could not but make any virtuous people happy.

21   A free government, which the good providence of God has preserved to us through innumerable dangers, is an invaluable blessing. And our ingratitude to him in abusing of it, must be great in proportion to the greatness of the blessing, and the providential deliverances by which it has been preserved to us. Yet the crime of abusing this blessing, receives further aggravation from hence, that such abuse always is to the reproach, and tends to the ruin of it. The abuse of liberty has directly overturned many free governments, as well as our own, on the popular side; and has, in various ways, contributed to the ruin of many, which have been overturned on the side of authority. Heavy therefore must be their guilt, who shall be found to have given such advantages against it, as well as theirs who have taken them.

22   *Lastly*, The consideration, that we are the servants of God, reminds us, that we are accountable to him for our behaviour in those respects, in which it is out of the reach of all human authority; and is the strongest enforcement of sincerity, as 'all things are naked, and open unto the eyes of him with whom we have to do'.[13] Artificial behaviour might perhaps avail much towards quieting our consciences, and making our part good in the short competitions of this world: but what will it avail us considered as under the government of God? Under his government, 'there is no darkness, nor shadow of death, where the workers of iniquity may hide themselves'.[14] He has indeed instituted civil government over the face of the earth, 'for the punishment of evil-doers, and for the praise', the apostle does not say the rewarding, but, 'for the praise of them that do well'.[15] Yet as the worst answer these ends in some measure, the best can do it very imperfectly. Civil government can by no means take cognizance of *every work*, which is good or evil: many *things* are done in *secret*; the

authors unknown to it, and often the things themselves: then it cannot so much consider actions, under the view of their being morally *good*, or *evil*, as under the view of their being mischievous, or beneficial to society: nor can it in any wise execute *judgement* in rewarding what is *good*, as it can, and ought, and does, in punishing what is *evil*. But 'God shall bring every work into judgement, with every secret thing, whether it be good, or whether it be evil.'[16]

Notes

1. The hypocrisy laid to the charge of the Pharisees and Sadducees, in *Matt.* xvi at the beginning, and in *Luke* xii. 54, is determinately this, that their vicious passions blinded them so as to prevent their discerning the evidence of our saviour's mission; though no more understanding was necessary to discern it, than what they had, and made use of in common matters. Here they are called hypocrites merely upon account of their insincerity towards God and their own consciences, and not at all upon account of any insincerity towards men. This last indeed is included in that general hypocrisy, which, throughout the gospels, is represented as their distinguished character; but the former is as much included. For they were not men, who, without any belief at all of religion, put on the appearance of it only in order to deceive the world: on the contrary they believed their religion, and were zealous in it. But their religion, which they believed, and were zealous in, was in its nature hypocritical: for it was the form, not the reality; it allowed them in immoral practices; and indeed was itself in some respects immoral, as they indulged their pride, and uncharitableness under the notion of zeal for it. See *Jer.* ix. 6, *Ps.* lxxviii.36, *Job* iii.19, and *Matt.* xv.7–14, and xxiii.13, 16, 19, 24, 26, where *hypocrite*, and *blind*, are used promiscuously. Again, the scripture speaks of the 'deceitfulness of sin'; and its deceiving those who are guilty of it: *Heb.* iii.13, *Eph.* iv.22, *Rom.* vii.11, of men's acting as if they could 'deceive and mock God': *Is.* xxix.15, *Acts* v.3, *Gal.* vi.7, of their 'blinding their own eyes': *Matt.* xiii.15, *Acts* xxviii.27, and 'deceiving themselves'; which is quite a different thing from being deceived: *I Cor.* iii.18, *I John* i.8, *Gal.* vi.3, *Jam.* i.22, 26. Many more coincident passages might be mentioned: but I will add only one. In *II Thess.* ii, it is foretold, that by means of some 'force', some 'energy of delusion', men should believe 'the lie' which is there treated of: this 'force of delusion' is not any thing without them, but somewhat within them, which it is expressly said they should bring upon themselves, by 'not receiving the love of the truth, but having pleasure in unrighteousness'. Answering to all this is that very remarkable passage of our Lord, *Matt.* vi.22, 23, *Luke* xi.34, 35, and that admonition repeated fourteen times in the New Testament, 'he that hath ears to hear, let him hear'. And the ground of this whole manner of considering things; for it is not to be spoken of as only a peculiar kind of phraseology, but is a most accurate and strictly just manner of considering characters and moral conduct; the ground of it, I say, is, that when persons will not be influenced by such evidence in religion as they act upon in the daily course of life, or when their notions of religion (and I might add of virtue) are in any sort reconcilable with what is vicious, it is some faulty negligence or prejudice, which thus deludes them; in very different ways, perhaps, and very different degrees. But when any one is thus deluded through his own fault, in whatever way or degree it is, he deludes himself. And this is

as properly hypocrisy towards himself, as deluding the world is hypocrisy towards the world: and he who is guilty of it acts as if he could deceive and mock God; and therefore is an hypocrite towards him, in as strict and literal a sense as the nature of the subject will admit.

2. *Rom.* viii.21.
3. *I John* iv.18.
4. *I Pet.* ii.13–15.
5. *I Pet.* ii.16.
6. *Eph.* ii.12.
7. *Prov.* xi.3.
8. *Isa.* v.20.
9. *Ps.* i.21.
10. *Prov.* xvii.14.
11. Nec vitia nostra, nec remedia pati possumus, Liv. Lib. i. c. I.*
12. *Jude* 8.
13. *Heb.* iv.13.
14. *Job* xxxiv.22.
15. *I Pet.* ii.14.
16. *Eccles.* xii.14.

A Selection from the Correspondence between Joseph Butler and Samuel Clarke

FROM BUTLER TO CLARKE, SEPTEMBER 30TH 1717

Sir, ...

Upon reading what you last published upon that subject,* I see great reason to be **3** satisfied that freedom and action are identical ideas, and that man is, properly speaking, an agent or a free being. But as the question concerning freedom is or is not of consequence just as it affects the purposes of religion, my not being able clearly to make out how freedom renders us capable of moral government perplexes me as much as tho' I was in doubt concerning freedom itself. I am satisfied that it is in our power to act or not to act in any given case, yet I do not see that it follows from thence that it is in our power to act virtuously, because the physical and the moral nature of an action comes under quite two different considerations. Virtue does not consist barely in acting, but in acting upon such motives, and to such ends; and acting upon such motives, etc. evidently supposes a disposition in our nature to be influenced by those motives, which disposition not being an action, does not depend upon us, but, like the rest of our affections, seems to proceed from our original frame and constitution. For instance; It is a virtue to relieve the poor, upon this account (suppose) that it is the will of God, and tho' the action be done, yet if it be not done upon this account, it is not a virtuous action. I own it's in my power to relieve the poor (*i.e.* to do the physical action); but I don't see that it's in my power to do it upon the account, that it's the will of God (i.e. to do the moral action), unless I have a disposition in my nature to be influenced by this motive; therefore this disposition may be considered as a *sine qua non* to the performance of every duty. Now that we have not this disposition when we neglect our duty is evident from this, that if we always had it, we should always certainly, though not necessarily, do our duty. How then can we be accountable for neglecting the practice of any virtue, when at what time soever we did neglect it we wanted that which was a *sine qua non*, or absolutely necessary to the performance of it, viz. a disposition to be influenced by the proper motive?

4   Thus the case seems to stand as to virtue; it's somewhat different in respect to vice, or the positive breach of God's law, because here must be action, and it's always in our power not to act; but in this case also there is a very great difficulty; for the reason why it's expected that we should avoid vice is, because there are stronger motives against it than for committing it; but then motives are nothing to one who is indifferent to them, and every man is at least indifferent to them who is not influenced by them in his actions, because if he was not indifferent, or, which is more, had not stronger dispositions to be influenced by contrary motives, it's morally certain that he would not act contrary to these. So that tho' a man can avoid vice, yet (according to this) he cannot avoid it upon that account, or for that reason, which is the only reason why he ought to avoid it.

5   Upon the whole such is the imperfection of our nature, that it seems impossible for us to perform any one more virtuous action than we do perform; and tho' we may always avoid vice, yet if we are indifferent to that which is the only proper motive why we should avoid it (i.e. cannot avoid it upon that motive), a bare possibility of avoiding vice does not seem a sufficient reason for the punishment of it from a good and equitable Governor. Tho' all that I have here said should be true, I don't think the foundation of religion would be at all removed, for there would certainly, notwithstanding, remain reasons of infinite weight to confirm the truth and enforce the practice of it; but upon another account I have cause to think that I am guilty of some mistake in this matter, viz. that I am conscious of somewhat in myself, and discern the same in others, which seems directly to contradict the foregoing objections; but I am not able at present to see where the weakness of them lies, and our people here never had any doubt in their lives concerning a received opinion; so that I cannot mention a difficulty to them. Upon which account, since it's a matter of great consequence, I hope for your excuse and assistance in it, both which I have formerly had to my great satisfaction in others.

I am, honoured Sir,

Your most obliged humble servant,

J. Butler

Oriel Coll.

REPLY FROM CLARKE TO BUTLER, OCTOBER 3RD 1717

1   If I apprehend your difficulty right, I think it may be cleared by the following consideration. A disposition in our nature (which disposition is no action, nor in our power any further than as 'tis affected by habits) to be influenced by right motives, is certainly a *sine qua non* to virtuous actions. In God, the disposition is essential and invariable. In angels and saints in heaven 'tis constantly effectual, but not essentially so. In men 'tis that which we call rationality, or the faculty of reason, which makes them capable of rewards or punishments, to be determined by the proportion or degree of every man's

rationality (which is the talent God has given him) [coupled?] with the degree of his use of that talent in acting.

To apply this to your instance:—'Tis the will of God that I should relieve the poor. 2 Being a rational creature is having a disposition to act upon this motive (and therefore you wrongly suppose that any man naturally, and without very corrupt habits, can be without that disposition). If I relieve the poor merely out of natural compassion, or any other motive that is not vicious, this is still freely obeying the will of God as made known by the law of nature. And it then only ceases to be a virtuous action when I do it upon a vicious motive, and without that vicious motive would not have done it, that is, would, by the use of my liberty, have overruled my rationality, or natural disposition to have obeyed the will of God, made known either by nature, or revelation, or both. If I have either mistaken, or not satisfied your difficulty, you will let me hear from you again.

LETTER FROM BUTLER TO CLARKE, OCT 3RD 1717
Reverend Sir,

I have long resisted an inclination to desire your thoughts upon the difficulty 1 mentioned in my last, till I considered that the trouble in answering it would be only carrying on the general purpose of your life, and that I might claim the same right to your instructions with others; notwithstanding which I should not have mentioned it to you had I not thought (which is natural when one fancies one sees a thing clearly) that I could easily express it with clearness to others. However, I should by no means have given you a second trouble upon the subject had I not had your particular leave. I thought proper just to mention these things that you might not suspect me to take advantage from your civility to trouble you with any thing, but only such objections as seem to me of weight, and which I cannot get rid of any other way.

A disposition in our natures to be influenced by right motives is as absolutely 2 necessary to render us moral agents, as a capacity to discern right motives is. These two are, I think, quite distinct perceptions, the former proceeding from a desire inseparable from a conscious being of its own happiness, the latter being only our understanding, or faculty of seeing truth. Since a disposition to be influenced by right motives is a *sine qua non* to virtuous actions, an indifference to right motives must incapacitate us for virtuous actions, or render us, in that particular, not moral agents. I do indeed think that no rational creature is, strictly speaking, indifferent to right motives, but yet there seems to be somewhat which to all intents of the present question is the same, viz., a stronger disposition to be influenced by contrary or wrong motives, and this I take to be always the case when any vice is committed. But since it may be said, as you hint, that this stronger disposition to be influenced by vicious motives may have been contracted by repeated acts of wickedness, we will pitch upon the first vicious action any one is guilty of. No man would have committed this first vicious action if he had not a stronger (at least as strong) disposition in him to be influenced by the motives of the vicious action, than by the motives of the contrary virtuous action; from whence I infallibly conclude, that since every man has committed some first vice, every man had, antecedent to the commission of it, a stronger disposition to be influenced by the vicious than the virtuous motive. My difficulty upon this is, that a stronger natural disposition to be influenced by the vicious than the virtuous motive (which every one has antecedent to his first vice), seems, to all purposes of the present question, to put the man in the same condition as though he was indifferent to the virtuous motive; and since an indifferency to the virtuous motive would have incapacitated a man from being a moral agent, or contracting guilt, is not a stronger disposition to be influenced by the vicious motive as great an incapacity? Suppose I have two diversions offered me, both of which I could not enjoy, I like both of them, but yet have a stronger inclination to one than to the other, I am not indeed strictly indifferent to either, because I should be glad to enjoy both; but am I not exactly in the same case, to all intents and purposes of acting, as though I was absolutely indifferent to that diversion which I have the least inclination to? You suppose man to be endued naturally with a disposition to be influenced by virtuous motives, and that this disposition is a *sine qua non* to virtuous actions, both which I fully believe; but then you omit to consider the natural inclination to be influenced by vicious motives, which, whenever a vice is committed, is at least equally strong with the other, and in the first vice is not affected by habits, but is as natural, and as much out of a man's power as the other....

I am, Rev. Sir,
Your most obliged humble servant,

J. Butler

Oriel

REPLY FROM CLARKE TO BUTLER, OCT 9TH 1717

1   Your objection seems indeed very dexterous, and yet I really think that there is at bottom nothing in it. But of this you are to judge, not from my assertion, but from the reason I shall endeavour to give to it.

2   I think then, that a disposition to be influenced by right motives being what we call rationality, there cannot be on the contrary (properly speaking) any such thing naturally in rational creatures as a disposition to be influenced by wrong motives. This can be nothing but mere perverseness of will; and whether even that can be said to amount to a disposition to be influenced by wrong motives, formally, and as such, may (I think) well be doubted. Men have by nature strong inclinations to certain objects. None of those inclinations are vicious, but vice consists in pursuing the inclination towards any object in certain circumstances, notwithstanding reason, or the natural disposition to be influenced by right motives, declares to the man's conscience at the same time (or would do, if he attended to it) that the object ought not to be pursued in those circumstances. Nevertheless, where the man

commits the crime, the natural disposition was only towards the object, not formally towards the doing it upon wrong motives; and generally the very essence of the crime consists in the liberty of the will forcibly overruling the actual disposition towards being influenced by right motives, and not at all (as you suppose) in the man's having any natural disposition to be influenced by wrong motives, as such.

LETTER FROM BUTLER TO CLARKE, OCT 10TH 1717
Rev. Sir,

I had the honour of your kind letter yesterday, and must own that I do now see a   1
difference between the nature of that disposition which we have to be influenced by virtuous motives, and that contrary disposition, (or whatever else it may properly be called,) which is the occasion of our committing sin; and hope in time to get a thorough insight into this subject by means of those helps you have been pleased to afford me. I find it necessary to consider such very abstruse questions at different times and in different dispositions; and have found particular use of this method upon that abstract subject of necessity: for 'tho I did not see the force of your argument for the unity of the divine nature when I had done writing to you upon that subject, I am now fully satisfied that it is conclusive. I will only just add that I suppose somewhat in my last letter was not clearly expressed, for I did not at all design to say, that the essence of any crime consisted in the man's having a natural disposition to be influenced by wrong motives....

I am with the greatest respect and gratitude for all your favours,   3

Reverend. Sir,
Your most obedient humble Servant,

J. Butler

Oriel Coll.

Editor's Notes

The referencing system is as follows. Following Bernard's edition, all paragraphs in the main text are numbered. References to the Preface to the *Sermons* begin with P, followed by the paragraph number. References to the *Fifteen Sermons* are by Sermon number and then paragraph number; e.g. S 3.4. References to the *Dissertation on Virtue* begin with D, followed by the paragraph number. References to the *Analogy of Religion* (except for the Introduction) are by part, chapter number, and then paragraph number; thus A II.1.3, refers to the third paragraph of the first chapter of the second part of that work; A Intro. 4 refers to the Introduction to the whole work, fourth paragraph. Page references to the *Analogy* (indicated by a colon after the paragraph reference) are to the edition by J. H. Bernard. References to the *Sermons Preached Upon Public Occasions*, as printed in Bernard's edition, are preceded by SPO, followed by sermon number and paragraph number, and then the page number in Bernard's edition.

In the main text, notes are indicated by an asterisk. In the Editor's Notes, the place in the text to which each note refers is indicated using the referencing system above; thus a note preceded by 'S 2.3' indicates that the note is on Sermon 2, paragraph 3. Where there is more than one note on a paragraph the words immediately preceding the asterisk are quoted at the beginning of the note. An 'n' following the paragraph number indicates that the editorial comment is on Butler's footnote.

The first reference to an historical text is by author and title, followed by Book, Part, Section, or Paragraph, as appropriate, followed by a page number in the edition cited in the Bibliography. Thus: Locke, *An Essay Concerning Human Understanding*, Book III, ch. 9, para. 6: vol. II, 78. Subsequent references will be shortened thus: Locke, *Essay* III, 9, 6: II, 78. In the case of Cicero's *Tusculan Disputations* translations and page references to Books III and IV are to Graver's edition. References to the other books are to the Loeb translation. References to Plato and Aristotle will also include the Stephanus and Bekker numbers, respectively, followed by the page number in the relevant translation. Contemporary works are cited using the Author–Date method.

Where an author's name or a topic is in small capitals, readers are invited to consult the section on Butler's Predecessors, immediately following these notes, for more detailed discussion.

All quotations from the Christian Bible are, following Butler, from the Authorized Version (AV) also known as the King James Version, with the exception of the Psalms, which are from the 1662 Book of Common Prayer (BCP). See 'Note on the Text' for further explication.

In compiling these notes, I have built on the work of previous editors, but I must here record my great debt to J. H. Bernard's edition, which gives by far the most comprehensive notes, references, and cross-referencing. Full references for all editions consulted are cited in the Bibliography.

P 1 The Preface was added in the Second Edition.

P 6 Locke makes a similar point: 'Men's names of very compound *ideas*, such as for the most part are moral words, have seldom in two different men, the same precise signification' (John Locke, *An Essay Concerning Human Understanding*, Book III, ch. 9, para. 6: vol. II, 78.)

P 8 'Thus' in the editions of 1729, 1736, 1749.

P 10 'auditories' = 'audiences'. It is perhaps worth recalling that these are Sermons preached at the Rolls Chapel, where Butler's original auditors would chiefly be lawyers and clerks, who would be familiar, for example, with classical authors. For a fascinating insight into why the topic of conscience would have been especially relevant for this audience, see Garrett (unpublished).

P 12 The author with whose method Butler is here primarily contrasting his own is SAMUEL CLARKE, who holds that moral truths are necessary, because founded in the nature of things. Certain actions are, in themselves, fit or appropriate responses to the circumstances in which an agent is placed.

> [T]here *are* therefore certain *necessary and eternal differences* of things, and certain conse-
> quent *fitnesses* or *unfitnesses* of the application of different things or different relations one
> to another; not depending on any positive constitutions, but founded unchangeably in the
> nature and reason of things. (Samuel Clarke, *A Discourse Concerning the Being and
> Attributes of God*, vol. II, Prop. 1, Section 1: 183.)

Clarke is thus opposed to Ethical Voluntarism, which maintains that what is right or wrong is determined by the will of God, or of some earthly sovereign. (For Butler's rejection of voluntarism, see A I.6.13n.) Clarke holds that the reason why ingratitude, for example, is wrong is that it is an inappropriate, or unfitting, response to receiving a benefit. The respective natures of a benefit and of gratitude are such that the second is the appropriate response to the first, in whatever circumstances they might be found, and independently of divine or human law.

Note that, far from rejecting or disparaging Clarke's approach to ethics, Butler makes a point of endorsing it, not only in this passage but in several places in the *Analogy*—e.g. the long footnote at A I 6.12: 112—and perhaps most forcefully at A II 8.11: 264–5.

> [I]n this treatise I... have omitted a thing of the utmost importance which I do believe, the
> moral fitness and unfitness of actions, prior to all will whatever; which I apprehend as
> certainly to determine the Divine conduct, as speculative truth and falsehood necessarily
> determine the Divine judgement.

Butler thus sees his approach as complementary to Clarke's, and not in competition with it.

Note also that, for Butler, the central point of agreement between the two approaches is that 'they both lead us to the same thing, our obligations to the practice of virtue'. That is, they both show that rational beings should govern their lives by the dictates of morality. (See also A I.3.3, 27–8; A II.3.13. There is a good discussion of these points in Bernard's edition of the *Analogy*, on p. 117.)

P 13 As Bernard points out, Butler alludes here to the STOIC claim that virtue consists in following nature. Diogenes Laertius reports that

> Zeno was the first (in his treatise *On the Nature of Man*) to designate as the end 'life in
> agreement with nature' (or living agreeably to nature), which is the same as a virtuous life,

virtue being the goal towards which nature guides us. (Diogenes Laertius, *Lives of Eminent Philosophers*, Book VII, Section 87: 195.)

Butler's phrasing echoes Cicero's:

Now then: for one man to take something from another and to increase his own advantage at the cost of another's disadvantage is more contrary to nature than death, than poverty, than pain, and than anything else that may happen to his body or external possessions. (Cicero, *On Duties*, Book III, Section 21: 108.)

See, for further discussion, Irwin 2003, and Long 2003.

P 13n The passage to which Butler alludes reads as follows:

They who place all in following nature, if they mean by that phrase acting according to the natures of things (that is, treating things as being what they in nature are, or according to truth) say what is right. But this does not seem to be their meaning. And if it is only that a man must follow his own nature, since his nature is not purely rational, but there is a part of him, which he has in common with brutes, they appoint him a guide which I fear will mislead him, this being commonly more likely to prevail, than the rational part. At best this talk is loose. (WOLLASTON *The Religion of Nature Delineated*, Section 1: 22–3.)

(The 1724 edition of Wollaston's *Religion of Nature Delineated* can be accessed in Google Books.)

P 14 '...reflection or conscience.' Note that Butler here identifies the principle of reflection with conscience. Indeed, throughout the Preface and the first three Sermons, Butler often makes a point of coupling the two. In P 24 he employs the phrase 'disapprobation of reflection' as synonymous with the judgement of conscience. He never identifies self-love with reflection. This suggests that Butler thinks of conscience as having ultimate authority in virtue of reflecting on the total nature of an action, whereas self-love reflects only on those features of the action that bear on self-interest.

P 14 '...adapted to measure time.' The analogy between the human constitution and a watch is not, of course, a new one. It had recently been employed by SHAFTESBURY to make a point very similar to Butler's.

If a passenger should turn by chance into a watchmaker's shop and, thinking to inform himself concerning watches, should inquire of what metal or what matter each part was composed, what gave the colours or what made the sounds, without examining what the real use was of such an instrument or by what movements its *end* was best attained and its perfection acquired, it is plain that such an examiner as this would come short of any understanding in the real nature of the instrument. (Shaftesbury, *Soliloquy, or Advice to an Author*, Part III, Section 1 in *Characteristics of Men, Manners, Opinions, Times*: 131.)

P 18 By 'principle' here Butler means merely any part of our psychology that motivates us.

P 25 'Above all else, reverence yourself' (ascribed to Pythagoras).

P 26 '...would be without remedy.' The passage to which Butler alludes reads as follows:

Now as to atheism, though it be plainly deficient and without remedy in the case of ill judgement on the happiness of virtue yet it is not, indeed, of necessity the cause of any such ill judgement. For without an absolute assent to any hypothesis of theism, the advantages of virtue may possibly be seen and owned, and a high opinion of it established in the mind. However, it must be confessed that the natural tendency of atheism is very different. (Shaftesbury, *An Inquiry Concerning Virtue or Merit*, Part II, Section 3 in *Characteristics*: 189.)

It is thus the specific case of the *atheist* who doubts that virtue and self-interest coincide that Shaftesbury says would be 'without remedy'. In omitting that detail, however, Butler does not markedly misrepresent Shaftesbury, since someone who believes that the world is, or may quite possibly be, under the moral governance of God is unlikely confidently to entertain scepticism about 'the happiness of virtue'.

To talk of 'a manifest *obligation*' to pursue one's own good may strike the modern reader as odd, since we tend to use the term only when thinking of morality. But, for both Shaftesbury and Butler, to say that someone has an obligation to act a certain way is merely to assert that that is what he ought to do; that he has good and sufficient reasons so to act.

In the remainder of this paragraph and the next, Butler asks what difference it makes when we take into account the authority of conscience as well as of self-love. In so doing, he develops a novel argument for the supremacy of conscience that is not to be found in the main body of the *Sermons*. This ingenious but, in my view, unsuccessful, argument has attracted surprisingly little attention. For an analysis see McNaughton (2013), and the next note.

P 26 '...appear no more than probable.' Compare A I. 7.11.

> For though it were doubtful, what will be the future consequences of virtue and vice; yet it is, however, credible, that they may have those consequences which Religion teaches us they will: and this credibility is a *certain obligation in point of prudence*, to abstain from all wickedness, and to live in the conscientious practice of all that is good (128, my emphasis).

This passage is in marked contrast to P 26. In the *Analogy* Butler allows that, though it is only probable that virtue will be rewarded and vice punished, yet that is sufficient to yield an obligation, from the point of view of prudence, that is itself *certain*. In P 26, however, he contrasts the obligation to virtue which is 'the most certain and known', with the obligation to promote one's self interest which can 'at the utmost appear no more than probable'. These claims in the two works appear at odds, and Butler's later view seems to me the correct one.

In P 26 he fails to distinguish clearly two questions:

(1) Will some course of action *in fact* turn out to be in our self-interest?
(2) Does prudence require that we do what seems most likely to promote our self-interest in the future?

The answer to the first, as he rightly points out, will always be a judgement about probabilities; we can clearly be mistaken in our beliefs about what will happen, or about what its value will be, so that our prediction may be falsified. But it does not follow, as Butler in P 26 seems to suppose, that the prudential *obligation* to do what will *most probably* best promote our interests is *itself* less than certain. If we have weighed the evidence carefully and determined that a certain course of action will be best for us, then prudence *requires* that we take that course. That judgement about what prudence requires cannot be falsified by how things in fact turn out even though, with the benefit of hindsight, we may wish we had done something different. In that respect, judgements about both moral and prudential obligations are invulnerable to refutation by future events. The only uncertainty to which both kinds of judgement are liable concerns how careful we were to discover and weigh all the relevant foreseeable factors before making the judgement. Butler seems to have come to see this point by the time he wrote the *Analogy*, but it undermines the argument of P 26, which relies on a supposed contrast between moral obligations, which are certain, and prudential ones, which are not.

A central argument of the *Analogy* rests, indeed, on denying the contrast that Butler draws in P 26. We are under 'an *absolute* and formal obligation, in point of prudence and of interest' to take what is most probably the best course, even where that probability is low. 'For surely a man is as *really bound in prudence* to do what upon the whole *appears, according to the best of his judgement*, to be for his happiness, as what he certainly knows to be so' (A Intro. 4: 3; my emphases).

P 27 It is unclear whether Butler had a specific passage in SHAFTESBURY in mind. Bernard cites the following passage from the Conclusion of the *Inquiry*, in which Shaftesbury does indeed discuss what he takes to be the greatest degree of scepticism imaginable.

> On the other side, the happiness and good of virtue has been proved from the contrary effect of other affections, such as are according to nature and the economy of the species or kind. We have cast up all those particulars from whence, as by way of addition and subtraction, the main sum or general account of happiness is either augmented or diminished. And if there be no article exceptionable in this scheme of moral arithmetic, the subject treated may be said to have an evidence as great as that which is found in numbers or mathematics. *For let us carry scepticism ever so far*, let us doubt, if we can, of everything about us, we cannot doubt of what passes within ourselves. Our passions and affections are known to us. They are certain, whatever the objects may be, on which they are employed. Nor is it of any concern to our argument, how these exterior objects stand—whether they are realities, or mere illusions, whether we wake or dream. For ill dreams will be equally disturbing. And a good dream, if life be nothing else, will be easily and happily passed. In this dream of life, therefore, our demonstrations have the same force, our balance and economy hold good, and our obligation to virtue is in every respect the same. (Shaftesbury, *Characteristics*: 229–30; my emphasis.)

Whether or not this is the passage Butler had in mind, it may seem at first sight to sit ill with Butler's criticism, since Shaftesbury here claims that 'the greatest scepticism' *cannot* undermine our obligation to virtue. This passage raises two questions. Can it be reconciled with Shaftesbury's earlier concession (alluded to by Butler in P 26) that scepticism or 'ill judgement' on the 'happiness of virtue' is possible and, in the case of atheism, 'without remedy'? Does it provide any grounds for thinking that Butler has misinterpreted Shaftesbury's view?

These two passages from Shaftesbury can be reconciled once we realize that he is talking about different kinds of scepticism in each. In the first (*Characteristics*: 189), he is considering the sceptic about the coincidence of happiness and virtue. In the second, he is considering a sceptic about the reality of the external world. The conclusion to which Shaftesbury is arguing in the *Inquiry* is that the sort of character you must have to be virtuous *is* the kind of character that will make you most happy. In that sense, virtue brings its own reward. The first kind of sceptic is someone who doubts this central claim of Shaftesbury's. In that first passage, therefore, Shaftesbury holds that we might hope to influence the conduct of this first kind of sceptic by appeal to the rewards and punishments meted out by an all-seeing Deity. If, however, the sceptic about the 'happiness of virtue' were also an atheist, then such appeals would be pointless and there would be no remedy for his scepticism. In the later passage, quoted above, Shaftesbury is dealing with a quite different sceptic: one who doubts the existence of the external world. His point is simply that, since he is basing his claim on what sort of character we need to be happy, doubts about the existence of the external world would not affect the force of his argument. In short, Shaftesbury admits he has no answer to the atheist who doubts the 'happiness of virtue', but claims that his argument is untouched by someone who is sceptical as to the reality of the objects of our experience.

Since Butler's criticism only concerns the first kind of sceptic as to the happiness of virtue, and not the sceptic about external reality, Butler has not misinterpreted Shaftesbury. What Butler asserts, and Shaftesbury denies, is that we have decisive reason to follow the dictates of conscience even if we are sceptical about the coincidence of virtue and interest.

P 30 This quotation comes from the following passage from Section 5 of Shaftesbury's 'A Letter Concerning Enthusiasm to My Lord ****'.

[I]f we have never settled with ourselves any notion of what is morally excellent, or if we cannot trust to that reason which tells us that nothing beside what is so can have place in the Deity, we can neither trust to any thing which others relate of him or which he himself reveals to us. We must be satisfied beforehand that he is good and cannot deceive us. Without this, there can be no real religious faith or confidence. Now, if there be really something previous to revelation, some antecedent demonstration of reason, to assure us that God is and, withal, that he is so good as not to deceive us, the same reason, if we will trust to it, will demonstrate to us that God is so good as to exceed the very best of us in goodness. And after this manner we can have no dread or suspicion to render us uneasy, for it is malice only, and not goodness, which can make us afraid. (Shaftesbury, *Characteristics*: 20–1.)

P 31 Since Sermons 7 and 10 are so closely related it is unclear why Butler decided not to print them consecutively.

P 34 Bernard suggests that the 'gentile moralists' may include Plato and Cicero. In *Crito*, 49d (44) Socrates says: 'One should never do wrong in return, nor mistreat any man, no matter how one has been mistreated by him.' Similar sentiments are voiced by Socrates in *Gorgias*; see, e.g., 469b (813).

Cicero writes:

Moreover, certain duties must be observed even towards those at whose hands you may have received unjust treatment. There is a limit to revenge and to punishment. I am not even sure that it is not enough simply that the man who did the harm should repent of his injustice, so that he himself will do no such thing again, and others will be slower to act unjustly. (*On Duties*, I.33: 14.)

See also Seneca's essay *On Mercy*: 129–64.

P 35 The reference is to the Duc de la Rochefoucauld (1613–80). The passage Butler refers to appears to be Maxim 173:

There are various forms of curiosity: one, based on self-interest, makes us want to learn what may be useful, another, based on pride, comes from a desire to know what others don't. (La Rochefoucauld, *Maxims*: 59.)

P 35n Books I and II of Cicero's *On Moral Ends* are a discussion of the views of the Epicurean school, with Epicurus' part being argued for by one Lucius Torquatus, who is implied to be a descendent of the illustrious Torquati. In the beginning of the discussion, the character in the dialogue named Cicero notes that these illustrious Torquati seem to be counterexamples to the Epicurean view that people pursue (only) their own pleasure. He cites specific examples of their heroic deeds performed, apparently, without any concern for their own interest.

In the following passage, which may be the one Butler had in mind, Torquatus explains the apparently self-sacrificial actions of his heroic ancestors on Epicurean principles.

> I maintain that if they performed those undoubtedly illustrious deeds for a reason, their reason was not virtue for its own sake. 'He dragged the chain from the enemy's neck.' Indeed, and so protected himself from death. 'But he incurred great danger.' Indeed, but in full view of his army. 'What did he gain from it?' Glory and esteem, which are the firmest safeguards of a secure life. 'He sentenced his son to death.' If he did so without a reason, I would not wish to be descended from someone so harsh and cruel; but if he was bringing pain upon himself as a consequence of the need to preserve the authority of his military command, and to maintain army discipline at a critical time of war by spreading fear of punishment, then he was providing for the security of his fellow-citizens, and thereby—as he was well aware—for his own. (Book I, Section 35: 15).

(I am grateful to my colleague, Nat Stein, for considerable help with this footnote.)
Butler's discussion of Hobbes' account can be found in a lengthy footnote to S 1.6.

P 37 See S 11.5–8.

P 39 This famous apothegm was chosen by G. E. Moore as the epigraph for *Principia Ethica*. The phrase is not, of course, original to Butler; WOLLASTON offers 'everything is what it is' as an example of a 'truth eternal' (*Religion* 14). It is Butler's use of it that is significant: it sums up his opposition to various kinds of reductionism.

P 40 That self-love can be too weak, as well as too strong, is frequently stressed by Butler. See also S 1.6, S 9.9, and A I. 5.13: 87n, where he writes: 'This reasonable self-love wants to be improved, as really as any principle in our nature.' On this matter, Shaftesbury and Butler are in agreement:

> If the want of such an affection as that towards self-preservation be injurious to the species, a creature is ill and unnatural as well through this defect, as through the want of any other natural affection. (Shaftesbury, *Inquiry* I, 2, 2 in *Characteristics*: 170.)

P 41 Butler says more about the relation between these three things—self-love, the religious life, and the moral life in the *Analogy*.

> Against this whole notion of moral discipline, it may be objected, in another way; that so far as a course of behaviour, materially virtuous, proceeds from hope and fear, so far it is only a discipline and strengthening of self-love. But doing what God commands, because he commands it, is obedience, though it proceeds from hope or fear. And a course of such obedience will form habits of it. And a constant regard to veracity, justice, and charity, may form distinct habits of these particular virtues; and will certainly form habits of self-government, and of denying our inclinations, whenever veracity, justice, or charity requires it. Nor is there any foundation for this great nicety, with which some affect to distinguish in this case, in order to depreciate all religion proceeding from hope or fear. For, veracity,

justice, and charity, regard to God's authority, and to our own chief interest, are not only all three coincident; but each of them is, in itself, a just and natural motive or principle of action. And he who begins a good life from any one of them, and perseveres in it, as he is already in some degree, so he cannot fail of becoming more and more, of that character which is correspondent to the constitution of nature as moral; and to the relation which God stands in to us as moral governor of it: nor consequently can he fail of obtaining that happiness, which this constitution and relation necessarily suppose connected with that character. (A I. 5.19: 95.)

P 43 Butler here refers to the dispute between Fénelon (1651–1715) and Bossuet (1627–1704) concerning the possibility of a disinterested love of God. That God should be loved for himself alone and not for the sake of eternal life or any other benefit was a part of the quietistic teaching of Madame Guyon, and was defended by Fénelon in his *Explication des Maximes des Saints sur la Vie Intérieure*. Passages from this book were condemned by Innocent XII in 1699.

For further details of the dispute, see Grean 1967: 188–91. A recent popular account is available in Chadwick 2002.

(I am indebted to two earlier editors of Butler, Matthews 1964: 26, note 2, and White 2006: 396 for some of this information.)

Butler's nuanced verdict is given in S 12.13. For Shaftesbury's somewhat similar view, see *Inquiry*, I, iii, 3, in *Characteristics*: 182–92.

Sermon 1

Originally, the first three sermons were grouped under the title 'Upon human nature, or man considered as a moral agent'; the sub-title of Sermon 1 was 'Upon the social nature of man', and of Sermons 2 and 3, 'Upon the natural supremacy of conscience'.

S 1.1 More is said of these 'extraordinary gifts' in *I Corinthians* xii: 7–11.

But the manifestation of the Spirit is given to every man to profit withal. For to one is given by the Spirit the word of wisdom, to another the word of knowledge by the same Spirit: to another faith by the same Spirit: to another the gifts of healings by the same Spirit: to another the working of miracles, to another prophecy, to another discerning of spirits, to another divers kinds of tongues, to another the interpretation of tongues: but all these worketh that one and the selfsame Spirit, dividing to every man severally as he will.

Which of these 'extraordinary gifts' might Butler have thought to have 'totally ceased'? Presumably not knowledge or wisdom, but almost certainly speaking in tongues, prophecy, performing miracles, and supernatural healing. Butler's view was fairly common in the Anglican Church in the eighteenth century. That he took the age of personal revelations from God to be over is amusingly illustrated by a conversation with Butler that John Wesley records in his diary. Wesley, who remained an ordained minister in the Church of England, was following his call to itinerant evangelism by preaching in the diocese of Bristol. Butler summoned him to explain his preaching without a licence from the Bishop. At one point in the conversation, Butler notes that George Whitefield (a fellow Methodist preacher) wrote in his Journal that 'there are promises [of God] still to be fulfilled in me'. Of this claim, Butler remarks. 'Sir, the pretending to extraordinary revelations and gifts of the Holy Ghost is a horrid thing, a very horrid thing!' (*Works of John Wesley*, 1872, vol. 13: 409; quoted in Gladstone, *Sermons*: 366).

S 1.4 '... illustrated by the former.' Bernard notes that the analogy of the body and its members was very common in antiquity, citing passages from Livy, Xenophon, Cicero, and Seneca in support.

S 1.4 '... to the whole body.' In the first edition this sentence reads:

> the latter shews us it is our duty to do good to others, as the former shews us that we are to take care of our own private interest.

Butler's alterations in the second edition, by stressing what the parts of the body and each individual in society were *intended* to do, reinforce the teleological note that we frequently find in the *Sermons*: God made us with a particular nature for certain purposes.

S 1.6 This is a matter on which Butler and SHAFTESBURY agree. Two of the theses Shaftesbury sets out to prove in the *Inquiry* are:

1. that *to have the natural, kindly or generous affections strong and powerful towards the good of the public is to have the chief means and power of self-enjoyment and that to want them is certain misery and ill;*
2. that *to have the private or self affections too strong or beyond their degree of subordinacy to the kindly and natural is also miserable* (*Inquiry* II, 2, 1 in *Characteristics*: 200).

Note also that Butler does not here distinguish, as he sometimes does, benevolence as a general principle of goodwill to all from the particular benevolent affections, e.g. pity, sympathy, that have the good of some particular person as their object.

S 1.6n The full reference is to HOBBES, *The Elements of Law*, Part I, 'On Human Nature', ch. 9, para. 17.

> There is yet another passion sometimes called love, but more properly good will or charity. There can be no greater argument to a man of his own power, than to find himself able, not only to accomplish his own desires, but also to assist other men to theirs: and this is that conception wherein consisteth charity. (Hobbes, *Human Nature and De Corpore Politico*: 56.)

Butler ignores the less contentious definition in *Leviathan*, Book I, ch. 6:

> Desire of good to another, benevolence, good will, charity. If to man generally, good nature. (Hobbes, *Leviathan*: 123.)

Bernard suggests that Hobbes may have here been influenced by Aristotle's account of the great-souled man.

> He is the sort of person who does good but is ashamed when he receives it; for doing good is proper to the superior person, but receiving it is proper to the inferior. (*Nicomachean Ethics*, Book IV, ch. 3, para. 24, 1124b 10–13: 58.)

It is agreed by most commentators that Butler's interpretation of Hobbes is at points, to say the least, unsympathetic. In one of the few unpublished fragments of his that remain Butler admits that there is an element of truth in HOBBES' account.

> Hobbes' definition of benevolence, that 'tis the love of power, is base and false, but there is more of truth in it than appears at first sight; the real benevolence of man being, I think, for the most part, not indeed the single love of power, but the love of power to be exercised in the way of doing good; that is a different thing from the love of the good or happiness of

others by whomsoever effected, which last I should call single or simple benevolence. (Bernard, *Sermons*: 306.)

S 1.8 Note that, as in the Preface, Butler starts by talking about a principle of reflection and then proceeds to identify this principle with conscience.

S 1.12 '... emulation and resentment being away.' The rather sanguine view that there is no such thing as disinterested malice was fairly common in the eighteenth century. HUTCHESON writes:

> As to malice, human nature seems scarce capable of malicious disinterested hatred, or a sedate delight in the misery of others, when we imagine them in no way pernicious to us or opposite to our interest. (*Inquiry into the Original of our Ideas of Beauty and Virtue*, Treatise II, Section 2, sub-section IV: 105.)

Hume agrees:

> Absolute, unprovoked, disinterested malice has never perhaps place in any human breast; or if it had, must there pervert all the sentiments of morals, as well as the feelings of humanity. (*An Enquiry Concerning the Principles of Morals*: 227.)

SHAFTESBURY, however, takes a different view. Speaking of what he calls the 'unnatural affections' he says:

> Of this kind is that unnatural and inhuman delight in beholding torments and in viewing distress, calamity, blood, massacre and destruction with a peculiar joy and pleasure.... [T]o delight in the torture and pain of other creatures indifferently, natives or foreigners, of our own or of another species, kindred or no kindred, known or unknown, to feed as it were on death and be entertained with dying agonies—this has nothing in it accountable in the way of self-interest or private good,... but is wholly and absolutely unnatural as it is horrid and miserable. (*Inquiry* II, 2, 3 in *Characteristics*: 226.)

It also seems strange that so acute an observer of human nature as Butler should deny the possibility of self-hatred. Perhaps what he means to deny is *causeless* self-hatred. Just as resentment and emulation can indeed provoke malice, so guilt and disgust at one's own failings or shortcomings may provoke self-hatred.

S 1.12 'by innocent means': see S 7.16.

S 1.12n Bernard points out that Aristotle distinguishes emulation and envy in a similar manner:

> Emulation is pain caused by seeing the presence, in persons whose nature is like our own, of good things that are highly valued and are possible for ourselves to acquire; but it is felt not because others have these goods, but because we have not got them ourselves. It is therefore a good feeling felt by good persons, whereas envy is a bad feeling felt by bad persons. Emulation makes us take steps to secure the good things in question, envy makes us take steps to stop our neighbour having them. (*Rhetoric* II, ii, 1388a 30–6: 120.)

See also HOBBES' admirably succinct definition in *Leviathan*:

> Grief, for the success of a competitor in wealth, honour, or other good, if it be joined with endeavour to enforce our own abilities to equal or exceed him, is called EMULATION: but joined with endeavour to supplant or hinder a competitor, ENVY. (I, 6: 126.)

S 1.14 In the first edition the last sentence of this paragraph makes a rather different claim:

So that from what appears, there is no ground to assert that cool self-love has any more influence upon the actions of men than the principles of virtue and benevolence have.

Sermon 2

S 2.1 Butler once again sounds a strongly teleological note. See also, e.g., S 1.4, S 4.7, and S 6.1.

S 2.2 See S 1.12.

S 2.4 See P 13.

S 2.8 See S 7.16, S 11.15, A I. 3. 16: 57.

S 2.10 See S 3.9, D 5.

S 2.12 '…and it will further appear…' The last part of this sentence was not in the first edition. Conscience or reflection, by its very nature, not only tells us what we ought to do, it reflexively judges itself to be superior and authoritative. See D 1n.

S 2.17 '…mischief to another for its own sake.' See S 1.12, S 2.2, and S 9.26.

S 2.17 '…nothing can be reduced to a greater absurdity.' Sturgeon 1976 raises an important question about Butler's crowning argument in this Sermon for the superiority of conscience. The function of conscience is to approve or disapprove of our actions. Its fulfilling this role seems separate from the issue of whether it is merely one principle in our psychology among others, or whether it has ultimate authority. So why, Sturgeon asks, would a lack of superiority prevent it from condemning parricide? For further discussion of Sturgeon's view and a possible response, see McNaughton 2013.

Sermon 3

S 3.2 For some of the ancient writers that Butler has in mind, see the note to P 13.

S 3.2n See S 12.13.

S 3.4 See S 5.15: 'In all common ordinary cases we see intuitively at first view what is our duty, what is the honest part'; and also S 7.14.

Sermon 4

S 4.3 'Humour' here means temperament, disposition, or mood. This use of the word comes from the medical theories of Hippocrates which were widely accepted in Europe in the Middle Ages. There were four basic humours or temperaments: sanguine (optimistic and social), choleric (short-tempered or irritable), melancholic (analytical and quiet), and phlegmatic (relaxed and peaceful). Strictly, the humours are not the temperaments themselves but the four underlying physiological conditions from which those temperaments sprang.

S 4.7 '…it was given us.' In several places, e.g. S 2.1, S 6.1, Butler contends that if any of our faculties has some obvious use or purpose, we may legitimately infer that such is its proper use, since they were given to us by God for that purpose. In S 9.9 Butler allows, as here, that every appetite and passion may be innocently gratified in ways that do not further its main end or purpose. That gratification is innocent provided it neither conflicts with the main purpose for which we were given the faculty, or with any moral obligation we are under. There are similarities here to Natural Law Theory as propounded by Aquinas and others.

S 4.7 '...he hath placed us in.' Butler means that, in giving us various faculties, God not only provided for our needs but also offered us a means of enjoyment.

S 4.17 *Mark* 12.38–40 reads:

And he said unto them in his doctrine, Beware of the scribes, which love to go in long clothing, and love salutations in the marketplaces. And the chief seats in the synagogues, and the uppermost rooms at feasts: Which devour widows' houses, and for a pretence make long prayers: these shall receive greater damnation.

S 4.19 Butler was fond of quoting from *Ecclesiasticus*, a book not given canonical status in the Hebrew scriptures and hence placed by the Protestant Reformers in the Apocrypha, even though it is canonical in the Roman Catholic Church.

Sermon 5

S 5.1n Hobbes, *Human Nature* ch. 9, para. 10: 53. The account in *Leviathan* I.6 is very similar:

'Grief, for the calamity of another is PITY; and ariseth from the imagination that the like calamity may befall himself; and therefore is called also COMPASSION, and in the phrase of the present time a FELLOW-FEELING' (126).

As with the earlier criticisms of HOBBES in Sermon 1, some of Butler's complaints rely on a very unsympathetic reading. For instance, Butler interprets Hobbes as claiming that fear and compassion are the same thing. This would indeed be absurd, but Hobbes claims that pity *for others* is really only at bottom fear *for ourselves*. It is illegitimate to leave out the italicized words and interpret Hobbes as identifying fear and compassion, so that to pity our friends is to fear them. Nor, I think, is Hobbes making the claim that these two phrases have the same meaning; rather, he is making the psychological claim that what really drives our so-called compassion is in fact a fear for our own skins. Butler is on stronger ground when he points out that the claim that we pity the distress of our friends more than that of strangers is not the same claim as that we fear more *for ourselves* when we observe our friends to be in distress than when we observe strangers to be in a similar plight. While the first claim is generally true, the second is clearly not equivalent and also much more doubtful. Even though Hobbes is not providing a verbal definition of pity, he does treat his 'definition' as axiomatic, when in fact it needs to be established by observation and argument.

S 5.2 It is unclear exactly what hangs on the claim that compassion is an 'original, distinct, particular affection' whereas rejoicing in another's good fortune is not, in part because Butler's distinction between general and particular affections is itself unclear. Indeed, Butler seems at various places to be drawing different distinctions in his use of this contrasting pair of terms. (For an attempt to enumerate and evaluate some of these, see McNaughton 1992: 269–91). Indeed Butler himself is less concerned with classificatory issues than with the underlying differences between compassion and 'delight in the prosperity of others'. Even if someone wished to classify both as distinct affections, the differences would still remain.

The main difference that Butler sees between compassion and rejoicing in the good fortune or achievements of others is that distress requires that we relieve it, whereas good fortune requires nothing of us in terms of practical action. Butler's view of the role of the particular affections seems to be this: they are given us to provide additional motivation towards some particular desirable end when the influence of conscience, self-love, or benevolence might be insufficient for that purpose (See, e.g., S 5.3, S 5.10). So, for example, we have the appetite of hunger because the recognition that food is required for sustenance might be insufficient on its own to motivate us. Similarly, Butler thinks, our natural goodwill ensures that we are pleased when others flourish and displeased when things go badly for them (provided that we have no personal animus against those individuals). Where we rejoice with those that rejoice, nothing more needs to be done. Since there is no further goal, there is no need of a particular affection to provide additional motivation. But in the case of those who have fallen on evil times, feeling sorry is not enough; action to relieve their distress is required. Our tendency to sympathize might be insufficient to achieve this end; compassion helps to move us beyond sympathy to offering practical help. This distinction is genuine and important; whether it is best articulated in terms of a distinction between general and particular affections is more doubtful.

S 5.3 See also S 8.4.

In this paragraph, Butler rejects the extreme STOIC doctrine that it would be better if we were not merely to moderate our passions but to extirpate them completely. The Stoic view of the emotions was opposed to that of the Peripatetics who, following Aristotle, thought that the emotions should be moderated through education and training. Butler here clearly sides with Aristotle.

St. Augustine has an interesting brief discussion contrasting the Christian and Stoic views of compassion in *City of God*, Book IX, ch. 5: 349–50.

S 5.11 See Cicero, *On Duties* III. 43: 116.

S 5.12 See also P 40.

S 5.13 See *Luke* xix.41: 'And when he came near, he beheld the city, and wept over it.' See also *John* xi.35 in the story of the raising of Lazarus.

S 5.14 See Sermon 6.

S 5.15 'no one of mere common understanding could.' See *Matt.* xi.25: 'I thank thee, O Father, Lord of heaven and earth, because thou hast hid these things from the wise and prudent, and hast revealed them unto babes.' See also the parallel passage in *Luke* x.21. Jesus here echoes *Isaiah* xxix.14.

Butler's defence of common sense, and his conviction that the plain honest man is less likely to go wrong in these matters than the intellectually sophisticated, extend beyond his belief that untutored conscience will not normally err about right and wrong, to the claim that common sense will often be a better guide *to human nature itself* than the sophisticated hypotheses of the learned. It is clear that, in the remainder of this final paragraph, Butler is returning to his attack on HOBBES, as exemplifying the errors of the learned.

S 5.15 'going beside or beyond it'. The Church of England viewed itself as occupying a middle position between, on the one hand, the superstitious idolatry of the Roman Church, with its devotion to the relics of saints etc. and, on the other, the enthusiasm of certain non-conformist Protestant churches that held that God could and did send special revelations to believers. (See Note to S 1.1 for Butler's remarks to Wesley about his fellow-preacher Whitefield.)

Sermon 6

For a brief account of observance during Lent in the early eighteenth century, see C. J. Abbey and J. H. Overton, *The English Church in the Eighteenth Century* (London: Longmans, 1906)

432–4 (Accessible at Google Books). The final grave and solemn paragraphs of this Sermon reflect the penitential nature of Lent in the Christian calendar.

S 6.1 The AV translation may obscure Butler's point. The New Revised Standard Version makes the point more clearly. 'All things come in pairs, one opposite the other, and he has made nothing incomplete.'

S 6.2 See also S 5.2.

S 6.7 Butler seems here to suggest that our whole nature, and not just conscience, is the voice of God within us. Presumably his thought is that, when rightly ordered, each particular affection, as well as conscience, urges us in the right direction (see S3.2n). He affirms this line of thought in the *Analogy*:

Our whole nature leads us to ascribe all moral perfection to God, and to deny all imperfection of him. And this will for ever be a practical proof of his moral character, to such as will consider what a practical proof is; because it is the voice of God speaking in us. And from hence we conclude, that virtue must be the happiness, and vice the misery, of every creature; and that regularity and order and right cannot but prevail finally in a universe under his government. But we are in no sort judges, what are the necessary means of accomplishing this end (A Intro. 10).

S 6.8 See S 9.27.

S 6.9 Bernard suggests that the contrast here is not between an affection and conscience or reflection, but between a 'blind' or unguided affection and that same affection under the direction of reason. Compare S 12.27 and A I. 5. 20.

S 6.10 Despite Butler's remonstrance against the STOICS for advocating the extirpation of emotions (see S5.3), there is here an almost Stoic tone, in that the highest form of life to which we can aspire is one in which we manage to achieve tranquillity of mind in the face of our sorrows and afflictions.

S 6.11n Butler is here quoting *Psalm* xxxix.5 in AV and not, as he usually does, in the Prayer Book version. There is a slight misquotation: AV reads 'state' rather than 'estate'.

S 6.12 This reference to the outward show of repentance during Lent shows, as Gladstone (*Works*, vol. II: 101) observes that 'there was still in Butler's day a general outward compliance with the ancient prescriptions touching Lent'.

S 6.13 This passage, which reflects a common view of heaven in Christianity, raises an interesting issue in moral theology: why are we called upon to make such efforts to develop on earth virtuous dispositions that will be useless in heaven? Butler briefly alludes to this problem and hints at a possible solution at A I.5.20 (96):

It is indeed true, that there can be no scope for patience, when sorrow shall be no more: but there may be need of a temper of mind, which shall have been formed by patience.

Sermon 7

S 7 This sermon, whose main topic is self-deception, should be read in conjunction with Sermon 10 and with *A Sermon Preached Before the House of Lords* (SPO 3) which is reprinted in this volume.

S 7.2 '... first lesson of the day.' The lesson appointed for Matins on the second Sunday after Easter was *Numbers* xxiii and xxiv. The preceding chapter of that book would have been read at Evensong on the previous Sunday, and the succeeding chapter would have been read at Evensong on the second Sunday after Easter.

S 7.2 '… there are parallels to.' The 'cavils' to which Butler refers might well have included scepticism about the story of Balaam's ass, which is temporarily given the power of speech by God and upbraids Balaam for his ill-treatment of it (see *Numbers* xxii. 22–35).

S 7.6 'he seeks… by "sacrifices" and "enchantments"'. On three occasions, Balaam asks Balak to build seven altars on each of which were sacrificed a bullock and a ram. Three times God repeats his injunction to Balaam not to curse Israel. After the third such sacrifice we read: 'And when Balaam saw that it pleased the Lord to bless Israel, he went not, as at other times to seek for enchantments, but he set his face toward the wilderness' (*Numbers* xxiv.1).

S 7.6 Philo wrote:

[H]e [Balaam] pressed forward even more readily than his conductor [Balak], partly because he was dominated by the worst of vices, conceit, partly because in his heart he longed to curse, even if he were prevented from doing so with his voice. (Philo *De vita Mosis*, I, Section 286.)

The whole story is related by Philo in chs. 48–55 (Sections 263–305).

Bernard ascribes a similar view to Origen, and some of the Latin fathers, viz. that Balaam was constrained by God to bless when his own desire was to curse.

S 7.7 The sin and punishment allotted to the children of Israel are recorded in *Numbers* xxv.1–9. The Israelites 'commit whoredom with the daughters of Moab', sacrifice to other gods, and 'join [themselves] unto Baal-peor'. God brings a plague upon Israel, in which 24,000 die before God is appeased. That Balaam was the 'contriver of the whole matter' is suggested in *Numbers* xxxi.16, which reads in part: 'These (i.e. the women) caused the children of Israel, *through the counsel of Balaam*, to commit trespass against the name of the Lord in the matter of Peor' (my emphasis).

Revelation ii.14 reads: 'But I have a few things against thee, because thou hast there them that hold the doctrine of Balaam, who taught Balak to cast a stumbling-block before the children of Israel, to eat things sacrificed unto idols, and to commit fornication.' There are two other unfavourable references to Balaam in the New Testament: *Jude* v.11, and *2 Peter* ii.15–16. The latter reads: 'which have forsaken the right way, and are gone astray, following the way of Balaam the son of Bosor, who loved the wages of unrighteousness, but was rebuked for his iniquity: the dumb ass speaking with man's voice forbad the madness of the prophet'.

S 7.14 See S 3.4. Berkeley makes the same point in *Alciphron*, Third Dialogue, Section 3 (*Works*, vol. III, 118.): 'Men's first thoughts and natural notions are the best in moral matters.' See also S 5.15.

S 7.15 'indulgences and atonements before-mentioned.' Bernard claims there is an inconsistency between this passage, which claims that the errors of superstition are occasioned by dishonesty, and the concession in S 3.4, that superstition may distort conscience without any dishonesty being involved. There is in fact no inconsistency between the passages, because Butler is talking about different ways of being superstitious. In S 7.15 Butler puts a specific gloss on the term 'superstition', depicting the superstitious as 'making a composition with the Almighty' to obey only some of his commands. Where such people disobey, they seek to placate God by seeking indulgences for their sins prior to their misdeeds, or making atonements after they have committed them, as if they could bribe God or appease him into overlooking their transgressions. But such conduct proceeds 'from a certain unfairness of mind, a peculiar inward dishonesty' (S 7.15). What makes their actions superstitious is that they believe they can buy God's favour, and thus get let off the punishment for what they know to be disobedience, by engaging in certain rituals or sacrifices. That is compatible with his allowing in S 3.4 that 'superstition', in the quite different sense of *sincerely held false* religious beliefs, may lead *honest* people astray.

S 7.15 *Matt.* xviii.3 reads: 'Verily I say unto you, except ye be converted, and become as little children, ye shall not enter into the kingdom.' See also S 5.15.

S 7.16 'state of an innocent man.' Bernard cites Cicero as making a similar point:

> However burning one's greed, however unbridled one's desires, there is no one today, nor was there ever, who would even dream of attaining some goal by an act of wickedness, when the same goal was achievable without such means, even if complete impunity was offered in the former case. (*On Moral Ends*, III. 36: 76.)

S 7.16 'upon which our whole being depends.' See S 2.8.

S 7.16 'peace at the last': *Ps.* xxxvii.38 (prayer book version). The equivalent verse in AV reads: 'Mark the perfect man, and behold the upright: for the end of that man is peace.'

Sermon 8

S 8.1 '...by which it is preserved': see S 12.2.

S 8.1 'any particular affection or passion leads us to': this is the method used in Sermon 6 and elsewhere.

S 8.1 'anything at all to do with': Butler frequently insists that we do not, and do not need to, know the answers to abstract questions about God's nature and purposes beyond what we require for immediate practical purposes. See especially Sermon 15.

S 8.2 A reference to the text for the sermon. It is not clear to whom Jesus is referring when he tells his listeners that they have formerly been taught to hate their enemies. *Leviticus* xix.18 enjoins love of neighbour, but not hatred of our enemies (see also *Exodus* xxiii.4–5, for a direct injunction to aid our enemy).

S 8.3 This is one of the rare places in the *Sermons* where Butler employs phrases reminiscent of the a priori ethics of Samuel Clarke. Such language is more common in the *Analogy*. Another example can be found in S 8.16.

S 8.4 Although Butler borrows much from STOICISM, here again he rejects the doctrine of *apatheia*: the teaching that we should seek to eradicate our passions. See also S 5.3.

S 8.7 '...is by no means malice': see S 1.7.

S 8.7 '...is at all too high amongst mankind': see S 9.2.

S 8.7 '...what concerns ourselves': see S 12.17.

S 8.10 This is the reading of all editions published in Butler's lifetime but, as Bernard points out, it is hard to see what Butler might have meant by this. The context surely suggests that he meant to say that peevishness, though less 'boisterous', is no *more* innocent than irascibility.

S 8.11 Note that Butler holds settled resentment to be perfectly licit unless it is excessive, given the severity of the offence. See also S 9.2.

S 8.13 'He hath also prepared for him the instruments of death; he ordaineth his arrows against the persecutors' (*Ps.* vii.13).

S 8.16 '...founded in the nature of things': see S 8.3.

S 8.16 'are to be the guide of his actions': Compare Shaftesbury in *The Moralists*, Part III, Section 2 where, after decrying the absurdity of feeling resentment for an accidental hurt, he writes:

> Therefore there is just and unjust; and belonging to it a natural presumption or anticipation on which the resentment or anger is founded. For what else should make the wickedest of mankind often prefer the interest of their revenge to all other interests, and even to life itself, except only a sense of wrong, natural to all men, and a desire to prosecute that wrong at any rate. (Shaftesbury, *Characteristics*, 329.)

Butler returns to this theme in D 1.

Sermon 9

S 9.2 '...anger, indignation, resentment, or by whatever name anyone shall choose': note that Butler here uses these terms interchangeably. Many writers on forgiveness now distinguish resentment and indignation; the former is typically personal whereas the latter is impersonal. One can feel indignant on anyone's behalf, whereas one can typically resent only injury to oneself or those with whom one is closely identified. One who resents is often typically aggrieved, feels betrayed, or has their feelings hurt, in a way that one who is merely indignant is not. Some have suggested that forgiveness requires the overcoming of resentment, but not necessarily of indignation. It seems fairly clear from the remainder of the paragraph that Butler is primarily talking of what we should now call indignation, since he holds that one can feel it on one's own behalf, or on behalf of others. It is only in the former case that it is liable to be excessive.

S 9.2 '...low enough in mankind': see S 8.7.

S 9.2 '...personal and private injury': Butler is often credited with recognizing that forgiveness requires the *forswearing* of resentment, but that is not what he says. He objects only to 'the excess and abuse of this natural feeling'. One abuse is retaliation or revenge. However, this common misreading of Butler may not distort his meaning as much as at first appears. For if, as I suggested in the first note to S 9.2, we distinguish indignation from resentment, it could be argued that a position like Butler's might imply that we should forswear resentment, but not indignation (see Garrard and McNaughton 2003).

S 9.5 '...for resentment itself...blameable than the aggressor' added in second edition.

S 9.5 '...letteth out water':

> The figure is taken from the great tank or reservoir upon which Eastern cities often depended for their supply of water. The beginning of strife is compared to the first crack in the mound of such a reservoir. At first a few drops ooze out, but after a time the whole mass of waters pour themselves forth with fury, and it is hard to set limits to the destruction which they cause. (Albert Barnes, *Notes on the Bible* accessed at <http://biblehub.com/commentaries/proverbs/17-14.htm>.)

S 9.6 '...it hath been shewn': at S 8.8.

S 9.8 '...is the sum of morals.' This remark might be taken to indicate that the *sole* purpose of morality is to promote the well-being of all. Although Butler is sometimes sympathetic to this view, he appears ultimately to reject it. (See, especially S 12.31 and accompanying footnote, and D 8.)

S 9.8 '…a member of it.' Butler's remarks about indignation and punishment here are similar to Bentham's famous later remarks:

> But all punishment is mischief: all punishment in itself is evil. Upon the principle of utility, if it ought at all to be admitted, it ought only to be admitted in as far as it promises to exclude some greater evil. (*Principles of Morals and Legislation* XIII. 2: 158.)

However, when considering divine punishment, Butler takes a more retributivist stance. God rewards and punishes according to desert. See D 9, and A I.2.3; A I.3.2, 3, 6, 9, 25; A II.5.3–4. At A I.3.12 (54) Butler elaborates his view that *civil* punishment does *not* consider moral desert:

> …civil government [is] supposed to take cognizance of actions in no other view than as prejudicial to society, without respect to the immorality of them.

However, he goes on to concede that our keenness to bring offenders to justice and our willingness to moderate or remit punishment are, in fact, affected by our assessment of the degree of *moral* guilt or innocence in the offender.

S 9.11 '…before mentioned': see also A I. vii. 7: 124–5.

S 9.13 If, as I earlier suggested, we distinguish indignation from resentment, then we might well allow that indignation is consistent with goodwill, while doubting that resentment is. (See again note to S 9.2.)

S 9.15 '…capable of happiness or misery.' Butler's position here differs from that of both Kant and Bentham. The former holds that we have direct obligations only to rational or moral agents; the latter holds that all that matters morally is the capacity to feel pleasure or pain. Butler's sensible view appears to be that we have an obligation of benevolence to all sentient creatures, but that other obligations only arise with respect to moral agents.

S 9.15 '…inconsistent with it.' Given the comparatively minor offences that were punishable by death at the time Butler wrote, one must suppose either that he was opposed to the severity of the law in such cases, or that he had an exaggerated estimate of the dangers posed by petty thieving. Nor does Butler's justification address the question of why the execution needed to be *public*.

S 9.17 '…self-partiality possessed of the very understanding': see S 10.11.

S 9.19 '…after which there will yet remain real good-will towards the offender': words added in second edition.

S 9.26 '…not…any such thing as direct ill-will in one man towards another': see S 1.8 and S 2.17.

S 9.26 Cato the censor of whom Sallust writes:

> Repeatedly, Members of the Senate, I have spoken at great length in this body; often I have deplored the extravagance and greed of our citizens, and for that reason I have many mortals opposed to me. Since I had never granted to myself, or to my impulse, indulgence for any transgression, I have found it quite difficult to pardon misdeeds on the part of a dissolute person. (*War with Catiline*: 121.)

S 9.27 '…of compassion': see S6.8.

S 9.27 '…a much greater to himself.' Butler here endorses Socrates' famous claim that it is better to suffer wrong than to do wrong (see, e.g., *Gorgias* 469b ff.; 813 ff.).

Sermon 10

This Sermon should be read in conjunction with Sermon 7.

S 10.2 'Know thyself': this ancient Greek aphorism was supposedly inscribed in the forecourt of the Temple of Apollo at Delphi. It has been ascribed to various early thinkers, but may well simply be a common saying or proverb. Plato represents it as playing an important role in Socrates' philosophical quest. It is mentioned in a number of Platonic dialogues, e.g.: *Charmides* 164d: 651, *Protagoras* 343b: 775, *Phaedrus* 229e: 510, *Philebus* 48c: 438, *Laws* XI. 923a: 1576, and *I Alcibiades* 124a: 580; 129a: 587; 132c: 591 (Plato, *Complete Works*).

S 10.3 Bernard reports that he can find no source for this, but that Butler may have had in mind a saying of Pliny the Elder.

He made extracts of everything he read, and always said that there was no book so bad that some good could not be got out of it. (Pliny the Younger, *Letters*, Book III, Letter v, 10–11: 177.)

S 10.6 See also St. Paul:

... who knowing the judgement of God, that they which commit such things are worthy of death, not only do the same, but have pleasure in them that do them. (*Romans* i.32.)

At A I. 6.14: 114, Butler remarks:

... that as speculative reason may be neglected, prejudiced, and deceived, so also may our moral understanding be impaired and perverted, and the dictates of it not impartially attended to.

S 10.10 See S 3.4 and S 12.8.

S 10.11 '... internal hypocrisy and self-deceit': Butler holds that, as well as deliberate external hypocrisy, where a person knows her own character but intentionally deceives others about it, there are cases where the agent herself is among those deceived. Where the agent is to some extent aware, or could and should be aware, of that self-deception, it can properly be called internal hypocrisy. For a much longer discussion, see also SPO 3.1–12 (included in this volume as *A Sermon Preached Before the House of Lords*).

S 10.11 '... being itself evil and vicious': the whole passage in *Matthew* reads:

The light of the body is the eye: if therefore thine eye be single, thy whole body shall be full of light. But if thine eye be evil, thy whole body shall be full of darkness. If therefore the light that is in thee be darkness, how great is that darkness! (*Matt.* vi.22–3.)

In NRSV 'single' and 'evil' are translated as 'healthy' and 'unhealthy' respectively.

S 10.11 '... the condition of them is bad.' Bernard compares this to a passage in Locke's:

We. know some men will not read a letter which is supposed to bring ill news; and many men forbear to cast up their accounts, or so much as think upon their estates, who have reason to fear their affairs are in no very good posture. (Locke, *Essay*, IV.20.6: vol. II, 300.)

S 10.13 See S 12.15.

S 10.14 See *Luke* xviii.9–14.

Sermon 11

S 11.1 The two philosophers who spring to mind in this connection are Hobbes and Mandeville. How much views similar to theirs were popular among Butler's congregation at the Rolls Chapel it is hard to tell. However, Bernard cites Berkeley in *Siris* 331 as making a similar complaint.

> Certainly had the philosophy of Socrates and Pythagoras prevailed in this age, among those who think themselves too wise to receive the dictates of the Gospel, we should not have seen interest take so general and fast hold on the minds of men, nor public spirit reputed to be . . . a generous folly, among those who are reckoned to be the most knowing as well as the most getting part of mankind. (Berkeley, *Works* vol. V: 151.)

S 11.8 See S 11.11.

S 11.9 Butler here enunciates what Sidgwick called 'the fundamental paradox of Hedonism . . . that the impulse towards pleasure, if too predominant, defeats its own aim' (1967b: 49). Sidgwick developed this line of reasoning to suggest that the best way to secure the general happiness, as well as individual happiness, might be not to focus continually on that goal, but to have more immediate and limited aims.

S 11.11 The passage beginning, 'But the cases' and ending 'Love of our neighbour then' replaces a passage in the First Edition that reads:

> And as it is taken for granted in the former case, that the external good, in which we have a property exclusive of all others, must for this reason have a nearer and greater respect to private interest than it would have if it were enjoyed in common with others; so likewise it is taken for granted that the principle of an action which does not proceed from regard to the good of others has a nearer and greater respect to self-love, or is less distant from it. But whoever will at all attend to the thing, will see that these consequences do not follow. For as the enjoyment of the air we breathe is just as much our private interest and advantage now as it would be if none but ourselves had the benefit of it, so love of our neighbour . . .

S 11.13 Paragraph 12, and Paragraph 13 down to the words 'any other', were not in the First Edition which had instead:

> But since self-love is not private good, since interestedness is not interest, let us now see whether benevolence has not the same respect to, the same tendency toward promoting, private good and interest, with the other particular passions; as it hath been already shewn that they have all in common the same respect to self-love and interestedness.

S 11.13 'is in a degree its own reward.' Butler's thoughts here again echo Cicero's: 'my claim and contention is that duty is its own reward' (*On Ends* II. 72: 50).

S 11.15 See S 2.8, S 7.16.

S 11.16 For a similar distinction between a principle and a natural affection, see S 1.8.

S 11.18 See S 1.7n.

S 11.19 The passage beginning '. . . seems, as hath already been hinted' and ending '. . . lessen your own happiness' replaces a passage in the First Edition that reads:

> is this which hath been already hinted, that men consider the means and materials of enjoyment, not the enjoyment of them, as what constitutes interest and happiness. It is the possession, having the property of riches, houses, lands, gardens, in which our interest or

good is supposed to consist. Now, if riches and happiness are identical terms, it may well be thought that, as by bestowing riches on another, you lessen your own, so also by promoting the happiness of another you lessen your own. And thus there would be a real inconsistence and contrariety between private and public good.

S 11.19 '...fully proved to be one.' The remainder of the paragraph was added in the Second Edition.

S 11.20 '...so far from disowning the principle of self-love.' Compare A I. 5.19: 95. This passage is quoted in the note to P 41.

S 11.20 '...are real as truth itself.' This is one of many points in Butler's writings where he appears to express his adherence to the moral realism of writers like SAMUEL CLARKE and WILLIAM WOLLASTON.

S 11.20 This notorious sentence has attracted much attention, for Butler *appears* to give a veto to self-love with respect to the deliverances of conscience.

S 11.21 '...private interest and self-love.' Compare Shaftesbury:

For though the habit of selfishness, and the multiplicity of interested views, are of little improvement to real merit or virtue; yet there is a necessity for the preservation of virtue, that it should be thought to have no quarrel with true interest and self-enjoyment. (*Inquiry* III. 3 in *Characteristics*: 188.)

S 11.22 The full Epistle for the Day was *Romans* xiii.8–14.

S 11.22 '...and was made man.' Part of the Nicene Creed.

Sermon 12

S 12.2 '...love to the whole universe': whether Butler holds that benevolence is the sole attribute of God is a difficult question. Relevant texts include D 8, A I. 2.3: 36, and A I. 3.3: 47.

S 12.2 Instead of the final sentence, the First Edition had:

Thus we are commanded to be 'perfect as our Father which is in heaven is perfect' (*Matt.* v.48.), *i.e.* perfect in goodness or benevolence as the preceding words determine the sense to be; to make the object of this affection as general and extensive as we are able.

S 12.9 Note that Butler here claims that *rationality* requires obeying conscience. For him, therefore, the question 'Why should I be moral?' understood as 'What reason is there to be moral?' does not arise.

S 12.13 See note to S 3.2.

S 12.14 In the First Edition this paragraph continues:

A comparison being made in the text between self-love and the love of our neighbour, and it being evident that the love of others which includes in it all virtues must necessarily be in due proportion to the love of ourselves; these joint considerations afforded sufficient occasion for treating here of that proportion. It is plainly implied in the precept, though it should not be thought the exact sense of the words *as thyself.*

S 12.15 See Cicero, *Tusculan Disputations* III. 73: 32.

S 12.17 See S 8.7 and S 11.20.

S 12.21 See A I. 3: 20.

S 12.27 See S 6.9.

S 12.31n See further D 8–10.

S 12.32 See S 8.1.

S 12.33 See S 13.7.

Sermon 13

In the original editions, Sermon 13 ran straight into Sermon 14, so that the two are meant to be read as one continuous discourse. Butler's summary (at S 13.3) covers both this and the following Sermon.

S 13.1 See my note to P 43.

S 13.3 Butler here raises, but does not pursue, the interesting question of what qualities of character and intellect we would need in a state of perfection, i.e. in heaven. As he remarks, it may seem as if at least some of the traits and attitudes we develop on our way to a more perfect world would not be needed once we arrived. See also S 6.13.

S 13.5 As Aristotle famously points out:

Suppose, then, that the things achievable by action have some end that we wish for because of itself, and because of which we wish for the other things, and that we do not choose everything because of something else—for if we do, it will go on without limit, so that desire will prove to be empty and futile. (Aristotle, *Nicomachean Ethics*, I. 2, 1. 1094a 18–21: 1.)

S 13.7n. St. Austin = St. Augustine. The passage reads:

We must, in fact, observe the right order even in our love for the very love with which we love what is deserving of love, so that there may be in us the virtue which is the condition of the good life. (Augustine, *The City of God*, Book XV, ch. 22: 637.

S 13.7 '...the objects of contemplation.' See A I. 3.13: 54–5.

S 13.11 See SHAFTESBURY:

For, if there be in nature such a service as that of affection and love, there remains then only to consider of the object whether there be really that supreme one we suppose; for, if there be divine excellence in things, if there be in nature a supreme mind or deity, we have then an object consummate and comprehensive of all which is good or excellent. And this object, of all others, must of necessity be the most amiable, the most engaging and of highest satisfaction and enjoyment. (*The Moralists*, vol. II, Part 2, Section 3 in Shaftesbury, *Characteristics*: 269.)

See also Hooker:

Nothing may be infinitely desired but that good which indeed is infinite; for the better the more desirable; that therefore most desirable wherein there is infinity of goodness; so that if anything desirable may be infinite, that must needs be the highest of all things that are desired (*Ecclesiastical Polity*, Book I, ch. 11, para. 2: 206.)

S 13.13 See P 43, 44.

Sermon 14

S 14.3 See A I. 3.18: 58–9 and A II. 3.8: 168–70.

S 14.5 '...be at peace.' A paraphrase of Job xxii.21: 'Acquaint now thyself with him, and be at peace.'

S 14.5 '...walk with God.' A common phrase in the Bible for following God. 'Enoch walked with God' (*Genesis* v.22); 'walk humbly with thy God' (*Micah* vi.8).

S 14.6 The dictates of conscience are, for Butler, the voice of God, implanted in our nature.

S 14.9 Butler's words are here reminiscent of the famous saying of St. Augustine: 'you have made us for yourself, and our heart is restless until it rests in you' (Augustine, *Confessions*, Book 1, ch. 1, Section 1: 3).

S 14.10 See A I. 5.13: 88. Somewhat similar thoughts are found in Cicero.

And as it is the fires of the flesh in our bodies which commonly enkindle us to almost all desires, and the flame is heightened by envy of all who possess what we desire to possess, assuredly we shall be happy when we have left our bodies behind and are free from all desirings and envyings; and as happens now, when the burden of care is relaxed, we feel the wish for an object of our observation and attention, this will happen much more freely then, and we shall devote our whole being to study and examination, because nature has planted in our minds an insatiable longing to see truth; and the more the vision of the borders only of the heavenly country, to which we have come, renders easy the knowledge of heavenly conditions, the more will our longing for knowledge be increased. (Cicero, *Tusculan Disputations* I, 19: 53, 55.)

For Butler's views on the nature and likelihood of life after death, see *Analogy* ch. 1; for his account of personal identity, see *Analogy* App. I.

S 14.12 '...which we discern': see S 15.5.

S 14.12 '...seeing all things in God': Butler may well be referring here to Malebranche.

S 14.14 '...the chief good of man': see S 15.16.

S 14.14 '...in which the moral attributes of God consist': see A I.6.12n.

S 14.16 Bernard cites a parallel here with St. Augustine:

In that contemplation, therefore, God will be all in all; because nothing else but himself will be required, but it will be sufficient to be enlightened by and to enjoy him alone. (*On the Trinity* 1. I. x. 20: 28.)

Sermon 15

S 15.5 '...power of exercising them depends': almost identical wording can be found at A I. 1.5.

S 15.9 '...resignation to the divine will.' See S 14.3 and A I. 5.20: 96–7.

S 15.9 '...insisted upon.' The suggestion that our epistemic limitations are both one of the evils of life that has to be explained, coupled with the thought that those very limitations form part of a theistic defence to the problem of evil, is currently fairly common. Opponents of theism claim that, if there were a God, he would have removed various evils for which there is no explanation or justification. Defenders of theism sometimes respond that our ignorance precludes our being certain that no explanation or justification of God's allowing those evils is available.

S 15.10 See A II. 5.23: 201–2 and II. 8.8: 260–2. See also Locke:

For, our faculties being suited not to the full extent of being, nor to a perfect, clear, comprehensive knowledge of things free from all doubt and scruple; but to the preservation of us, in whom they are; and accommodated to the use of life: they serve to our purpose well enough, if they will but give us certain notice of those things, which are convenient or inconvenient to us. (*Essay* IV. 11.8: vol. 2, 232.)

S 15.14 See P 27.

S 15.15n See A I. 7.12: 128 and A II. 7.21: 233–4.

S 15.16n The verse alluded to reads: 'he that increaseth knowledge increaseth sorrow.'

S 15.16n Butler here slightly emends *Ecclesiastes* xii.13, which ends 'the whole duty of man'.

S 15.16 Butler here dissents from a famous saying of Cicero:

Socrates on the other hand was the first to call philosophy down from the heavens and set her in the cities of men and bring her also into their homes and compel her to ask questions about life and morality and things good and evil. (*Tusculan Disputations*, Book V. 4. 10–11: 435.)

S 15.16n *Proverbs* iv.23 reads 'Keep thy heart with all due diligence: for out of it are the issues of life.'

A Dissertation of the Nature of Virtue

D 1n 'two epithets, δοκιμαστική and ἀπεοδοκιμάστική': these terms mean 'self-approving' and 'self-disapproving' respectively. They are found in the opening of *The Discourses* of Epictetus which were taken by Arrian from Epictetus' lectures.

Concerning what is in our power and what is not

[1] In general, you will find no art or faculty that can analyse itself, therefore none that can approve or disapprove of itself. [2] The art of grammar is restricted to analysing and commenting on literature. Music is confined to the analysis of harmony. [3] Consequently neither of them analyses itself. Now, if you are writing to a friend, the art of grammar will help you decide what words to use; but it will not tell you whether it is a good idea to write to your friend in the first place. Music is no different; whether this is a good time to sing and play, or a bad one, the art of music by itself cannot decide.

[4] So what can? The faculty that analyses itself as well as the others, namely, the faculty of reason. Reason is unique among the faculties assigned to us in being able to evaluate itself— what it is, what it is capable of, how valuable it is—in addition to passing judgement on others. (*Discourses* I. 1. 1: 5.)

D 1 '...HOBBES says. 'Fifthly, irrational creatures cannot distinguish between *Injury* and *Damage*' (*Leviathan* II. 17: 226.) The remainder of this sentence is a sally against Hobbes, who denies that there can be justice prior to human law. See also S 8.7 and S 8.16.

D 1 '...as including both.' Nearly every commentator has remarked on this striking phrase, which reverses the expectation of the reader who would anticipate seeing sentiment ascribed to heart, and perception to the understanding. Since Butler is both cautious and deliberate, he may here be hinting at a dissatisfaction with the very terms of the debate that continued to rage throughout the eighteenth century between rationalists and sentimentalists. He may also be echoing Aristotle: 'This is why decision is either understanding combined with desire [*orektikos nous*] or desire combined with thought [*orexis dianoêtikê*] (*Nicomachean Ethics* VI. 2. 1139 b2–5: 87). This whole phrase could possibly be translated as 'either desiderative understanding, or thoughtful desire.' (I owe this point to Nat Stein.)

D 2n 'just as his virtue too and his vice lie in activity and not in being acted upon.' Marcus Aurelius, *Meditations* IX. 16: 243; 'all the praise that belongs to virtue lies in action' (Cicero, *On Duties* I. 19: 9.)

D 3 Butler may have taken this illustration from Shaftesbury: 'We do not however say of anyone that he is an ill man, because he has the plague-spots upon him' (*Inquiry* I. 2.1; *Characteristics*: 169).

D 5 'the nature and capacities of the agent': see also S 2.10 and S 3.9. This claim is, in my view, the key to understanding Butler's argument at the end of Sermon 3 (see McNaughton 2013).

D 5 'our moral faculty determines to be vicious': see also A I. 6.12n (112).

D 6 Butler may have HUTCHESON's denial of this claim in mind:

Prudence, if it was only employ'd in promoting private Interest, is never imagin'd to be a Virtue. (*Inquiry*, Treatise II, Section 2.1: 102).

Butler's inclusion of prudence as part of morality may indicate a change from the *Sermons*, where conscience appears to restrict itself to judgements of right and wrong, leaving matters of self-interest and prudence to the faculty of self-love. See McNaughton 2013.

D 7 This objection is also raised and answered at A I. 5.19: 95–6.

D 8 '...in no sort the whole of virtue and vice': see S 12.25–32, and A I. 3.3: 47.

D 8 '...all consideration of distant consequences': see S 1.6n.

D 8 '...procure to himself as great advantage': it is clear that Butler is here assuming, as utilitarianism indeed does, that impartial benevolence requires the agent to give his own happiness the same weight as anyone else's.

D 8 '...a temper of mere general benevolence': here Butler seems willing to take seriously a theological version of what is sometimes dubbed 'indirect utilitarianism'. As finite beings, were we to directly seek the general happiness, we would be liable to err in a number of ways. It may be better from a utilitarian perspective, therefore, that we should follow the kinds of rule envisaged in traditional deontological systems, as a means of promoting the general happiness. If God were a utilitarian, he would foresee these problems, and give us a moral nature that rejects utilitarianism. If we are meant to take this suggestion seriously, it raises problems for Butler's view. It seems to conflict with his avowed adherence to CLARKE's moral theory, which supposes that all rational agents, God as well as humans, can grasp the same eternal fitnesses of things, and should guide their conduct thereby. It also raises questions about how we are to understand Butler's claim that conscience or reflection is *authoritative*.

D 10 Butler probably has in mind HUTCHESON:

In the same manner, the moral evil, or vice, is as the degree of misery, and number of sufferers; so that, that action is best, which procures the greatest happiness for the greatest numbers; and that, worst, which, in like manner, occasions misery. (*Inquiry* II. 3.8: 125.)

A Sermon Preached Before the House of Lords

This is the third of the six *Sermons Preached Upon Public Occasions*, all of which can be found in Bernard's edition of the *Sermons*.

The date is given in both Old and New Style. 'From the 12th century to 1752, the civil or legal year in England began on 25 March (Lady Day); so, for example, the execution of Charles I was recorded at the time in Parliament as happening on 30 January 1648 (Old Style). In modern English-language texts this date is usually shown as "30 January 1649" (New Style)' (<http://en.wikipedia.org/wiki/Old_Style_and_New_Style_dates>).

The 1662 Prayer Book contains a special service for this day (see Cummings 2011: 655–60). Butler's text is taken from the Epistle for that Day. The service expresses the nation's sorrow and penance for its sins that led to this terrible divine judgement, thanksgiving for the restoration of the monarchy, and imprecations against the regicides. An extract from the first sentence of the concluding Collect will suffice to give the flavour of this solemn, not to say sombre, occasion.

> We acknowledge it thy special favour, that though for our many and great provocations thou didst suffer thine Anointed to fall this day into the hands of violent and bloud-thirsty men, and barbarously to be murthered by them; yet thou didst not leave us for ever as sheep without a shepherd, but by thy gracious providence didst miraculously preserve the undoubted heir of the Crown, our most gracious Sovereign King *CHARLES* the Second, from his bloudy enemies, hiding him under the shadow of thy wings, until their tyranny was overpast, and bringing him back in thy good appointed time to sit in peace upon the throne of his Father, and to exercise that authority over us, which of thy special grace thou hadst committed unto him. (Cummings 2011: 660.)

SPO 3.2n Butler's biblical citations in this footnote are to the following passages:

> The Pharisees also with the Sadducees came, and tempting desired him that he should shew them a sign from heaven. He answered and said unto them, When it is evening, ye say, It will be fair weather: for the sky is red. And in the morning, It will be foul weather to day: for the sky is red and lowering. O ye hypocrites, ye can see the face of the sky: but can ye not discern the signs of the times? (*Matt.* xvi.1–3).

The parallel passage at *Luke* xii.54–7 describes Jesus as talking to the people, rather than to the Pharisees and Saducees. It ends: 'Yea, and why even of yourselves judge ye not what is right?

> Thine habitation is in the midst of deceit: through deceit they refuse to know me, saith the Lord. (*Jer.* ix.6.)

> Nevertheless they did flatter him with their mouth, and they lied unto him with their tongues. (*Ps.* lxxviii.36.)

> Ye hypocrites, well did Esaias [Isaiah] prophesy of you, saying, This people draweth nigh unto me with their mouth, and honoureth me with their lips; but their heart is far from me. But in vain they do worship me, teaching for doctrines the commandments of men. And he called the multitude, and said unto them, Hear, and understand: Not that which goeth into the mouth defileth a man; but that which cometh out of the mouth, this defileth a man. Then came his disciples, and said unto him, Knowest thou that the Pharisees were offended, after

they heard this saying? But he answered and said, Every plant, which my heavenly Father hath not planted, shall be rooted up. Let them alone: they be blind leaders of the blind. And if the blind lead the blind, both shall fall into the ditch. (*Matt.* xv.7–14.)

But woe unto you, scribes and Pharisees, hypocrites! for ye shut up the kingdom of heaven against men: for ye neither go in yourselves, neither suffer ye them that are entering to go in. Woe unto you, ye blind guides, which say, Whosoever shall swear by the temple, it is nothing; but whosoever shall swear by the gold of the temple, he is a debtor! Ye fools and blind: for whether is greater, the gift, or the altar that sanctifieth the gift? Ye blind guides, which strain at a gnat, and swallow a camel. Thou blind Pharisee, cleanse first that which is within the cup and platter, that the outside of them may be clean also. (*Matt.* xxiii.13, 16, 19, 24, 26.)

... lest any of you be hardened through the deceitfulness of sin. (*Heb.* Iii.13.)

... which is corrupt according to the deceitful lusts. (*Eph.* iv.22.)

For sin, taking occasion by the commandment, deceived me, and by it slew me. (*Rom.* vii.11.)

Woe unto them that seek deep to hide their counsel from the LORD. (*Is* .xxix.15.)

But Peter said, Ananias, why hath Satan filled thine heart to lie to the Holy Ghost? (*Acts* v.3.)

Be not deceived; God is not mocked: for whatsoever a man soweth, that shall he also reap. (*Gal.* vi.7.)

For this people's heart is waxed gross, and their ears are dull of hearing, and their eyes they have closed. (*Matt.* xii.15.)

This last quotation from *Matthew* is a paraphrase of *Isaiah* vi.10. The whole verse is repeated word for word at *Acts* xxviii.27.

Let no man deceive himself. (*I Cor.* iii.18.)

If we say we have no sin, we deceive ourselves, and the truth is not in us. (*I John* i.8.)

For if a man think himself to be something, when he is nothing, he deceiveth himself. (*Gal.* vi.3.)

But ye be doers of the word, and not hearers only, deceiving your own selves. If any man among you seem to be religious, and bridleth not his tongue, but deceiveth his own heart, this man's religion is vain. (*James* i.22, 26.)

For *Matt.* vi.22–3 and *Luke* xi.34–5, see note on S 10.11.

Butler also cites *Job* iii.19, but this seems to be an error; it occurs in a passage in which Job wishes that he had never been born and reads: 'The small and great are there; and the servant is free from his master.'

SPO 3.6 Note Butler's insistence that self-deception is voluntary, and thus blameable. Some have contended that much, if not all, self-deception is involuntary. Robert Adams 1985 argues that we can nevertheless be blamed even if our character defects were not within our voluntary control.

SPO 3.7 See A I. 3.12: 53–4.

SPO 3.8 Butler here extends the concept of hypocrisy yet further to include professions of virtue, even where neither the speaker nor others expect them to be believed.

SPO 3.10 This topic is extensively discussed in Sermon 7.

SPO 3.16 Butler here prefigures some of Edmund Burke's arguments for conservatism.

SPO 3.17 See SPO 5.5: 261–2.

SPO 3.18n 'When we can endure neither our vices nor their cure' (Livy, *History of Rome*, Book 1: 7.).

SPO 3.19 See A I. 3.15: 56–7.

Notes to Correspondence

The complete extant correspondence is reprinted in Bernard's edition of the *Sermons*. The first part, not reprinted here, concerns CLARKE's arguments about the being and attributes of God. The selection printed here begins at what, in Bernard's edition is Butler's Seventh Letter, and continues to the end (Bernard *Sermons*: 331–9). I have omitted sections of the correspondence of merely historical interest, but retained Bernard's paragraph numbering for ease of reference.

The work to which Butler alludes in the first paragraph of his letter of 30 September 1717 is Clarke's *Letters to Leibnitz, with remarks on Collins' Philosophical Enquiry Concerning Human Liberty* (London 1717).

Butler's Predecessors

In this section there are very brief summaries of the views, insofar as they relate to ethics, of some of those who most influenced Butler, either by way of agreement or disagreement.

The entries are as follows:

Stoicism
Hobbes
Shaftesbury
Clarke
Wollaston
Hutcheson

Butler was, like all learned people of his time, deeply influenced by Plato and Aristotle, but a *brief* summary of the views of either is beyond my powers. In any case, there is a mass of material available in various media on these two great thinkers, pitched at varying levels of difficulty.

Stoicism

Stoicism was a widespread philosophical movement in the Hellenistic period (following the death of Socrates) and subsequently in the Roman Empire. Its many exponents differed in a number of respects, so what follows is a very general characterization of their views on human nature and ethics.

Stoics, in common with all the Greek schools, held that the goal of life is happiness or flourishing (*eudaimonia*). The various schools differed, however, with respect to what constituted human flourishing. In Stoicism, whatever is intrinsically good must benefit its possessor under all circumstances: health and wealth are not unconditionally good, since money can be misused, and health can lead one to excesses. The only unconditionally good things are the virtues: excellences of character, such as wisdom, justice, courage, and moderation. To possess them is not only to be an admirable person but also to be living the best kind of life for a human, and thus to be living as well as possible. The virtuous person not only possesses the character that makes their life go best: whatever else others may take from them, virtue is a prize that cannot be prised from one's grasp.

Stoics typically claimed that we should not merely moderate our passions but extirpate them completely. For the Stoic, virtue requires *apatheia*, lack of passion. There are two primary passions, appetite and fear, which result in two further passions, pleasure and distress, depending on whether or not we attain our goals. But why should we seek to eliminate them? What is distinctive of passions, as their name suggests, is that they are *passive*: they are states 'which one undergoes and are to be contrasted with actions or things that one does'. The attainment of virtue requires autonomy: 'you should not be psychologically subject to anything—manipulated and moved by *it*, rather than yourself being actively . . . in command of your reactions and responses' to present and to anticipated events (Baltzly, 'Stoicism', *Stanford*

Encyclopedia of Philosophy 2013). Calmness and control go together. We need to distinguish what we can change from what we cannot, and learn to accept the latter with equanimity. Frequently, we cannot change the events, but only our responses to those events.

The passions of hope and fear are not only turbulent and upsetting; they mislead us as to what is genuinely good or bad. Only virtue is unconditionally good, and only vice is bad. Other things, the things that we typically hope for and fear, including wealth and success, or pain and death, are in reality indifferent—neither good nor bad, strictly speaking. (Some Stoics, however, distinguish between those indifferents that are normally appropriate to our natures, and are thus to be preferred, such as health, and those that are inimical to our natures, such as pain, which are normally to be avoided.) The passions represent various indifferents to us as good or bad, when they are not. Since the passions are thus inclined to lead us into false beliefs, we should strive to eliminate them. The Stoic sage, who has attained perfection, will thus be immune to misfortune, since no-one can take your virtue away from you. Stoicism is thus not simply an intellectual theory but a way of life: a therapy that, if successfully followed, will transform your life.

Cicero sums up the life of the Stoic sage thus:

> [The virtuous person] will be free not only of distress but of all the other emotions as well. And it is the mind free of emotions that makes a person completely and absolutely happy, while the mind agitated by emotions and cut off from solid and secure reasoning loses not only its consistency but even its health. (Graver 2002: 52.)

The popular view of the Stoic as, well, stoical, is thus not too far from the truth. But the claim that we must strive to eliminate the passions can easily be misunderstood. Stoics need not be dour, as Johnson's friend supposed: 'You are a philosopher, Dr. Johnson. I have tried too in my time to be a philosopher; but, I don't know how, cheerfulness was always breaking in' (Boswell, *Life*, 17 April 1778). Nor need they withdraw from public life because they are above the fray. (One famous Stoic, Marcus Aurelius, was a Roman Emperor.) Stoics do not typically claim that one should not *care* about anything, just that one should not allow the mind to be disturbed by emotions or passions that cloud the judgement. Reason is the right guide to life. This Stoic view of the emotions was opposed to that of the Peripatetics who, following Aristotle, thought that the emotions were necessary to the moral life. They should not be eliminated but moderated through education and training.

For the Stoics, we should live according to nature. We are rational creatures; thus we can reflect on our impulses, and choose how to govern our own lives; in so doing we fulfil our human nature. But we must also follow nature in a wider sense. The whole cosmos is governed by reason: we can detect order in the universe, and events unfold as they should. In accepting what happens to us, and not kicking against the pricks, we conform our rational wills to the rational universe.

Among the most widely read Stoics today are Epictetus, Marcus Aurelius, and Cicero. For further details see 'Stoicism' by Dirk Baltzly, in the *Stanford Encyclopaedia of Philosophy* (<http://plato.stanford.edu/entries/stoicism/>) to which I am deeply indebted.

Thomas Hobbes (1588–1679)

Hobbes' political philosophy is so well known that this summary can be very brief. He is concerned with the nature and justification of political obligation. To this end, he imagines human life in what he calls the state of nature, without any form of government. Because of fear, ambition, and covetousness, each would have to be on guard against the rapine and plunder of their neighbours. There would, in effect, be a war of all against all. From the perspective of self-interest, each of us has reason to wish the war to end, while no-one can risk making the first move towards peaceful co-existence, lest others take advantage of him. The solution is for everyone to agree to invest sovereignty in some person, or group of persons. The Sovereign will both issue laws and enforce them, with the aid of the citizenry. Once a judicial system is in place disputes can be arbitrated and law-breakers punished. That removes the threat from our neighbours and allows us to live peaceably with them. Since living in civil society is obviously preferable to the state of nature, each of us has good reason to obey the Sovereign in all things. The Sovereign must have absolute power and authority. If the Sovereign's authority were limited there would be the perpetual danger of Sovereign and citizenry disagreeing as to whether those limits had been breached. (It is noteworthy that Hobbes wrote his main work, *Leviathan*, during and immediately after such a civil war between Charles I and Parliament.)

Hobbes' views were regarded as scandalous by most of his contemporaries, for a number of reasons. Some, such as John Locke, rejected his claim that the Sovereign should be absolute, though others, most famously Bishop Bramhall, thought he had not gone far enough, describing *Leviathan*, as a 'rebels' catechism'. Hobbes was seen as subscribing to the view that 'might makes right'. We ought not to rebel against any government, however tyrannical, so long as it is performing its basic function of protection. However, if there is a successful rebellion, the former government would no longer be protecting us and we should immediately switch allegiance to the rebels. Hobbes would regard any claim that a successful government was an *illegitimate* government as absurd, since that would imply that there was some higher law than that of the Sovereign.

This brings us to a second objection: for Hobbes there can be no question of whether something is just or unjust in the state of nature. In that condition, there are no restrictions on what we may do to defend ourselves; everyone has a right to everything. Justice arises only with the setting up of civil society and the establishment of property and personal rights. But what these are depends on the Sovereign's will. His opponents thus classified him as a *voluntarist*: one who makes morality depend on the arbitrary will of some sovereign. Theological voluntarism, in the form of Divine Command Theory, is much discussed, but Hobbes' opponents found what we might term civic voluntarism just as obnoxious, and for the same reasons: it made the content of morality contingent, because dependent on the arbitrary dictates of whoever held power. Clarke is representative of those who thought that there were immutable and necessary moral laws, and he devotes considerable space to arguing against Hobbes on this point.

A third concern was his perceived atheism. Whether he held this view has been a matter of some scholarly dispute, but since Hobbes was also a materialist (yet another of his doctrines that alarmed his opponents) it is clear that he could not have an orthodox conception of the deity.

Butler, of course, rejected all these views, but it was the fourth scandalous aspect of Hobbes' philosophy against which he fulminates in the *Sermons*: his moral psychology. Hobbes was taken to be a psychological egoist: someone who maintains that humans are motivated *solely* by considerations of self-interest. Whether that interpretation is correct is dubious, but that was more or less the universal view. In particular, Hobbes' method is to define various psychological traits, and from those to develop a view of human nature on which to found his account of why the state of nature would be so awful. In doing so, Hobbes seems at times to delight in displaying a degree of cynicism about human motivation that appalled Butler. Hobbes seems to have delighted in stirring up controversy, so it is unclear how seriously we should take some of these 'definitions'. Indeed, the remarks to which Butler takes exception in Hobbes' infamous accounts of pity and of benevolence in the earlier *Human Nature* should not, perhaps, be read as part of the definition at all, but as somewhat barbed asides about what provokes these passions in many people. This is clearer in *Leviathan* which is considerably toned down from the earlier work. Benevolence is defined simply as the 'desire of good to another' (*Leviathan* 123) without further qualification, and the definition of pity is itself very brief: '*Griefe*, for the calamity of another, is PITTY.' Hobbes then moves on to the question of what typically *causes* pity: 'the imagination that the like calamity may befall himselfe'. In similar vein, he goes on to remark that 'those have least Pitty, that think themselves least obnoxious to the same' (*Leviathan* 126). There is a degree of truth in this as an account, not of what pity is, but of the circumstances in which people are *actually* likely to feel it, whatever they might say, or whatever we might wish. That Butler spends so much time concentrating his fire on the earlier work reveals how much Hobbes was regarded as a dangerous subversive, rather than someone to be interpreted charitably.

Anthony Ashley Cooper, Third Earl of Shaftesbury (1671–1713)

Shaftesbury's main publication, *Characteristics of Men, Manners, Opinions, Times* is an extensive collection of works in various styles addressing a wide range of topics. It was very influential throughout the eighteenth century, and went through numerous editions. For Shaftesbury, following Plato and the Stoics, the universe is a well-ordered intelligible system, in which each part has some role to play. By far his most systematic work on ethics is *An Enquiry Concerning Virtue or Merit*, in which he discusses what makes for a good life. The goodness of any creature is to be judged by its contribution to the system of which it is a part; the most immediate system to which it relates is the species of which it is a part. Creatures, including humans, are only good or bad in virtue of their characters: whether their affections (desires, motives, and enjoyments) tend to the good or ill of the species and the wider whole.

Animals can be good or bad—a dog can be aggressive or affectionate—but only humans can be virtuous or vicious, because only humans are self-conscious, capable of reflecting on their affections and approving or disapproving of them. We have no direct control over our approval and disapproval, but we can use them to control which of our affections we should foster or discourage, and which ones we should act on. Thus Shaftesbury rejects theological voluntarism: the view that what is right or wrong is determined solely by God's commands, which can be accessed only by revelation. Rather, how we should live is determined by the nature of the reality in which we live, and can be discovered by rational reflection.

Having defined what virtue is, Shaftesbury proceeds to ask 'what obligation there is to virtue; or what reason to embrace it' (*Inquiry* II.i.1 in *Characteristics*: 192). Shaftesbury thus denies, as Butler complains, that the deliverances of our moral sense have intrinsic authority. Like Plato, Aristotle, and most of the ancient philosophers, Shaftesbury is a eudaemonist: that is, he holds that there is reason to be virtuous only if that way of life is the happiest. There are, for Shaftesbury, three kinds of affections: the natural affections, which lead to public good; the self-affections, which are conducive to private good; and unnatural affections, which promote neither, and may even have a deleterious effect. Virtue consists in having no affections of the third kind, and having those of the first two in due proportion to each other. Why is having this kind of character going to make us happiest?

Shaftesbury begins by arguing that the mental pleasures are vastly superior to the bodily or sensual ones in offering us deeper and longer-lasting satisfaction. He then proceeds to argue that the natural affections, such as sociability or beneficence are, or give rise to, mental pleasures. Indeed, even the pleasures of the table or the bed are not purely sensual; both involve the social affections and it is this, and not fleeting physical sensations, that make them so delightful. The pleasures of the intellect are classified as natural because disinterested; the accomplished mathematician delights in the elegance of proofs for its own sake. Self-affections obviously aim at one's own good, and their gratification will help achieve this, provided that they do not crowd out the social affections. And an excessive concern for one's own welfare, to the exclusion of that of others, fosters timidity and anxiety. The unnatural affections, which include malice, envy, and misanthropy, breed misery. They are universally abhorred by others and, since the reflective judgement of the moral sense cannot be extinguished, by the agent herself.

Shaftesbury's use of the term 'moral sense' has led some to claim that he is the founder of the 'sentimental school' in ethics (Hutcheson and Hume being prominent members). The sentimentalists held that moral distinctions (between right and wrong, virtuous and vicious) spring from feeling or desire, whereas the rationalists held that they were founded in reason and the nature of things. This division is itself suspect, since many thinkers of the time fall into neither category. But insofar as it is sound, it is a mistake to classify Shaftesbury as primarily a sentimentalist. For Shaftesbury, the universe is comprehensible through and through, and our moral sense is simply our reason in another guise. He is firmly in the Platonist tradition.

Samuel Clarke (1675–1729)

Clarke's work covers many areas, including theology, free will, philosophy of science, and philosophy of religion. A staunch defender of Newtonianism, he famously corresponded with Leibniz about the nature of space and time, among other things. He upheld theism, against deists and sceptics, arguing that matter could not move of itself but only by divine power, and that miracles are not only possible but actual. His views on the Trinity were regarded as possibly heretical by some, though they do not now appear very unorthodox.

His major works were the two volumes of Boyle lectures, delivered in 1704 and 1705. The first, entitled *A Demonstration of the Being and Attributes of God*, was followed by a second set entitled *A Discourse Concerning the Unchangeable Obligations of Natural Religion and the Truth and Certainty of the Christian Revelation*. Clarke is a foremost representative of what is sometimes known as the rationalist school of ethics. He holds, in opposition to ethical voluntarism, that moral truths are independent of the will or command of any sovereign, whether God or the government. Theological voluntarism takes the form of Divine Command Theory, which holds that God's commands and prohibitions determine what is morally obligatory and forbidden, respectively. On this view, the wrongness of some act, such as child sacrifice, does not depend on its own nature, but on the commands of God. Had God not forbidden it then it would not have been wrong. As the first part of his title indicates, Clarke rejects this view, since it makes morality contingent and arbitrary. Rather, the fundamental principles of ethics are necessarily and eternally true. They arise from what Clarke describes as the eternal and necessary reasons of things. Some things essentially agree or disagree with one another; some responses or reactions to various events are fitting and others unfitting.

Described in this abstract manner, Clarke's view may seem puzzling, but his underlying conception is both clear and plausible. Rightness and wrongness, for Clarke, are relations, involving (at least) three elements: an agent, some morally salient facts, and an action or attitude. So, for example, it may be right for Xander to obey Yuan, given that Xander is a child and Yuan his parent. No doubt some background needs filling in that explains why parents have (limited) authority over their children. But once we have specified the relation between Xander and Yuan in virtue of which the former should obey the latter then, so Clarke claims, any two people who stand in this relation are such that the former should obey the latter. Necessities of this sort are going to hold with respect to any moral duty, such as the duty to keep promises, or the duty not to lie. Equally, of course, some attitudes are suitable or fitting in response to some actions, while others are unfitting. Thus, the proper response to someone who does you a good turn is gratitude. To illustrate his position Clarke compares moral to mathematical relations, which he takes to be necessary truths grasped by reason. This comparison appears to have confused unsympathetic critics, who have focused on the disanalogies between ethics and mathematics, ignoring the fact that Clarke is only maintaining that they are alike in these two respects.

The eternal reasons of things—the moral law—is logically prior to the will of any being. God chooses to act according to this law, and we should, and indeed would, so choose were we fully governed by reason. It follows, of course, that the moral law precedes, both logically and temporally, any human interaction, and is antecedent to any question of reward or punishment. Clarke uses this claim to launch an attack on Hobbes, especially on his contention that justice and injustice do not exist in the state of nature, but come into existence only in civil society where they are determined by the will of the Sovereign. Likewise, Clarke asserts, it makes no sense to suppose that we have an obligation to obey the social contract, unless there were already an obligation to obey contracts.

William Wollaston (1659–1724)

Wollaston is now remembered, if he is remembered at all, as the butt of an amusing but dismissive footnote in Hume's *Treatise*.[1] Hume wrongly takes Wollaston to be claiming that what makes an action wrong is that it *may* occasion a false belief in a spectator. Someone who saw me having sex with my neighbour's wife might be so simple as to suppose she is my own. But

> if I had used the precaution of shutting the windows, while I indulg'd myself in those liberties with my neighbour's wife, I should have been guilty of no immorality; and that because my action, being perfectly conceal'd, wou'd have had no tendency to produce any false conclusion. (Hume, *Treatise*: 462.)

Wollaston's view is much more subtle than Hume suggests and his major work, *The Religion of Nature Delineated*, was well received on its first publication in 1724 and sold more than 10,000 copies in just a few years. We know that Butler read and respected it, and there are interesting points of similarity, and of dissimilarity.

A proposition is true, Wollaston maintains, when it expresses things as they are, i.e. when the words or signs used to express the proposition conform or correspond to the things themselves. While assertions state some proposition, actions, other than linguistic ones, can *imply* some proposition. To illustrate: suppose I tell you that I am not leaving, but shortly thereafter I put on my coat and pick up my umbrella. You might reasonably say 'I thought you said you were not leaving'. You thus take my action to have denied, or contradicted, my previous assertion. Actions can thus have meaning, even when no words are uttered. If my action declares something to be the case when it is not, then I have denied the truth just as much as if I had done so by uttering a falsehood. I have acted *as if* it were true, when it is not. If, to take an example of Wollaston's, I promise you that I will do something, but intentionally omit to do it, then—Wollaston claims—my omission denies that we have an agreement. Wollaston recognizes that actions fall under different descriptions, and that an act can deny a proposition under one description but not under another. Thus, if I steal a horse, my act implies that I have a right to ride the horse, which is false, but it does not deny such truths as that this is a bay horse, or that I am riding it.

It is now a philosophical commonplace that actions can speak, if not louder than words, at least as clearly. For example, it is often claimed that when someone wrongs another she thereby conveys a non-verbal message to the person she has wronged: she implies that this person can be treated in this way, that her well-being is of little or no account, and so on. But how does Wollaston propose to get a theory of right and wrong from this shrewd point about actions?

He does not claim, as is sometimes supposed, that all wrongdoing is a form of lying. For we can act wrongly even when we do not have an audience; so Hume's objection misses its mark.

> No act (whether word or deed) of any being, to whom moral good and evil are imputable, that interferes with any true proposition, or denies any thing to be as it is, can be right.... Things cannot be denied to be what they are, in any instance or manner whatsoever, without contradicting axioms and truths eternal. (*Religion*, 13, 14; italics omitted.)

What are these 'axioms and truths eternal'? Examples include 'everything is what it is', and 'that which is done, cannot be undone'. To deny evident truths is not only absurd but may also be reprehensible, as the following example is meant to show:

> To talk to a post, or otherwise treat it as if it was a man, would surely be reckoned an absurdity... because this is to treat it as being what it is not. And why should not the converse be reckoned as bad; that is to treat a man as a post. (15; italics omitted.)

And why is it wrong to treat a person as a post?

> Because we are treating him as if he had no sense, and felt not injuries, which he doth feel; as if to him pain and sorrow were not pain; happiness not happiness. (15.)

To deny such truths is contrary both to reason and to morality. It is also, in a significant sense, unnatural. Truth is determined and fixed by the nature of things themselves and to 'interfere' with truth is to interfere with the very nature of things. It is a mistake, therefore, to think that following nature means acting in accord with our immediate inclinations.

We can thus see in Wollaston echoes of Clarke, with this twist: that all wrongdoing shares a common form—explicitly or implicitly denying some truth. Wollaston's claims raise two questions. First, just which truths does Wollaston think that the wrongdoer denies? Wollaston's example of treating a person as a post suggests that he takes the wrongdoer to be denying *non*-normative truths, such as the thing before me is a man, has feelings, etc. But this seems implausible as a general claim, though it is certainly true in some cases. There are, I would hold, two relevant truths that a wrongdoer might be implicitly denying by his actions. Suppose I *never* help the poor, though I can afford to (another of Wollaston's examples). I might thereby be denying that these people really are poor (which can easily be shown to be false), or I might be denying that I have an *obligation* to help them. Wollaston takes it that I am denying the former proposition, which does indeed seem absurd. But a certain kind of ethical or political libertarian is surely best understood as denying the latter, normative claim. Similarly, an oppressor can deny the humanity of the oppressed, not by denying that they *have* feelings or desires, but by treating them *inappropriately*: by not giving *proper* weight to ways in which people differ from posts.

If I am right about this, then Wollaston has no quick riposte to the libertarian who denies we have a moral obligation to help the poor, since the libertarian is not denying that the poor are poor. So why does Wollaston think that they are denying this? He may suppose that the intrinsic nature of each thing determines the correct response; normative truths are, as it were, built into the nature of things. On this view, since the appropriate response is entailed by the thing's intrinsic nature, anyone who denies that we *should* help the poor is thereby denying something about the intrinsic nature of what it *is* to be poor.

The second question is this. Even if all wrong actions implicitly deny some evident truth, is that what *makes* any action wrong? Surely, what is wrong with not helping the poor is that they stand in need of help which I can supply. In other words, is Wollaston offering a character-ization of what all wrong acts have in common, or is he claiming that truth-denying is the only wrong-making feature of an action? (An analogy with a question in Kantian ethics may make the point clearer. All wrong acts fail the Categorical Imperative test: but is that failure what *makes* them wrong. Is it wrong to lie *because* I cannot will a universal law permitting lying?)

Since morality concerns how we treat ourselves and others, one of the most important truths to which Wollaston draws our attention is that it is in the nature of persons to seek happiness and to avoid unhappiness. So,

> If a man does not desire to prevent evils and to be happy, he denies both his own nature and the definition of happiness to be what they are. (16; italics omitted.)

But now, what guarantee is there that the agent who avoids immorality will eventually find happiness? That guarantee is provided by God:

> For that, which contradicts nature and truth, opposes the will of the Author of nature . . . ; and to suppose, that an inferior being may in opposition to His will break through the constitution of things, and by so doing make himself happy is to suppose that being more potent than the Author of nature . . . which is absurd. (38; italics omitted.)

Wollaston is a hedonist; he identifies happiness with pleasure, and offers a kind of felicific calculus, of the sort later made famous by Bentham. Our obligation to make ourselves and others happy is the 'religion of nature' of Wollaston's title. Religion is, for him, nothing but our being under moral obligations in virtue of the natures of the things that God has created.

Francis Hutcheson (1694–1746)

Although Butler and Hutcheson were almost exact contemporaries, and must have been familiar with each other's work, there is no extant correspondence and it is extremely doubtful that they ever met: Butler never left England and Hutcheson never ventured into it. Hutcheson published a number of works but the two most likely to have influenced Butler are *An Inquiry into the Original of Our Ideas of Beauty and Virtue in Two Treatises* and *An Essay on the*

Nature and Conduct of the Passions and Affections, with Illustrations of the Moral Sense, the first of which was published in 1725 and the second in 1728. Although Butler never mentions Hutcheson explicitly, there can be little doubt that Butler took his work into account, especially in his later work. The first of Hutcheson's works almost certainly came out too late to influence the substance of the first edition of the *Sermons* (except, conceivably, in the long footnote that Butler added to S 12.31) but both works were out by the time Butler came to revise the *Sermons* for the second edition of 1729, and will almost certainly have influenced Butler in the *Analogy*, especially in the sections on utilitarianism in the *Dissertation of Virtue*.

For Hutcheson, our moral judgements are generated by a moral sense. To think of 'sense' here on analogy with the traditional five senses might well lead to misunderstanding. He does not think we have a 'sixth sense' which can somehow detect an external moral reality, though without the aid of any discoverable sense organ. Rather, for Hutcheson, a sense is any capacity our minds have to receive ideas independently of our will: there are many such, including a sense of honour and a sense of beauty. These capacities, including the moral sense, are implanted in us by God. Certain objects please us, while others displease, and we lack voluntary control as to what arouses these feelings, and we lack *direct* voluntary control over their continuance, though we may train them over time. Each sense pleases and displeases in a particular manner and is directed to certain objects. All kinds of events in nature can be good or bad, but only the motives and actions of agents can be morally good or bad. Moral goodness is 'our idea of some quality in actions, which procures approbation, attended with desire of the agent's happiness' (*Inquiry* II, Introduction: 85); moral evil is that quality that elicits the opposite reaction. Hutcheson holds that the primary objects of the moral sense are qualities of character. To discover what moral goodness is we must consider what character trait(s) we approve of. Hutcheson (following Shaftesbury) takes it that benevolence is that trait, where benevolence is a concern for the good or happiness of others.

Hutcheson, like Butler, Clarke, and so many others, asserts the reality of disinterested benevolence and is vehemently opposed to the psychological egoism of Hobbes and Mandeville, which he thinks both false and dangerous. False, because the existence of benevolent impulses is evident to anyone not in the grip of a theory; dangerous, because it may encourage selfishness in those who can see no gain in helping others. Indeed, for Hutcheson, only actions motivated by benevolence are virtuous; self-interest is not a morally worthy motive. Further, like Butler, he thinks that, as well as a general sense of benevolence or goodwill, there are also particular affections that aim at the good of others.

Talk of a moral sense might lead one to think that Hutcheson conceives of all moral judgements as inherently immediate and unreflective, but that would be a mistake on two counts. First, we may need to reflect on the salient features of the situation in order to ascertain what benevolence requires. Additionally, when judging the moral worth of the actions of others we need to determine whether those actions were motivated by benevolence or some other impulse. Second, our judgement may be distorted by passions which can preoccupy us unduly, and exercise a power disproportionate to their importance. Benevolence, by contrast, is a calm affection that is more far-sighted than passion, and it is to the calm affections that we typically look when we are reflecting on what we should do. It is what we approve of on reflection that we typically think of as the rational choice, and it is that reflective evaluation that grounds moral judgements.

In the somewhat confused debate between rationalists and sentimentalists as to the source or grounds of morality, Hutcheson clearly sides with the latter. Reason does not discern moral truth, nor can reason motivate us. To take the latter point first: he distinguishes between justifying and exciting reasons (a distinction sometimes expressed by contemporary philosophers as one between normative and motivating reasons). What moves us to action must always be desires, which spring from instincts or affections. In the case of morality motivation springs, not from the judgement made by the moral sense, but from our benevolent impulses. Nor can reason discern what is worth pursuing. It can determine what means to take to our ends, but it cannot determine our ends, i.e. which goals are worthy of pursuit.

Although the primary object of the moral sense is moral goodness—our benevolent impulses (or lack of them)—we need also to determine, when deliberating about what to do, which acts are right and which wrong. Since benevolence is the object of moral approval, we will approve of those actions that a wholly benevolent person would do were he fully informed about the best means to his goal—namely, the act that best promotes the general welfare. Hutcheson is thus an early utilitarian; indeed, it is Hutcheson, and not Bentham, who coined the phrase 'the greatest happiness for the greatest numbers' (*Inquiry* II, 3, 8: 125). However, he acknowledges that our moral sense does not always apply the utilitarian standard directly, either in deciding what to do, or in judging the actions of others. He thus foreshadows the popular distinction between a standard of rightness and a decision procedure. We approve of various *kinds* of action, and disapprove of others, without going through the excessively complex and uncertain calculations that a direct application of the standard would require.[2] God, in his wisdom, recognizes that such calculations would be a poor guide and has given us both a moral sense that enables us to judge more surely and more swiftly, and powerful affections that will motivate us to act on those judgements:

> The Author of Nature has much better furnished us for a virtuous conduct than our moralists seem to imagine, by almost as quick and powerful instructions as we have for the preservation of our bodies. He has made virtue a lovely form, to excite our pursuit of it, and has given us strong affections to be the springs of each virtuous action. (*Inquiry*, Preface: 9.)[3]

Does Hutcheson's theory allow our moral sense to have that authority which Butler ascribes to the verdicts of conscience? There are other senses and other motivations, including self-love which may lead us in other directions. Our moral sense may, as Hutcheson claims above, offer us *powerful* instructions, and most of us may be furnished with *strong* affections that will prompt us to do the right thing. But these are remarks only about *power*. Hutcheson's theory may be vulnerable to the objection that Butler raises to Shaftesbury's views, namely that it ignores the *authority* of the verdicts of the moral sense.

Notes

1. I am deeply indebted to Tweyman 1976 for much that I say here.
2. This appeal to general rules is the foundation of Hutcheson's account of rights.
3. It is hard not to think that Butler had this passage, or one like it, in mind in his discussion of 'divine utilitarianism' in D 8.

Bibliography

Works by Butler Published during his Lifetime

Several Letters to the Reverend Dr. Clarke, from a Gentleman in Gloucestershire Relating to the First Volume of the Foregoing Sermons; with the Dr.'s Answers Thereto. London: James Knapton, 1716, pp. 42. 1716. (Subsequently appended to Samuel Clarke, *A discourse concerning the being and attributes of God*, 4th edn., corr. London: printed by W. Botham for James Knapton, 1716, 344p.)

[Only the first five letters and replies were printed with Clarke's works and included in early editions of Butler's works. The four additional letters to Clarke that have survived were published much later, and were included in the Gladstone and Bernard editions of the *Works*.]

Fifteen Sermons Preached at the Rolls Chapel

First edition: London: Printed by W. Botham, for James and John Knapton, 1726, 312p.

Second edition: London: James and John Knapton, 1729, xxxiv, 318p.

Third edition: London: James, John, and Paul Knapton, 1736, xxxiv, 318p.

Fourth edition: To which are added six sermons preached on public occasions. London: John & Paul Knapton, 1749, xxxiv, 480p.

The Analogy of Religion, natural and revealed, to the constitution and course of nature. To which are added, Two Brief Dissertations: I. Of personal identity. II. Of the nature of virtue.

First edition: London: James, John, and Paul Knapton, 1736, x, 11–320p.

Second edition (corrected): London: John and Paul Knapton, 1736, xvi, 17–467p.

Third edition: London: John and Paul Knapton, 1740, xvi, 17–467p.

Fourth edition: London: John and Paul Knapton, 1750, xvi, 17–467p.

A Charge deliver'd to the Clergy, at the primary visitation of the Diocese of Durham, in the year, MDCCLI. Durham: I. Lane, 1751, 29p.

Modern Editions of Butler's Works

The Works of Joseph Butler, D.C.L., Sometime Lord Bishop of Durham. Edited by the Right Hon. W. E. Gladstone (Oxford: At the Clarendon Press, 1896), vol. 1. The Analogy of Religion xxxvii, 461p.; vol. 2. Sermons, etc. x, 464p.

The Works of Bishop Butler. A new edition with introduction and notes by J. H. Bernard, D.D. (London: Macmillan and Co., 1900), vol. 1. Sermons, Charges, Fragments and Correspondence. xxxii, 352p.; vol. 2. Analogy of Religion, xxi, 313p.

Fifteen Sermons Preached at the Rolls Chapel and a Dissertation on the Nature of Virtue. With introduction, analyses, and notes by W. R. Matthews (London: George Bell and Sons, 1914), xxvii, 257p.

Butler's Fifteen Sermons Preached at the Rolls Chapel; and, a Dissertation of the Nature of Virtue. Edited with an introduction and additional notes by T. A. Roberts (London: Society for Promoting Christian Knowledge, 1970), xxiv, 168p.

Five Sermons Edited with an introduction by S. Darwall (Indianapolis: Hackett, 1983).
The Works of Bishop Butler, edited by D. White (Rochester, NY: University of Rochester Press, 2006).

Biographical Works

Bartlett, T., 1839. *Memoirs of the Life, Character and Writings of Joseph Butler* (London: John W. Parker).
Cunliffe, C., 1992. 'The "Spiritual Sovereign": Butler's Episcopate', in C. Cunliffe (ed.), *Joseph Butler's Moral and Religious Thought: Tercentenary Essays* (Oxford: Clarendon Press).
Cunliffe, C., 2008. 'Butler, Joseph (1692–1752)', in the *Oxford Dictionary of National Biography* (online edition) (Oxford: Oxford University Press).

Works by Butler's Predecessors and Contemporaries

Aristotle, *The Rhetoric and the Poetics of Aristotle*, eds. W. Roberts, I. Bywater, and E. Corbett (New York: McGraw-Hill, 1984).
Aristotle, *Nicomachean Ethics*, ed. T. Irwin (Indianapolis: Hackett, 2nd edn. 1999).
Augustine, *A Select Library of the Nicene and Post-Nicene Fathers of the Christian Church. vol. III St. Augustine on the Holy Trinity, Doctrinal Treatises, Moral Treatises*, ed. Philip Schaff (Buffalo: The Christian Literature Co., 1887).
Augustine, *Concerning the City of God, Against the Pagans*, ed. Henry Bettenson (London: Penguin Books, 1972).
Augustine, *Confessions*, ed. H. Chadwick (Oxford: Oxford University Press, 1991).
Aurelius, Marcus, *Meditations*, ed. C. R. Haines (Cambridge MA: Harvard University Press, 1916).
Berkeley, G., *The Works of George Berkeley: Bishop of Cloyne*, 9 vols., eds. A. A. Luce and T. E. Jessop (London: Thomas Nelson and Sons, 1948–57).
Cicero, *Tusculan Disputations*, ed. J. E. King (Cambridge MA: Harvard University Press, 1945).
Cicero, *On Duties*, eds. M. T. Griffin and E. M. Atkins (Cambridge: Cambridge University Press, 1991).
Cicero, *Cicero on the Emotions*, ed. M. Graver (Chicago: Chicago University Press, 2002). [Books III and IV of *Tusculan Disputations* with commentary.]
Cicero, *On Moral Ends*, ed. J. Annas (Cambridge: Cambridge University Press, 2011).
Clarke, S., *A Discourse Concerning the Being and Attributes of God, the Unchangeable Obligations of Natural Religion, and the Truth and Certainty of the Christian Revelation* (London: James and John Knapton) [7th edn.1728]. (Extracts can be found in Raphael 1969: 192–225.)
Diogenes Laertius, *Lives of Eminent Philosophers*, 2 vols., ed. R. D. Hicks, Loeb Classical Library (Cambridge, MA: Harvard University Press, 1925).
Epictetus, *Discourses and Selected Writings*, ed. R. Dobbin (London: Penguin Books, 2008).
Fénelon, *The Best of Fénelon*, ed. H. J. Chadwick (Gainesville FL: Bridge-Logos Publishers, 2002).
Hobbes, T., 1985. *Leviathan* [1651], ed. C. B. McPherson (London: Penguin Classics).

Hobbes, T., *Human Nature and De Corpore Politico* [1640], ed. J. C. A. Gaskin (Oxford: Oxford University Press, 1994).

Hooker, R., *Ecclesiastical Polity*, vol. I (Indianapolis IN: Online Library of Liberty, 2015.)

Hume, D., *An Enquiry Concerning the Principles of Morals*, ed. P. Nidditch (Oxford: Clarendon Press, 1975).

Hume, D., *A Treatise of Human Nature*, ed. P. Nidditch (Oxford: Clarendon Press, 1978).

Hutcheson, F., *An Essay on the Nature and Conduct of the Passions and Affections, with Illustrations of the Moral Sense* [1728], ed. A. Garrett (Indianapolis: Liberty Fund, 2002).

Hutcheson, F., *An Inquiry into the Original of Our Ideas of Beauty and Virtue in Two Treatises* [1725], ed. W. Leidhold (Indianapolis: Liberty Fund, 2008).

La Rochefoucauld, *Maxims*, ed. L. Tancock (London: Penguin Books, 1959).

Livy, *History of Rome*, vol. I, Books 1–2. trans. B. O. Foster, Loeb Classical Library 114 (Cambridge, MA: Harvard University Press, 1919).

Locke, J., *An Essay Concerning Human Understanding* [5th edn.1706], ed. J. Yolton (London: J. M. Dent, 2 vols. 1965).

Philo, *De vita Mosis*, 1, in *Works of Philo*, vol. VI, trans. F. H. Colson, Loeb Classical Library (Harvard University Press, 1935).

Plato, *Complete Works*, ed. J. M. Cooper (Indianapolis IN: Hackett, 1997).

Pliny the Younger, *Letters, vol. I: Books 1–7*, trans Betty Radice, Loeb Classical Library (Cambridge, Massachusetts: Harvard University Press, 1969).

Sallust, *The War with Catiline; the War with Jugurtha*, trans J. C. Rolfe, revised by John T. Ramsey, Loeb Classical Library (Cambridge, Massachusetts: Harvard University Press, 2013).

Seneca, *Moral and Political Essays*, eds. J. M. Cooper and J. F. Procopé (Cambridge: Cambridge University Press, 1995).

Shaftesbury, *Characteristics of Men, Manners, Opinions, Times* [1714], ed. L. E. Klein (Cambridge: Cambridge University Press, 2003).

Wollaston, W., *The Religion of Nature Delineated* (New York and London: Garland Publishing, 1978) [Reprint of 1724 edition].

Books about Butler's Moral Philosophy

Carlsson, P. (1964), *Butler's Ethics* (The Hague: Mouton & Co.).

Cunliffe, C. (ed.) (1992), *Joseph Butler's Moral and Religious Thought: Tercentenary Essays* (Oxford: Clarendon Press).

Duncan-Jones, A. (1952), *Butler's Moral Philosophy* (Harmondsworth: Penguin).

Mossner, E. C. (1990), *Bishop Butler and the Age of Reason* (New York: Macmillan).

Penelhum, T. (1985), *Butler* (London: Routledge & Kegan Paul).

Tennant, R. (2011), *Conscience, Consciousness, and Ethics in Joseph Butler's Philosophy and Ministry* (Boydell Press: Woodbridge).

Articles and Chapters about Butler

Akhtar, S. (2006), 'Restoring Butler's Conscience', in *British Journal for the History of Philosophy* 14: 581–600.

Anscombe, G. (1958), 'Modern Moral Philosophy', *Philosophy* 33: 1–19.

Arrington, R. (1998), *Western Ethics: An Historical Introduction* (Oxford: Blackwell), 211–30.

Brinton, A. (1991), '"Following Nature" in Butler's Sermons: Reply to Millar', in *Philosophical Quarterly* 41: 325–32.

Brinton, A. (1993), 'The Homiletical Context of Butler's Moral Philosophy', in *British Journal for the History of Philosophy* 1: 83–107.

Broad, C. D. (1930), *Five Types of Ethical Theory* (London: Kegan Paul, Trench, Trubner & Co.), 53–83.

Brownsey, P. (1995), 'Butler's Argument for the Natural Authority of Conscience' in *British Journal for the History of Philosophy* 3: 57–87.

Darwall, S. (1992), 'Conscience as Self-Authorizing in Butler's Ethics', in Cunliffe 1992, 209–42.

Darwall, S. (1995), *The British Moralists and the Internal 'Ought'* (Cambridge: Cambridge University Press), 244–84.

Frey, R. (1992), 'Butler on Self-Love and Benevolence', in Cunliffe 1992, 243–68.

Garrett, A., 'Bishop Butler on Bullshit' (unpublished).

Garrett A. (forthcoming), 'The History of the History of Ethics and Emblematic Passages', in volume honouring Knud Haakonsenn (Cambridge: Cambridge University Press).

Garrett, A. (2012), 'Reasoning about Morals from Butler to Hume', in R. Savage (ed.), *Philosophy and Religion in Enlightenment Britain: New Case Studies* (Oxford: Oxford University Press), 169–86.

Grave, S. (1952), 'The Foundation Of Butler's Ethics', in *Australasian Journal of Philosophy* 30: 73–89.

Hebblethwaite, B. (1992), 'Butler on Conscience and Virtue', in Cunliffe 1992, 197–208.

Henson, R. (1988), 'Butler on Selfishness and Self-Love', in *Philosophy and Phenomenological Research* 49: 31–57.

Irwin, T. (2008), *The Development of Ethics*, vol. II (Oxford: Oxford University Press), 476–557.

Jackson, R. (1943), 'Bishop Butler's Refutation of Psychological Hedonism', in *Philosophy* 18: 114–39.

Kleinig, J. (1969), 'Butler in a Cool Hour', in *Journal of the History of Philosophy* 7: 399–411.

Louden, R. (1995), 'Butler's Divine Utilitarianism', in *History of Philosophy Quarterly* 12: 265–80.

Martin, M. (1977), 'Immorality and Self-Deception: A Reply to Bela Szabados', in *Dialogue* 16: 274–80.

McNaughton, D. (1992), 'Butler on Benevolence', in Cunliffe 1992, 269–91.

McNaughton, D. (1996), 'The British Moralists: Shaftesbury, Butler, Price', in S. Brown (ed.), *British Philosophy and the Age of Enlightenment* (London: Routledge), 203–27.

McNaughton, D. (2013), 'Butler's Ethics', in R. Crisp (ed.), *Oxford Handbook of the History of Ethics* (Oxford: Oxford University Press), 377–98.

McPherson, T. (1948), 'The Development of Bishop Butler's Ethics Part I', in *Philosophy* 23: 317–31.

McPherson, T. (1949), 'The Development of Bishop Butler's Ethics Part II', in *Philosophy* 24: 3–22.

Millar, A. (1988), 'Following Nature', in *Philosophical Quarterly* 38: 165–85.

Millar, A. (1992), 'Butler on God and Human Nature', in Cunliffe 1992, 269–92.

Millar, A. (1992), 'Reply to Brinton', in *Philosophical Quarterly* 42: 486–91.

Newberry, P. (2001), 'Joseph Butler on Forgiveness: A Presupposed Theory of Emotion', in *Journal of the History of Ideas* 62: 233–44.

O'Brien, W. (1991), 'Butler and the Authority of Conscience', in *History of Philosophy Quarterly* 8: 43–57.

Phillips, D. (2000), 'Butler and the Nature of Self-Interest', in *Philosophy and Phenomenological Research* 60: 421–38.

Platt, T. (1972), 'Self-Love and Benevolence: In Defense of Butler's Ethics', in *Southwestern Journal of Philosophy* 3: 71–9.

Pritchard, M. (1978), 'Conscience and Reason in Butler's Ethics', in *Southwestern Journal of Philosophy* 9: 39–49.

Raphael, D. (1949), 'Bishop Butler's View of Conscience', in *Philosophy* 24: 219–38.

Riddle, G, (1959), 'The Place of Benevolence in Butler's Ethics', in *Philosophical Quarterly* 9: 356–62.

Roberts, T. A. (1973), *The Concept of Benevolence: Aspects of Eighteenth-Century Moral Philosophy* (London: Macmillan).

Rorty, A. (1978), 'Butler on Benevolence and Conscience', in *Philosophy* 53: 171–84.

Scott-Taggert, M. (1968), 'Butler on Disinterested Actions', in *Philosophical Quarterly* 18: 16–28.

Sober, E. (1992), 'Hedonism and Butler's Stone', in *Ethics* 103: 97–103.

Sidgwick, H. (1967a), *Outlines of the History of Ethics* (London: Macmillan), 191–8.

Stewart, R. (1992), 'Butler's Argument Against Psychological Hedonism', in *Canadian Journal of Philosophy* 22: 211–21.

Sturgeon, N. (1976), 'Nature and Conscience in Butler's Ethics', in *Philosophical Review* 85: 316–56.

Szabados, B. (1974), 'The Morality of Self-Deception', in *Dialogue* 13: 25–34.

Szabados, B. (1976), 'Butler on Corrupt Conscience', in *Journal of the History of Philosophy* 14: 462–9.

Wedgwood, R. (2007), 'Butler on Virtue, Self-Interest and Human Nature', in P. Bloomfield (ed.), *Morality and Self-Interest* (New York: Oxford University Press), 177–204.

White, A. (1952), 'Conscience and Self-Love in Butler's Sermons', in *Philosophy* 27: 329–44.

Worthen, J. (1995), 'Joseph Butler's Case for Virtue', in *Journal of Religious Ethics* 23: 239–61.

Zellner, H. (1999), 'Passing Butler's Stone', in *History of Philosophy Quarterly* 16: 193–202.

Internet Entries about Butler

Frey, R., 'Butler, Joseph', *Routledge Encyclopedia of Philosophy* <https://www.rep.routledge.com>.

Garrett, A., 'Joseph Butler's Moral Philosophy', *Stanford Encyclopedia of Philosophy* <http://plato.stanford.edu>.

White, D., 'Joseph Butler', *Internet Encyclopedia of Philosophy* <http://www.iep.utm.edu>.

White, D., 'Joseph Butler: His Life, Writing and Theology' <http://bishopbutler.deviousfish.com>.

Other Works Cited

Adams, R. (1985), 'Involuntary Sins', in *The Philosophical Review* 94: 3–33.

Bentham, J. (1996), *Principles of Morals and Legislation*, in J. Burns and H. Hart (eds.), *The Collected Works of Jeremy Bentham*, vol. 9 (Oxford: Oxford University Press).

Cummings, B. (ed.) (2011), *The Book of Common Prayer: The Texts of 1549, 1559, and 1662* (Oxford: Oxford University Press).

Garrard, E. and McNaughton, D. (2003), 'In Defence of Unconditional Forgiveness', in *Proceedings of the Aristotelian Society*: 39–60.

Grean, S. (1967), *Shaftesbury's Philosophy of Religion and Ethics* (Ohio: Ohio University Press).

Holton, R. (2001), 'What Is the Role of the Self in Self-Deception?', in *Proceedings of the Aristotelian Society* 101: 53–69.

Inwood, B. (ed.) (2003), *The Cambridge Companion to the Stoics* (Cambridge: Cambridge University Press).

Irwin T. (2003), 'Stoic Naturalism and its Critics', in Inwood 2003.

Long, A. (2003), 'Stoicism in the Philosophical Tradition', in Inwood 2003.

Newman, J. (1959), *Apologia Pro Vita Sua* (London: Collins).

Prichard, H. (1912), 'Does Moral Philosophy Rest on a Mistake?' in *Mind* 21: 21–37.

Railton, P. (1984), 'Alienation, Consequentialism, and the Demands of Morality', in *Philosophy and Public Affairs* 13: 134–71.

Raphael, D. (1969), *British Moralists 1650–1800*, vol. I (Oxford: Oxford University Press).

Ross, W. D. (1939), *Foundations of Ethics* (Oxford: Clarendon Press).

Sidgwick, H. (1967b), *The Methods of Ethics* (London: Macmillan).

Tweyman, S. (1976), 'Truth, Happiness, and Obligation: The Moral Philosophy of William Wollaston', in *Philosophy* 51: 35–46.

Williams, B. (1985), *Ethics and the Limits of Philosophy* (Harvard: Harvard University Press).

Index

Printed in the USA/Agawam, MA
February 15, 2024

861195.001